Hormuzd Rassam

Narrative of the British Mission to Theodore, King of Abyssinia

Salzwasser

Hormuzd Rassam

Narrative of the British Mission to Theodore, King of Abyssinia

1. Auflage | ISBN: 978-3-84605-364-5

Erscheinungsort: Frankfurt, Deutschland

Erscheinungsjahr: 2020

Salzwasser Verlag GmbH

NARRATIVE

OF THE

BRITISH MISSION TO THEODORE,

KING OF ABYSSINIA;

WITH NOTICES OF THE COUNTRIES TRAVERSED FROM MASSOWAH,
THROUGH THE SOODÂN, THE AMHÂRA, AND BACK TO
ANNESLEY BAY, FROM MÁGDALA.

By HORMUZD RASSAM, F.R.G.S.,

FIRST ASSISTANT POLITICAL RESIDENT AT ADEN, IN CHARGE OF THE MISSION.

IN TWO VOLUMES.—Vol. I.

WITH MAP, PLANS, AND ILLUSTRATIONS.

LONDON:
JOHN MURRAY, ALBEMARLE STREET.
1869.

The vignette on the cover represents Theodore's seal. The surrounding inscription is bi-lingual, Amharic and Arabic. The former runs thus:—

Negûs Nĭgăset, [King of kings] Tĕôdros, of Ethiopia.

The Arabic as follows:—

The victorious King, Tâôdrôs, King of Abyssinia.

LONDON: PRINTED BY WILLIAM CLOWES AND SONS, DUKE STREET, STAMFORD STREET,
AND CHARING CROSS.

PREFACE.

I DEEM it desirable, by way of introduction to the following Narrative, to say a few words, in the first place, on my appointment to the charge of the British Mission to King Theodore.

The appointment took me by surprise while engaged in my official duties at Aden. Of course, when the order came directing me to convey a letter from her Most Gracious Majesty to the King of Abyssinia, I was bound to obey. Nevertheless, I need hardly say that I felt highly honoured by the distinction which the order implied.

The undertaking at the outset involved no higher functions than the delivery of a letter to the Abyssinian Sovereign. It was generally believed, and with good reason, that a courteous reply from her Majesty to Theodore's letter would effect the immediate liberation of the captives, and put an end to all our difficulties in that quarter.

One strong ground for that opinion was the statement contained in Consul Cameron's first note, reporting his imprisonment, in chains, together with several other Europeans:—" No release until civil answer to King's letter arrives." If such was the conviction of the persons on the spot, most interested in the measures to be adopted for their liberation, those at a distance were justified in inferring that a reply from her Majesty the Queen was all that was necessary to conciliate the haughty Monarch who held a British Consul in his power.

And yet, what actually happened? King Theodore was aware of my being the bearer of a polite answer to his letter for nearly a year before he deigned to take any notice of my communications to him on the subject. He kept the Mission waiting at Massowah during that long period, and it was only after the receipt of my third letter, wherein I informed his Majesty that unless I received a reply within a given time I should return to my post at Aden, that he sanctioned my proceeding to his Court.

What was the cause of this reticence on the part of the King? The captives could not account for it; they had evidently been constrained to modify their opinions about the good effect which a letter from her Majesty would produce, for they repeatedly dissuaded me, in the strongest terms, against attempting to visit Theodore, either with or without a safe-conduct; and it was not until about the time when the Mission was preparing to start inland that they were led to believe that unless I went up their lives would be endangered.

For my own part, I feel almost as much at a loss as they were to assign any obvious cause for the King's reserve on the occasion. The motive which he subsequently expressed to me, namely, that he acted as he did in order to test my character, was, of course, a mere complimentary subterfuge. It is my firm belief, however, formed on the concurrent testimony of those who were highest in the royal confidence, that Theodore's chief reason for deferring his assent to our proposed visit to him was his inability to insure the Mission a safe passage through his intermediate territories—then in open revolt against him—a fact which pride alone made him anxious to conceal. Even when induced at last to grant me the necessary permission, he was obliged, owing to the rebellion on the more direct route, to request that I would come to him *viâ* Matámma.

Theodore's eventual reception of the Mission, however, was all that could be desired. The captives were to be set at liberty, and a letter of apology was drawn up by him addressed to her Majesty.

During the interval which elapsed between that announcement and the release of the old captives from Mágdala, nothing could exceed the King's courtesy to the Mission, and especially to me personally. As will be seen from his letters at this period, he wrote unreservedly of my speedy departure out of the country, taking the liberated captives with me; and my firm conviction is, notwithstanding what after-experience taught me of the fickleness of his character, that Theodore fully intended, at that time, to act up to his promises.

Suddenly, however, about the middle of March, 1866, I observed a change in his views. First, he intimated a desire to "consult" me, and, then, to have "a chat with me," on the arrival of the released captives at Korâta. Shortly after, these hints developed into an order that I should try them on a list of charges which he preferred against them, and which he wound up with these significant words, "If I am in fault, do you tell me, and I will requite them; but if you find that I am wronged, I wish you to get them to requite me." It was quite clear now that Theodore demanded an indemnity for what he considered the injuries which he had received at the hands of the old Captives.

I have endeavoured, to the best of my ability, to set forth in these volumes the cause or causes of this unexpected alteration in the King's conduct, after he had unreservedly forgiven the alleged wrongs, and made the Captives over to me to be conveyed out of Abyssinia.

Theodore's claim to compensation eventually took the form of a demand for English artisans, and in the mean time he determined to retain us as hostages. Whether he would have liberated us had the artisans been forwarded to him from Massowah, I cannot venture to say. That the Government acted with becoming dignity in not sending them up until he had set us at liberty, is unquestionable.

As to the rest, the proceedings of the Mission, its variable phases while in Abyssinia, its alternate successes and failures, and its final liberation by the Army of Rescue, are so fully detailed in this Narrative, that I shall leave the reader to form his own judgment of the manner in which the Author conducted it.

There is another topic also which I must likewise refer to public opinion—I mean the character of King Theodore. I have attempted here and there to portray some of the psychical features of that extraordinary man; but so fickle was his temper, so intermingled his good and bad qualities, so inscrutable his motives, that the attempt to draw a full and correct portrait of him has always baffled me. The revelations of himself, however, made in his numerous authentic letters and messages, his intimate relations with me, together with frequent notices of his eventful career from childhood till the day of his death, to be found in this work, may serve to correct some exaggerated notions of his vices, as well as of his virtues, which have obtained currency in this country and elsewhere. The frontispiece to the first volume is a very characteristic likeness of him.

As regards the tenor of my letters to the King, the reader is requested to bear in mind, in the first place, the critical circumstances under which most of them were written; and, secondly, that the religious expressions frequently used were adopted in deference to the usages of the people.

The account given of the journey of the Mission from Massowah round the entire circuit of Abyssinia proper, comprising a large extent of territory on its northern borders comparatively little known, will, I trust, prove generally interesting. The route is laid down on the Map at the end of this Volume; but with the exception of the portion extending from Mágdala to Annesley Bay, which has been adopted from the Government survey, it has no claim to scientific accuracy. The position of the principal localities between Massowah and Kedârif are copied principally from Petermann's recent 'Original Karte von Nord-Abessinien und den Ländern am Mareb, Barka, und Anseba,' and the intermediate places and stages have been fixed at the estimated rate of our mules' pace, due allowance being made for the nature of the ground traversed. The route, including the physical features of the country between Matámma and along the western and southern borders of Lake Tâna, has been filled in from my own personal observations, aided by a rough sketch kindly placed at my disposal by my late companion Dr. Blanc. The detention of the Mission at Zagê enabled me to ascertain the proximate extent of that peninsula, and its relative position to the affluence of the Abai, or Blue Nile, into Lake Tâna on the north-west, and its efflux out of the Lake to the south-east.

Some pains have been taken to give a correct rendering of the proper and other names occurring in these volumes. A separate Note on the system attempted, and the spelling adopted in carrying it out, will be found on a succeeding page.

For the Plan and Views of Mágdala I am indebted to the courtesy of the War-Office authorities.

I cannot conclude the Preface without expressing my thanks to my friend the Rev. George Percy Badger, not only for the kind manner in which he looked over and revised my Journal, but also for his valuable assistance in carrying it through the press.

LONDON, *March*, 1869.

NOTE

On the Spelling and Accentuation of foreign Names occurring in these Volumes, and also along the Mission route on the Map, exclusive of the portion between Mágdala and Annesley Bay.

THE rule which it has been attempted to preserve is this :—Foreign names already familiar to the general reader, such as Mohammed, Massowah, Jiddah, &c., have been allowed to retain their ordinary English form, however imperfectly expressed.

Names less commonly known have, in most cases, been given as pronounced by the natives using them, modified occasionally by the more correct literary form, whenever the difference between the two is slight.

With regard to the alphabet:—the *Consonants* generally to have the same power as in English ; the *g* always hard, as in gun ; *ch* as in chat. The *Vowels* as follows :—*a* as in far ; *e* as in beg; *i* as in pit; *o* as in store; *u* as in lunar.   The vowels *ai*, in conjunction (as in the Amharic " Aito ") to be pronounced like *ie* in pie; *aw* like *ow* in how.

Accents :—the acute (´) denotes the syllable to be accentuated.   Attention to this mark will prevent such mis-pronunciation as Magdála instead of Mágdala.   The circumflex (^) over a vowel prolongs it : thus *ê* becomes like the *e* in the French même; *î* is equivalent to ee ; *û* to oo.   The sign ˘ shortens the vowel over which it is placed.

The apostrophe (') before a vowel is intended to express the guttural 'ain of the Arabic and other Eastern languages.

ERRATA IN VOL. I.

Page 64, *line* 2, *for* Dabra, *read* Debra.

Page 87, *line* 6.   The spot encamped at was called Hozât.

Page 129, *line* 17, *for* Taërarait, *read* Tacrarait.

Page 130, *line* 18, *for* Awhai, *read* Awhê.

Page 148, *line* 16, *for* Sheep's-skin, *read* Water-skin.

Page 185, *line* 16, *for* Dinkee, *read* Denké.

CONTENTS OF VOLUME I.

CHAPTER I.

ADEN TO MASSOWAH.

CHAPTER II.

MASSOWAH AND ITS NEIGHBOURHOOD.

CHAPTER III.

PRELIMINARY DIFFICULTIES.

CHAPTER IV.

PRELIMINARY PROGRESS.

CHAPTER V.

MASSOWAH TO CÁSALA.

CHAPTER VI.

CÁSALA TO MATÁMMA.

CHAPTER VII.

MATÁMMA.

CHAPTER VIII.

MATÁMMA TO THE PLAIN OF DÁMBĔA.

CHAPTER IX.

ONWARD TO THE ROYAL COURT.

CHAPTER X.

THE MISSION REACHES THEODORE.

CHAPTER XI.

WITH THEODORE AND HIS ARMY.

CHAPTER VIII.

MATÁMMA TO THE PLAIN OF DÁMBĔA.

CHAPTER IX.

ONWARD TO THE ROYAL COURT.

CHAPTER X.

THE MISSION REACHES THEODORE.

CHAPTER XI.

WITH THEODORE AND HIS ARMY.

CHAPTER XII.

OVER LAKE TÂNA TO KORÂTA.

LIST OF ILLUSTRATIONS

IN THE FIRST VOLUME.

THE
BRITISH MISSION TO THEODORE,
KING OF ABYSSINIA.

CHAPTER I.

ADEN TO MASSOWAH.

The Author's appointment to the Mission — Dr. Blanc — Arrival at
Massowah — Reception by Turkish Authorities — Purtoo Effendi's opinion
of the Mission — Difficulty of obtaining Messengers — Letters to King
Theodore and the Abûna — Inhabitants of Massowah — Harkíko —
Trade with the Interior — Revenue — Slave Trade — Water — Language
— Marriage Ceremonies — Imports — Food — Climate and its effects on
cattle — British Consulate — An Armenian's adventure with King Theodore — Moncûlu and adjacent villages — Khoja Bedrôs's opinion of
Theodore — Mr. Coffin's widow — 'Omar 'Ali, the Interpreter — Mr.
Munzinger's view of the Abyssinian difficulty — An expert native
sportsman — The Emperor Napoleon's birthday — Purtoo Effendi's
idea of Massowah — Contradictory reports about Consul Cameron and
the Missionaries.

IN the month of April, 1864, the startling news reached
Aden that Consul Cameron and the Protestant Missionaries
had been imprisoned by Theodore, King of Abyssinia. The
native version ascribed the cause to the jealousy and malice
of one party of the resident Europeans against the other.

Various rumours were afloat, some days after, of the means
which her Majesty's Government intended to adopt for the
liberation of the captives. These were set at rest on the
26th of June, when a telegram was received by Lieutenant-
Colonel Merewether, the Political Resident, from Sir Charles
Wood, then Secretary of State for India, directing that I

should hold myself in readiness to convey a letter from the Queen to the King of Abyssinia. Her Majesty's letter, however, did not reach Aden till the 20th of the month following; owing, I believe, to the difficulty of finding a competent person in Egypt—where it was sent in the first instance—to translate it into Amharic. As a last resource, the British authorities there had it rendered into Arabic—a language which the King of Abyssinia was said to understand.

Deeming that it would be advantageous, in many respects, that a medical officer should be associated with the Mission, and finding that Dr. Henry Blanc, then on staff employ at Aden, was willing to accompany me, I applied to Colonel Merewether for his services. The request was promptly acceded to, and the appointment eventually received the sanction of the Government of India.

The Home Government having directed that a man-of-war should convey me to Massowah, in order to enhance the importance of the Mission in the eyes of the natives, and no such vessel being available, the Resident ordered the Government steamer 'Dalhousie,' commanded by Lieutenant Morland, formerly of the late Indian Navy, which was then at Aden, to proceed with us to Massowah.

I embarked in the afternoon of the 20th of July, 1864, escorted to the vessel by numerous friends. Dr. Blanc came on board shortly after, and at six o'clock precisely we bade our friends farewell, and steamed for the Red Sea. A stiff breeze had been blowing all day from the south-west, and on getting clear of the harbour we encountered a heavy swell, but scarcely any wind.

21st.—The night was pleasant, and, as is generally the case at this season, the wind blew fresh towards morning. We passed the Straits of Bâb-ul-Mandeb in the forenoon, and at sunset were abreast of the Island of Hárnish, which was just visible on our right as we steamed close to the African coast.

22nd.—At 6·30 P.M., we anchored off the Island 'Ajûz, it being thought dangerous to proceed during the night to Massowah, in consequence of the numerous reefs in that part of the Red Sea. We steamed away early the following morning, reached Massowah a little before noon, and anchored between the island and the mainland, just below the custom-house. As soon as the 'Dalhousie' was properly berthed, she saluted the Turkish flag with twenty-one guns, the fort on the Island returning the compliment.

Shortly after, Purtoo Effendi, the Governor of the place, sent the harbour-master on board to inquire about the object of our visit and to offer his services. I begged him to thank his Excellency for his courtesy, and, after satisfying his curiosity, he returned to report what he had heard and seen to his superior officer.

The weather was intensely hot, so much so that even Aden seemed a paradise compared with Massowah. Towards sunset I left the vessel, accompanied by Dr. Blanc and Lieutenant Morland, under a salute of fifteen guns, to make an official call on the Kâyim-Makâm, or lieutenant-governor, the fort returning the compliment as soon as we landed. We found his Excellency ill in bed, but he did his best to show us every civility. He was delighted to find that there was an experienced medical man in our party, and the bare prospect of a cure under his treatment made him quite cheerful. On informing him that I wished to proceed into the interior to deliver a letter from her Majesty the Queen of England to King Theodore, he remarked that it would be dangerous to make the attempt, and as a friend of the English and an admirer of the British Government, he deemed it his duty to do all in his power to prevent our further progress. The King, he said, was mad, and as he had been ill-treating the representatives of foreign powers for years past, he did not think that I should fare better at his hands than others. He predicted that I should be well received, and be treated with great honour for a time, but that eventually the nature of "the beast," as he designated his Abyssinian Majesty, would show itself, and I should find myself a prisoner in chains, or debarred from quitting the country. "If your Government," he went on to say, "intend to leave you to end your days in bondage, you are mad to go; but if they intend to adopt coercive measures for your liberation in the event of your incarceration, they had better begin to make preparations at once. I advise you to reflect before placing yourself in the power of that treacherous man."

On replying that I must obey orders, but at the same time assuring him that neither Dr. Blanc nor I had any anxiety about the result, he said: "Then, do as you please; as an official of the Sublime Porte, the ally of the British Government, I shall be most happy to render you every assistance in my power. Let me know your requirements, and they shall be promptly attended to."

I record what passed at this interview, in order to show in what light the character of King Theodore was regarded by the Turkish representative at Massowah.

The Governor was not slow to fulfil his promise. He immediately directed the harbour-master to assist in procuring water and other supplies for the 'Dalhousie,' and he also placed the services of the Nâyib of Harkîko and the Mudîr of the Danâkil at my disposal. The Commissioner of Customs was ordered not to interfere with anything which we might wish to land either on the Island or the mainland, and further, that none of the local taxes were to be levied on any purchases made for the use of the Mission or the ship's company.

His Excellency also promised to assist me in procuring trustworthy messengers to King Theodore; but he sent word the day after that, although he had offered handsome rewards for the service, he could find none willing to undertake it. I had also commissioned two other influential persons to aid me in this matter; but it was not till the evening of the 24th that two Mohammedan Abyssinians engaged to convey a letter to the dreaded monarch. They, however, insisted on my assurance beforehand that the epistle contained nothing which could in any way compromise them. They undertook to go up to Góndar, and return with an answer in the course of a month, if the rise in the Tăkkăzê river did not impede their progress.

The following is a translation of my first letter to the King, which was written in Arabic, as I had heard that he understood that language; besides, it was known that he had several Egyptian writers at his Court:—

After compliments—

"I have the honour to inform your Majesty that I arrived at this port yesterday, bearing a letter to your address from her Majesty the British Queen (may God protect her!), and, as I am desirous to deliver the said letter into your hands, I shall await your answer here.

"Should your Majesty acquiesce in my coming to your parts for the purpose of consigning the letter to you personally, my desire would be fulfilled, as I am most anxious for the honour of seeing you, and of enjoying the gratification of being at your happy Court. In that case, I shall feel obliged if you would send one of your followers to escort me to your city, the defended [of God].

"But should you not deem it advisable for me to come to you at present, owing to the rains and the consequent difficulty of travelling, I hope that you will oblige me by releasing Consul Cameron and his imprisoned companions, and sending them under your protection to this place.

"Will you be pleased, further, to send a trustworthy person with the Consul, to whom I may deliver the Queen's letter above mentioned.

"I am directed to acquaint you that in the event of your wishing to send an embassy to England, as you intimated in your letter addressed to our Queen, her Majesty will be glad to receive it. If you are able to send the Mission down before my return to Aden, I shall take care that it is forwarded to England in safety.

"I enclose herewith three letters—one addressed to your Majesty from the Patriarch of the Copts in Egypt, and two to the address of Abûna Salâma, the Metropolitan of Abyssinia; one of these is from the aforesaid Patriarch, and the other from myself. If you send the replies to me, I will transmit them to their destination.

"I trust that your Majesty will favour me with an answer, as I long to have the pleasure of perusing its gratifying and gracious contents. May you be evermore preserved!"

Consul Cameron had written on the 4th February, 1864, "no release until civil answer to King's letter arrives;" and on reaching Massowah I had heard from different sources that the Abyssinian Autocrat had determined not to allow any foreign official to enter his territories without his special permission. Some persons further alleged that I should not be allowed to proceed into the interior owing to the repugnance which the King now entertained for all European travellers. Weighing these several opinions, I judged it advisable, in writing to his Majesty, to adopt a style calculated to elicit a civil reply, even if he refused my request to pay him a personal visit.

I subsequently discovered that a serious mistake had been made at the outset by our communicating with the Patriarch of the Copts and the Metropolitan, Abûna Salâma; for, on the receipt of my letter, the King remarked, with reference to me, "So he has already made friends with my enemies, the priests." Unluckily, when I started for Massowah, it was not known either in Egypt or at Aden that the Abûna was in disgrace; nevertheless, I was on my guard in writing to him, and, as already stated, took the precaution of sending the letter to the King, whom I also requested to transmit the reply. The following is a translation of the Arabic original :—

After compliments—

"I have the honour to inform your Lordship that I have arrived here [Massowah] bearing a letter from her Majesty the British Queen (may God defend her!) to his gracious Majesty King Theodore, Emperor of Abyssinia.

"As I cannot proceed to Góndar without his Majesty's protection, I have written requesting him to send some one to accompany me to your parts. My object is to confer with his Majesty respecting the release of Consul Cameron and his imprisoned companions; and, God willing, as soon as I receive an answer I shall come to you, under the protection of our Heavenly Father.

"I trust, through the mercy of the Most High, to succeed in beholding the light of your countenance, to have the pleasure of seeing you personally, and of meeting with the august King.

"I forward you an epistle from the venerable father, the Patriarch of your Church in Egypt. Should it call for an answer, be pleased to deliver the answer to the King, that he may transmit it by the bearer of this letter.

"I trust that you will remember me in your devout prayers."

I instructed the messengers not to receive any letters to my address, unless they were delivered to them through the King; at the same time they were to endeavour to communicate with Consul Cameron, or with any of the captives, if the attempt could be made without risk.

These precautions were suggested by the following considerations :—It was judged that if I communicated directly with the European captives, and the fact should come to the King's knowledge, he might be led to distrust me and to vent his displeasure on the unfortunate prisoners. Moreover, I was unable for a long time to find an Abyssinian who would venture up to Góndar with a communication to the captives—the general conviction being that, if apprehended, any such messenger would be condemned to death by the King. Therefore, before making the attempt, I judged it prudent to send messengers to Tigrê, in order, if possible, to obtain reliable information regarding the cause of the imprisonment of our Consul and the other Europeans. Among others, Mircha Warkee, a native of Adwa, was indicated as a most likely person to supply it. He was said to have been educated at an English school in Bombay, and to have been employed in the British Consulate at Massowah. I accordingly applied to him, but was sadly disappointed. The mere arrival at his house of a messenger from " the English " frightened him out of his wits, and he forbade a second attempt of the kind, on the plea that, if discovered in holding any correspondence with the Europeans, he would inevitably suffer for it. His message to me was, that he would reply to my queries as soon as he judged that it would be safe to do so.

The 24th of July being Sunday, prayers were read in the morning by Lieutenant Morland on the deck of the 'Dalhousie.' We found Massowah much hotter than Aden. Throughout the first night we spent there the thermometer stood at 95°, and the atmosphere was so close that sleep was out of the question. A vapour, which seemed to spring from the tepid sea in the harbour, mingling with the little air in circulation, made breathing on board unpleasant.

25th.—Having brought a letter of introduction from the Roman Catholic chaplain at Aden to the Vicar-Apostolic, Monsignor Biancheri, the Italian Bishop of Eastern Abyssinia, I dispatched it to Haibo, situated on the borders of that country, about two days' journey from Massowah, where he had gone to spend the summer months, and where a Roman Catholic mission had been established. I inquired of him, at the same time, whether it would be safe for Dr. Blanc and myself to repair thither for a few days, while waiting for a reply from the King. We felt the heat more and more every day, and dreaded lest, by remaining at Massowah, we might be seized with sickness, and incapacitated thereby for undertaking the journey inland when summoned by his Majesty. It appears that my letter so terrified the venerable prelate, that he forthwith dispatched his deputy, Padre Delmonte, to dissuade me from penetrating into Abyssinia, intimating that, as the English were at present under the King's displeasure, some of his soldiers might seize and detain us until they consulted his Majesty about our disposal. Padre Delmonte further expressed his own opinion that it would be highly dangerous for us to proceed to the King's Court, as Theodore was a most difficult man to deal with, and was commonly reported to be both unscrupulous and treacherous.

A terrific dust-storm occurred this afternoon. It was so dense that objects were invisible ten feet off, and when it passed over every one looked as if he had been dug out of a dust heap. Nevertheless, a very pleasurable sensation is felt after these tropical hurricanes, which cool the atmosphere and clear it of that oppressive sultriness which generally precedes them. These storms only occur after a heavy fall of rain in the mountains. The natives, whether at Aden or Massowah, seldom complain of the temporary discomfort, knowing that the heavier the dust the better is the prospect of a plentiful harvest.

Massowah is a very peculiar place, both as regards its situation and the manners and customs of its inhabitants. Although geographically pertaining to Africa, the natives are more Arab than Abyssinian or negro in character. In dress, food and domestic habits, they resemble the people of Jiddah; and I imagine there is as much African blood mixed with that of the Arabs of the seaboard of the Hijâz, as there is Arab blood in the veins of the Africans at Massowah. Both are strict Mohammedans of the Sunnî sect, and would not hesitate to give every Christian visiting their country the alternative of the Korân or the sword, were they free to follow their inclinations. They regard the Shî'ahs with as much detestation as they do Christians or Jews, although bound to believe that those schismatics from their own community will be saved at the last day, whatever their demerits may have been; but woe betide the reprobates who die without the mark of the Prophet on their foreheads!

The small Island of Massowah contains a population of about five hundred families, the majority of which reside at the villages of Hittimlo, Moncûlu, and Harkîko. Hittimlo is two miles distant from the Island, and Moncûlu one mile farther, in a north-westerly direction. Harkîko stands upon the mainland beach, about five miles to the south-west, and is the most important place in the neighbourhood; for, besides being the largest, it is also the residence of the hereditary Nâyibs, and contains a citadel and garrison to keep the marauding Abyssinians on the frontier in check. Whenever these come down from the table-land, the inhabitants of the other villages abandon their dwellings and take refuge on the Island.

Of late years, however, the unfortunate villages around Massowah have been so harassed by these freebooters that many families—some during our stay—have left to join the nomad tribes. Had the natives of Moncûlu and other hamlets been allowed to erect stone houses, they might have protected themselves against the brigands; but, owing to some unaccountable prejudice on the part of the Jiddah authorities, no substantial building was permitted beyond the Island, and a similar veto prohibited the erection of a hut on Jarâr, a neck of land opposite, across the harbour, towards the north. The prohibition was made to extend to us by Purtoo Effendi's successor, so that when Dr. Blanc and Lieutenant Prideaux occupied that spot they lived in tents, but were not allowed to erect huts there for their servants; for although the Kâyim-Makâm expressed his readiness to serve me in any other way, nothing could induce him to give way on that point. The order, he said, was peremptory, and must be obeyed; and, on my reasoning that a mere shed, removable in a few minutes, could by no possibility become a nuisance, and, moreover, that Purtoo Effendi had authorised me to build whatever I chose, either in or beyond Massowah, he replied that every man should act according to the dictates of his own conscience, and that his predecessor had taken upon himself a responsibility which he, 'Abdallah Effendi, could not assume.

The traffic between Massowah and Harkiko is carried on by boats, which ply throughout the day. The traders also use the same means of transit, but such as dislike the longer sea voyage ride round to the nearest point of embarkation on mules. The principal trade of the place is with the interior of Abyssinia, and is carried on mainly by barter— coin being seldom given in exchange for the articles disposed of. The Abyssinians, who bring down gold, ivory, coffee, musk, wax and grain, barter those articles for prints, calicoes and coarse silks—chiefly of Indian manufacture—beads, spices, &c. Two caravans arrive every year; the first and larger about the end of June, and the second, consisting of Abyssinian and Galla commodities, in October or the beginning of November. The former assembles in Tigrê just before the rains, and the latter starts from different parts of the interior towards the middle of September, when the rains cease and the rivers are fordable.

The Turkish authorities informed me that the revenue derived from the trade at Massowah scarcely covered the civil charges. The entire exports and imports during my time did not exceed three hundred thousand dollars (65,000l.) per annum, or a little above what it was in 1853, according to the report of Consul Plowden; and, bearing in mind that the Abyssinian merchants travel to Massowah from the remote province of Gójjam, it is obvious that the trade with the interior must be very insignificant. Formerly the traffic in slaves was the most lucrative speculation with the Massowah merchants; but the Sublime Porte having discountenanced it, this abominable trade can only be carried on clandestinely; nevertheless, during my stay at Massowah,

I discovered beyond doubt that it was still prosecuted to a considerable extent between the African coast and Arabia. The Turkish authorities at Massowah did their best to stop it, and were snubbed by the Governor-General of the Hijâz for their pains.

There is abundance of water in the neighbourhood of Massowah, which might easily be made available for irrigation; and if the natives possessed energy enough to dig wells and to cultivate the soil, they might grow their own grain, which they are now obliged to import from the interior and from several ports in the Red Sea. The most capacious well I met with was not more than thirty feet in depth, while those excavated near the bed of a torrent were rarely above ten feet. During the rains in the interior, when the water finds its way to the sea, these wells are replenished, and some of them, especially those at Harkîko, become full to overflowing. The Turkish Commandant of the garrison there had a very good garden, yielding several kinds of vegetables and flowers. All seemed to thrive so well that I thought of showing the natives how to raise water easily by means of a Persian wheel, and of cultivating a piece of ground myself as an example for their imitation. But I was told that if the King of Abyssinia heard of it, he would conclude that I was either a trader or one obliged to work for his livelihood, and should thereby lower myself in his estimation. Unwilling to risk anything which might damage the Mission entrusted to me, I abandoned the experiment.

There are three kinds of water at Massowah. First, rain-water, which is collected in reservoirs on the Island during the rainy season: this is mostly used by the resident Banian merchants, who, being Hindoos, object to drinking the water brought in skins from the adjacent villages. The second quality, which is the best, is obtained from wells excavated near the bed of a torrent at Moncûlu. The third is brought chiefly from Harkîko, and being brackish is used by the natives for culinary purposes. The tank water is seldom sold, being the property of private individuals who keep it for their own use. Moncûlu water fetches one piastre per skin, or about two shillings the hundred gallons; and that from Harkîko, which is conveyed to the island in boats, half that price. All the water obtained at Moncûlu is carried by females of the Hibâb tribe of all ages, from the girl of twelve years old to decrepit old women in their dotage. Sometimes the skins are so large, that one wonders they do not succumb under the heavy burden. Not unfrequently these unfortunate creatures have to make two trips a-day between Moncûlu and Massowah, a distance of four miles each way; and during the summer months, when the thermometer rises to 130° in the sun, the task must tax their strength to the utmost. All this fatigue, however, does not quench the tender passion; on the contrary, often when apparently utterly worn out with physical exertion, they enliven the monotony of their miserable existence by singing amorous duets, provided they are beyond the hearing of the learned Kâdhi or other over-religious critic.

The prevailing language on the Island is a mixture of Arabic and Tigrêan of the lowlands of northern Abyssinia. The male inhabitants of the mainland, however, with the exception of a few who have had intercourse with Arabs, only understand the latter dialect; and the same is true of the women in both localities, of whom I doubt whether one in ten understands a single Arabic word. Of course both men and women know the meaning of some few expressions in their Arabic prayers, which they learn by rote ; but they are quite indifferent to comprehending the whole, being assured that the simple enunciation of the sentences will suffice for their justification at the last day.

One of their marriage ceremonies is, I believe, unique, and has much to recommend it to intending Benedicts. All the guests invited to a wedding are expected to make a present in money to the bridegroom. The several sums contributed are placed to the credit of the respective donors, on whose marriage, or that of their sons, the amount is repaid, as if it had been a loan. Hence, when a man takes a wife he finds himself at the same time provided with capital to set up in business. Sometimes, when a man is in prosperous circumstances, he not only repays the sum he had received, but advances something more to be repaid at a future time to himself or to his son. The collections among the wealthier classes frequently exceed one thousand dollars, about 200*l*. ; and on one occasion when I was among the invited guests, and had to contribute to the bridegroom's fund—which, of course, has been placed to my credit—the amount reached three thousand dollars. The fortunate possessor of such a sum is regarded as a millionaire at Massowah.

I may mention another peculiar wedding custom which prevails at Massowah, scarcely as worthy of imitation as that just described. When the bride is conducted to the house of her affianced husband, the father of the husband, however advanced in years, is bound to dance before the procession with a drawn sword in his hand. If the bridegroom happens to be fatherless, then his nearest male relative must go through the ceremony. On the occasion already referred to, when I was one of the guests, the father of the boy—the latter was nothing more, for his age and that of his betrothed combined did not exceed twenty-two years—a man of dignified demeanour, could not help smiling when he saw me among the spectators. After he had gone through the performance, he apologised for having made himself ridiculous, alleging as an excuse the tyranny of a national custom which had been bequeathed to the true believers by the dark ages. It was his pious belief, indeed, that this and all other vain ceremonies which prevailed among the faithful had been handed over to them by the heathen, and that consequently in the day of judgment the sins, which had thus been inherited by the followers of the Prophet, would be laid to the charge of the unbelievers.

The trade of Massowah with India is carried on chiefly by Banian merchants, of whom there are about ten resident at that port. Bengal supplies rice; Surat, silk and tobacco; Bombay, sugar, spices and cotton goods. In exchange for these commodities, they export gold, ivory, pearls and hides. Thus, British possessions engross about two-thirds of the entire trade of the place, and the same remark applies to all the ports in the Red Sea, whether on the African or Arabian coast.

Beef and mutton at Massowah are of a very inferior quality, and the lower classes are so wretchedly poor that they seldom partake of either except on some grand occasion. The mutton was so scraggy and insipid, that the sight of a cooked joint of it sufficed to blunt our appetites. We obtained a few goats from the large neighbouring island of Dahlac, the flesh of which was tolerably good, but in a short time we nearly expended the stock. Twice we procured sheep from Abyssinia, which when first brought down looked in much better condition than those obtainable in the vicinity of Massowah, but when killed and exposed to the air, shrank so much that the carcasses resembled mummies. Butter was as much beyond our reach as strawberries, and milk was very scarce, owing to the fact that the cows brought from the interior either ceased to yield any, or died a few days after their importation into Massowah. The little milk we managed to secure was obtained from goats.

The climate of the plain around Massowah is most fatal to all kinds of cattle. It is so difficult to keep horses, that the best steed in the world, if offered for ten dollars, would not find a purchaser who wanted an animal for use in the lowlands. Mules, also, feel the deleterious effects of the climate when first brought down from the highlands.

26th.—My companion and I landed this afternoon on the Island, and visited the British Consulate. The building, if it deserves the name, was in a most dilapidated condition, but, thanks to the care of an Armenian, called Margôs, who was in charge of it, the two upper rooms were kept clean. Like all the houses at Massowah, with the exception of one rented by the Governor, the Consulate is a mere shed, hardly fit for a stable.

When the Armenian heard of my intended visit to Theodore, he remarked, " May the Lord deliver you from that treacherous man! " He himself, it appears, had had some experience of his malevolence. His story was as follows :—He was a native of Erzeroom, had travelled in Russia, Turkey, Persia and India, and hearing that there existed a country in the land of the negroes—as Africa is generally designated in Asia—whose people professed the same creed as the Armenians, and where gold might be had for the bare asking, he thought he could not do better than go to the king of the country and obtain from him a few handfuls of the dust of the precious metal. On reaching Abyssinia he was sadly disappointed, for he found the people so wretchedly poor that they could scarcely boast of having houses to live in—their best dwellings being mere hovels hardly fit for dogs. The chiefs were no better off than the peasants in his own country. Cleanliness was held in such low estimation, that excessive dirt generally indicated superior rank; and "will you believe it," he added, "the man who ventured to wash his face and hands would be taken for a Mussulman, whereas the dirtier his appearance the greater claims he would have to being considered a good Christian. However, having got thus far, I thought I might as well see what could be obtained from the King, who was reputed to be generous. Wah! no sooner was it my misfortune to behold the countenance of that son of a dog, the tormentor of his species, than I began to regret ever having seen a black face. The fellow who calls himself a King, but who would certainly not fetch a para [a Turkish farthing] if exposed for sale in the slave-market at Constantinople, asked what business had brought me to his country. In reply, I stated that I was an Armenian, professing the same doctrine as himself, and that I had visited the Holy Sepulchre at Jerusalem, in proof of which I showed him the tatooing on my arms—the sign of a Christian pilgrim; that I was a poor man with a large family, and, having heard that there was a great king in Abyssinia who was very charitable, had left my own country to solicit aid from his Majesty. He forthwith consigned me to one of his followers to be lodged and fed, but sent for me a few days after and again inquired what had induced me to come to his territories. On repeating my former statement, he called me a liar and a Turk, declaring that I was an Egyptian spy. I protested my innocence, swearing most solemnly that I had nothing whatever to do with the Egyptians, and had come exclusively on my own account. Whereupon he ordered me to be seized and imprisoned, and I fully expected decapitation before the day was over. Accordingly, I commenced crying and shrieking as loud as I could, and the place of my confinement being near the royal tent the King heard me. This led to my being summoned before him once more, when he called me a madman, bade me leave his country at once, and not let him see my face again. Never in my lifetime did I welcome an order with so much delight, and I solemnly assured him that once safe out of his territory, nothing in the world would induce me to return. Such," he concluded, " was the upshot of my delusive dream, and were you to offer me one thousand piastres a month to go and face that devil again, I would decline the proposal."

27th.—There was another sand-storm this afternoon, so violent that a number of native boats were stranded, and about a score of huts near the Custom-house were greatly damaged. It began at 7 P.M. and lasted two hours.

The thermometer ranged between 94° and 98° day and night. We tried sea-bathing to alleviate an outbreak of prickly-heat, or rash, but it rather intensified our sufferings. On testing the temperature of the sea one afternoon, we found it stood at 95°—as high as that of the surrounding atmosphere.

1st August.—At 5 P.M. I started for Moncûlu to see what kind of a house the late Consul Plowden had erected there. Instead of a fine building, which I had been led to expect, I found a miserable old fabric, constructed entirely of rafters and native matting ; the former corroded through and through by a worm bred in the wood, and the latter damaged by the hungry rats which infested the place. The shed—it is nothing better—was surrounded by a grove of *Parkinsoniæ*, with a few palms, henna shrubs, and a species of juniper, bearing a red berry. The former had been planted by Signor Barroni, late British consular agent at Massowah, who had previously acted as Mr. Plowden's private agent. Worse trees could not have been selected, for besides affording very little shade—the object aimed at—their thorny branches formed a *chevaux-de-frise* most unpleasant to come in contact with. These trees, it appears, were obtained from Aden, where the *Parkinsonia* has been found to thrive. I was informed that Consul Plowden had a good garden here, and managed to rear various kinds of fruit and vegetables; but no vestige of it remains.

There are two villages between the Island and Moncûlu, one called Yanbo' and the other Hittimlo, the latter containing the majority of the Massowah traders. Both have been formed quite recently, and owe their existence to the discovery of sweet water in the locality by an old sheikh, who on digging within two miles of the harbour, after several futile attempts, fortunately came upon good water. He was so delighted with his success, that he caused a small house to be built near the spot, which he dedicated, together with the well, to the free use of destitute travellers. The Mohammedans are eminently philanthropic in the matter of water, supplying it in the most out-of-the-way places, where its lack would be severely felt. Even at Yanbo', Hittimlo and Moncûlu, jars of water are set near the places of worship for the benefit of wayfarers.

Apart from these villages and a few scattered shrubs, the country between Moncûlu and the sea is dreary and monotonous. The ride is over heavy sand, and along a portion of the distance there is not the semblance of a road. A stranger attempting the route by night is almost sure to go astray. My mule was so done up that it took me an hour and a half to ride back four miles, and I was glad to find myself on board the 'Dalhousie' once more. The water at Monculu is wholesome, though not perfectly sweet, and is considered the best obtainable within fifteen miles of Massowah.

6th.—All the Banian merchants called upon me to-day, the Kâyim-Makâm having told them that I was the proper person to apply to in case they had any grievance to complain of. They were succeeded by a party of native merchants, including the ex-Kâdhi, the landlord of the Consulate, who asked me to pay him the arrears of rent due for several months. They all spoke in the strongest terms against King Theodore, advising me not to place myself in his clutches, and ridiculed the idea of my trusting to his safe-conduct. An Armenian merchant, however, named Khoja Bedrôs, who had resided long at Massowah, told me afterwards not to rely implicitly on the report of the Mohammedan traders, who were generally prejudiced against the King. He allowed that his Majesty's word was not to be depended upon; at the same time he counselled me not to be swayed either one way or another by what I might hear at Massowah. There was no doubt, he said, that the English had been unfortunate in Abyssinia for years past. Mr. Coffin had died of a broken heart, and his sons had been tortured by Dajjâj Oobê. Consul Plowden and Mr. Bell had fallen by the hands of the rebels, and now Theodore had seized and imprisoned Consul Cameron and all British subjects within his reach. "Had you been going on a pleasure excursion," he subjoined, "I should certainly have advised you to abandon the adventure; but as your sole object is to obtain the release of your Consul and others whose lives are in danger from day to day, do not hesitate to proceed after receiving a safe-conduct from the King. Trust in God and He will deliver you." This gentleman placed his services at my disposal, and was ever ready to assist me. He was carried off by cholera a few days before we started for Abyssinia, in the beginning of October, 1866.

I was subsequently visited by the Abyssinian widow of Mr. Coffin, bringing her two children—a boy and girl—aged nine and ten years respectively. She informed me that her husband had died leaving her utterly destitute, and that she had made her way from Adwa intending to proceed to Aden in the hope of enlisting the sympathies of her husband's countrymen in behalf of his children.

Soon after our arrival at Massowah, I engaged the services of a native of that place, named 'Omar 'Ali, to act as interpreter to Dr. Blanc, finding that he knew a little French. This man's integrity and honesty were so conspicuous throughout the duration of the Mission that he earned the respect of all, whether Christians or Mohammedans; and if a man in his position may lay claim to be styled a gentleman, 'Omar 'Ali unquestionably deserved the title as much as any individual in that part of Africa. I introduce him here because his name will frequently occur in the course of this narrative, Theodore having conceived a great liking for him, although he was then a rigid Mussulman. Eventually, he became a Christian, at Mágdala, under the tuition of the Rev. Mr. Stern, to whom he resorted for instruction. His great desire was to be baptized by a Protestant missionary, and not "by one of those ignorant priests who worship idols." That, however, was judged unadvisable, for fear of exciting the jealousy of the native clergy, who might have made a handle of it to do us mischief both with the King and the bigoted Abyssinians. I employed him subsequently as my confidential interpreter, as, not being an Abyssinian, he was more trusted by those who dreaded that their intercourse with us might be reported in suspicious quarters. I had intended to engage 'Abdallah Effendi, the Arabic writer of the Consulate—a man universally respected—in that capacity, whenever we went up to Abyssinia; but unfortunately cholera broke out at Massowah just as we were about to start for Matámma, and, as he had a large family to look after, I thought it would be cruel to take him away at that critical time when, at any moment, he might be deprived of some cherished relative.

9th.—Mr. Munzinger, the acting vice-consul for France, called on me this morning. He had been staying at his summer residence at Bogôs, two days distant from Massowah, and gave a most captivating account of that district. He informed me that he had resided in the country ten years, and would not object to remain in it ten years longer, provided he was able to spend the summer months in the highlands. As he spoke very little English, our conversation was carried on in Arabic, which he knew tolerably well. He was the first to give me any authentic information about the captives, who, he said, were still in chains. His impression was that the King would release them, on hearing that I had brought a letter for him from her Majesty. He was not so severe upon the King as others; on the contrary, he was of opinion that his Majesty had not been treated with due respect and consideration by the Europeans generally. Mr. Munzinger was most affable and courteous, and gladly assisted me on all occasions during our sojourn at Massowah.

Hearing that we should find a cooler climate at Moncúlu, Dr. Blanc, Lieut. Morland and I left the ship in the afternoon to spend a few days there. We had made arrangements to start immediately on landing, but one delay and another—the normal condition of things in these countries —so detained us that it was late before we arrived at our destination. However, we found our tents ready pitched within the inclosure of the British Consulate.

The following morning my companions went out very early for a little shooting, but found the fatigue so great, owing to the scorching heat, that they only bagged a guinea-fowl between them. A native soldier of Massowah, whom the Kâyim-Makâm had given us as a guide, brought down three guinea-fowl, a hare and a mousedeer. This man, who subsequently accompanied us on many other excursions, excited our admiration by the quickness of his sight and the agility of his movements, which, rather than a steady aim, were the secret of his success.

We fancied that the first night spent at Moncûlu was somewhat cooler; but it is doubtful whether it was really so, for the thermometer was not lower than it had been at Massowah. The heat was so intense during the day that we were obliged to abandon our double-fly tents and take shelter under the porch of the Consulate, where by keeping the ground well watered we reduced the temperature to 103°—ten degrees less than it was under the tent. We therefore judged that we might as well return to the steamer.

The European society of the place was now increased by the arrival of M. Gastineau, a French *savant*, who had come from Jiddah with the intention of proceeding to Abyssinia, but abandoned the project on hearing of the disturbed state of the interior and the imprisonment of British subjects.

Early on the 15th the Turkish fort fired a royal salute in honour of the Emperor Napoleon's birthday. Morland also contributed to the celebration by dressing the 'Dalhousie' with every available flag on board, and giving a grand entertainment to all the European community in the evening. The dinner was most sumptuous, comprising delicacies of endless variety, with claret and champagne *ad libitum.* The heat was kept under by punkahs and other appliances, and every art employed by the liberal host to gratify his guests, who, for the time, must have forgotten that they were at such an outlandish place as Massowah. Of course, as a loyal subject, he did not omit to propose the health of her Most Gracious Majesty, which was followed by another toast for her faithful ally, the Emperor of the French.

The only Christian church on the Island, which belongs to the Roman Catholic mission, joined in honouring the occasion by celebrating high mass in commemoration of the "fête Napoléon." My friend the Armenian merchant, who was a Monophysite, but from prudential motives had temporarily attached himself to the Latin Church, somewhat puzzled at the title given to the festival, inquired of me who "Saint Napoleon" was, as he had never found any saint of that name in the calendar.

The kind Kâyim-Makâm endeavoured to assuage our sufferings from the continued heat and dust by sending us presents of *Râhat-ul-Halkûm* and pomegranate syrup; the former, as the name implies, a sedative for the throat. He himself, though improved in health, was daily becoming more disgusted with the place and everything connected with it. His idea was that it was only fit for the abode of blacks, monkeys and hyenas, and would eventually serve as an appropriate suburb of Gehenna. Purtoo Effendi was one of those dainty Osmanlis whose appetite is upset at the bare sight of a dirty person handling his dinner-service, and through having been so long a victim to low fever his fastidiousness in that respect knew no bounds. On one occasion Dr. Blanc had sent him a bottle of quinine mixture by the harbour-master, and there being no domestic servant present at the time, his Excellency requested the latter to wash a tumbler and pour a dose of the medicine into it. The officer obeyed with alacrity, rinsing the glass over and over again, and then, in order to show how highly he appreciated the honour of waiting upon his superior, wiped it with the shirt he was wearing. On witnessing this, the patient flew into a rage, and assailed the unconscious offender with a shower of Turkish invectives, driving him from the house in disgrace. Luckily, Purtoo Effendi was unable to rise, otherwise a severer castigation would have been the reward of the over-obsequious subordinate.

After the 20th of August, the "Cocoa-nut Day" of the Hindoos, the masters of native craft venture out to sea, not expecting to meet with high winds. I took this first available opportunity of sending a boat to Aden, as nothing had transpired hitherto to warrant the dispatch of the steamer. The reports respecting Consul Cameron and the other captives had been vague and contradictory, and were so still. As regards the former, no two accounts agreed; but as regards the Missionaries, all concurred that they were in prison and badly treated by the King, who had been told that they had abused him. The Abyssinians, who thought to gratify me, reported that all the captives were well provided for, and, with the exception of being chained, were tolerably comfortable. Those, on the other hand, who wished me to share their bad opinion of the King, and to abandon the idea of visiting him, came to me daily with accounts of his barbarous treatment of the Europeans. To obtain authentic information on the subject seemed impossible; the most liberal terms offered to any one who would communicate with the captives invariably met with the rejoinder—" What will money avail a man when his life is forfeited?" The conviction was general that any Abyssinian attempting to befriend the detested Europeans would have his hands and feet chopped off. I began also to be anxious about our messengers to the King, as the time drew near for their return, and no tidings had reached us respecting them. Padro Delmonte did tell me on one occasion that they were still at the Tăkkăzê on the 11th August, eleven days after their departure from Massowah. This was very likely, but the intelligence was far from satisfactory.

CHAPTER II.

MASSOWAH AND ITS NEIGHBOURHOOD.

Monsignor Biancheri's opinion of Theodore — H.M.S. 'Pantaloon' — Death of the Vicar-Apostolic — A Góndar merchant's tale of his lost wife— European adventurers in Abyssinia — Purtoo Effendi leaves Massowah — Superstitious belief in Theodore's knowledge of the absent — Sack of Góndar — Return of messengers without trustworthy information — Anarchy in the interior — Dissee Island — Visit to the Nâyib of Harkîko — Rival Nâyibs — Contrast since Bruce's time — Nâyib Mohammed's experience of Theodore — Reasons against proceeding to the Court without a safe-conduct — Author's second letter to Theodore — Supposed spies sent to Massowah — Raid of Barca Muslims on the Christians of Bogôs — Count du Bisson's projected colony in Hamasên — A waggon-nette astounds the Natives — Visit to the ex-Nâyib Idrîs — Decay of prejudice — Residence at Moncûlu — False reports about the Captives — Night-revel among the hyænas — The Captives stated to have been sent to Mágdala — Reliable intelligence of receipt of Author's first letter by Theodore — A shrewd Abyssinian Mussulman — Information sought from Messrs. Flad and Schimper respecting the Captives — Ailât — A nomad encampment — Portable huts — Sport — Dasta, the Interpreter — Arrival of a new Kâyim-Makâm — False reports about the Captives — Repression of the Slave Trade discouraged.

MONSIGNOR BIANCHERI, having returned to Massowah, sent to say that he wished to call upon me, but I judged it becoming to pay him the first visit. Accordingly, Dr. Blanc and I called upon him the following day at his house adjoining the new Latin church, situated at the south-eastern extremity of the island. His lordship and Padre Delmonte received us very civilly. He told us that he had been obliged to leave the delightful climate of Haibo, owing to a report that the governor of one of the neighbouring districts was in league with the royal troops to seize and send him to Góndar. He declared that if I persisted in going to the "crazy Theodore," I should only get mal-treated for my pains; that he was not amenable to reason, and the only way of bringing him to his senses was to chastise him. To impress this upon us more forcibly, the right reverend prelate clenched his fists and struck them together repeatedly, signifying that if he had the power he would pound the despot to atoms.

On the 25th H.M.S. 'Pantaloon' arrived from Aden, from whence she had been dispatched by Colonel Merewether, in consequence of a report made by the master of a native boat that the 'Dalhousie' had not reached Massowah when he left that port on the 28th of July. Having on former occasions spent many happy days with Captain Purvis and the officers serving under him, I hailed their advent with unmingled gratification, and soon found myself once more " at home " in their agreeable society. The heat on board the 'Pantaloon,' however, was much greater than on the ' Dalhousie,' owing to the height of her bulwarks, which effectually prevented the free circulation of the little air there was stirring. A vessel so constructed is better fitted for the North Pole than the Red Sea.

27th.—Monsignor Biancheri and Padre Delmonte hon-oured us with a visit in the morning; and in the afternoon Dr. Blanc and I took up our residence at the Consulate on the Island. It was important that I should be easily accessible to the natives, to whom I looked for information; but the change from the comfort and luxury of the ' Dalhousie ' to the inconveniences and scarcity of Massowah was immense. The commonest necessaries of life, such as meat, bread, milk, butter, &c., were procured with the greatest difficulty; and, as to furniture, it was not obtainable at any price. In these straits, the Commander and officers of the 'Pantaloon,' with their wonted kindness, liberally supplied us with such stores as they could spare. Their return to Aden, on the 2nd of September, left a great blank in our little community; and we regretted still more not being able to make them the bearers of any reliable account of the captives. As already observed, there was no lack of reports, both favourable and unfavourable; but we had no means of tracing them to any trustworthy source.

Monsignor Biancheri, the Vicar-Apostolic, died suddenly on the 11th, of heart disease. He had been suffering for some time from palpitation, and the intense heat probably hastened his death. Dr. Blanc and I attended the funeral the following day. The body was to be interred in the Latin church; but the grave was not ready, owing to the difficulty of excavating in the madrepore and sandstone, of which the Island is composed. Padre Delmonte celebrated high mass and read the burial service, leaving the body to be interred after the dismissal of the congregation.

The shock of an earthquake was felt here at 11·15 P.M. of the 14th, and another on the following day at 1·45 P.M.

As the contradictory rumours which had hitherto reached us from the interior began to lull, I dispatched several messengers to Tigrê to try and collect some intelligence respecting the King and the condition of the captives; also, to discover what had become of the former messengers whom I had sent to his Majesty. The delay was most irksome, and we longed for the time when we should be free to start on our journey.

At this period I made the acquaintance of one Hajj Âdam Korman, an Abyssinian, formerly the principal Mohammedan merchant at Góndar. This man hated Theodore so intensely that a word spoken in his favour made him mad with rage. According to his own account, a love affair was the cause of his bitter enmity to his liege lord. To listen to his eulogies of his lost wife, one would scarcely believe that he had found a substitute in a purchased Galla slave; but such was the fact. His wife, he told me, was reckoned one of the handsomest women of the Abyssinian capital. He had known her from childhood, and had married her from pure affection. Her charms, however, coming to the knowledge of the King—that "scourge of human kind"—he forthwith coveted her, although already possessed of more than a hundred wives. Taking advantage of his absence at the coast, whither he had repaired for the annual fair, his Majesty had taken his beauty to live with him, and, what was worse, had made her abjure the religion of her fore-fathers. He further averred that the King had become so enamoured of her attractions, that he had raised her to the dignity of his favourite consort. On expressing my surprise that, with such ardent reminiscences of his lost love, he could ever have thought of marrying again, the Hajj devoutly replied: "You Christians are unable to appreciate the religious obligations of us Mussulmans; besides, without a wife, who would cook my food and wash my feet?"

I learnt the real facts of this case during my subsequent residence at the Abyssinian Court. It appears that shortly after Hajj Âdam's departure from Góndar, the King was informed that he had been intriguing with the rebels, and had supplied them with fire-arms. Some muskets and pistols being discovered in the house which he occupied, Theodore ordered all his property to be confiscated; and as a wife in Abyssinia is reckoned among a husband's goods and chattels, she was removed into the royal establishment, not as a consort to the King, but as a kitchen domestic, in which capacity she was serving when ·I visited his Majesty in the beginning of 1866.

This Góndar merchant was very useful during my sojourn at Massowah, supplying me generally with the most trustworthy information, and also procuring messengers for me. The latter service he affected to render somewhat unwillingly, deeming it a sin to promote a meeting between one of his friends and " the arch-enemy of the human race."

16*th*.—Three German naturalists arrived from Egypt with the intention of proceeding into Abyssinia, to collect zoological specimens of the country. They brought scarcely any money with them, expecting to live on the game which they shot, and to return to Europe with sufficient spoil to enrich themselves. It is a curious fact that, during the reign of Theodore, a number of European adventurers had made their way into Abyssinia with the sole object of gain. Even some foreign officials had gone there with very limited resources—a circumstance by no means calculated to give the Abyssinians or their haughty Sovereign a high opinion of their visitors. It was probably owing to his previous experience in this respect, that his Majesty, whose policy it was to exalt the dignity of our Mission to him in the eyes of his subjects, was most anxious, during my subsequent stay with him, that I should be well supplied with money, insisting on my receiving large sums from him rather than that I should be driven to borrow from them.

Purtoo Effendi, the Governor, to our sincere regret, left to-day for Jiddah. He was quite recovered from his late malady, but owing to the intense heat and poor living at the place could not regain tone, which he hoped the sea voyage, and a short residence in the hills of the Hijâz would restore. Before his departure, he appointed 'Abdallah-Khalîl, the principal merchant at Massowah, with the sanction of the Mecca authorities, to act for him until the arrival of a successor, and strongly recommended us to him, as also to the members of the local council and to the Turkish officials. Blanc and I accompanied him to the native vessel, where we bade him farewell.

One of the Germans who came to Massowah on the 16th died two days after, from sun-stroke. We saw him from the deck of the 'Dalhousie,' at about ten in the morning, crossing with his comrades from the Island to the mainland, on their way to the interior, dressed in a black suit of clothes. It appears that he fell after walking a few hundred yards in the scorching sun. He was carried back to Massowah, and expired immediately at Mr. Munzinger's house. Dr. Blanc hastened to his assistance, but before his arrival the poor fellow was beyond medical aid. He was buried the same afternoon on the islet to the west of Massowah, the only spot where Christians are allowed to bury. An exception had been made in the case of the late Vicar-Apostolic, who was interred in the church; but that was owing to the enlightened and liberal views of Purtoo Effendi. The Italian Mission had met with great difficulty in obtaining permission to erect the church, the fanatics of Massowah protesting against such an encroachment of the "infidels" on holy ground—for such they traditionally regard their island, though on what historical basis I could never discover. Purtoo Effendi, however, is stated to have cut the matter short by saying, that as Mussulmans were bound to call a Christian church "the house of God," there could be no sin in allowing one to be built at Massowah; and the work was accordingly commenced under his auspices.

The enterprise of the German naturalists was brought to a sudden termination by the death of their chief. The remainder, after disposing by auction of what little property they had, left the place in disgust.

19th.—T'issoo Hailo, the head of the Abyssinian merchants trading with Massowah, who had come down with the last caravan from Góndar, paid me a visit. This was the first time that an Abyssinian Christian, who intended to return home, had mustered up courage to come and see me. He brought me, as an introductory present, a horn of *téj*—mead, the common beverage of the upper classes in Abyssinia—which, by the way, was as sour as vinegar. I treated him in return with a glass of Curaçoa, which he admitted to be superior to anything he had ever tasted in his own country. On asking him to give me some information respecting the cause of Consul Cameron's imprisonment, he well-nigh went off in a fit, through excessive fear; and the only answer I could elicit from him was a faltering—"A—a—alawkim! alawkim!"—I don't know! In fact, he was so upset, that he did not collect his senses until I had repeatedly assured him that my interpreter was a trustworthy person, who would not repeat what had passed between us. A superstitious belief prevailed among the ignorant, both at Massowah and in the interior, that Theodore possessed the faculty of knowing what was said of him miles away; hence, such of his detractors as intended returning to his territories were very cautious not to utter a word against him. Purtoo Effendi had been so vexed with the insuperable reticence of T'issoo Hailo, that he assured him no spirits would dare to approach his residence, or carry any report to Góndar. This man was afterwards chained and sent a prisoner to Mágdala by order of the King, after surrendering to him all he possessed, and was ultimately one of those who were released when that fortress fell into the hands of the British.

News reached us from the interior that, under the pretext of the inhabitants of Góndar having refused to pay the usual taxes, the King had ordered that city to be sacked, and the houses of the principal families to be destroyed; that this outrage, combined with small-pox and typhus fever, had well-nigh ruined the capital; and that most of the residents had fled the place and sought shelter elsewhere. It was further reported that the King's treachery and cruelty, apparently dictated by sheer caprice, had alienated all his friends, and that his soldiers were deserting him by hundreds.

2nd October.—Our Abyssinian visitors began to increase daily, and T'issoo Hailo was always agreeable, provided nothing was said about our Mission, and no allusion made to his Sovereign. To-day, the messengers whom I had despatched to Tigrê in quest of intelligence respecting the captives and my previous couriers returned without any reliable information. They had heard that the latter had reached the King, and that Cameron and the Missionaries were still in prison; that, owing to the spread of rebellion on all sides against his Majesty, travellers found it difficult to pass from one district to another, and that nothing short of the King himself coming as far as Tigrê to meet us would ensure our safe advance into the country; that T'issoo Gobazê, the chief rebel of Walkaït, was encamping with a large force on the Tăkkăzê, whilst the Wakshum Gobazê, the leader of the rebellion in Lasta, had stopped the other highroad on the eastern borders of Abyssinia.

As the Góndar merchants were beginning to feel more

at their ease with me, and had expressed a wish to see a steamer in motion, I invited them to accompany us on a short cruise to the neighbouring island of Dissee, where I was going to return the visit of a native chief. I was glad to have it in my power to gratify T'issoo Hailo, especially as he was one of the merchants who had contributed towards the ransom of the late Consul Plowden, when the latter was wounded and taken prisoner by the rebels under the King's relative, Gárad, a few days before his lamented death. Everything was prepared for the entertainment of my expected guests in the Abyssinian style; but just as the 'Dalhousie' weighed anchor—about noon of the 4th of October—intelligence reached us that they had changed their minds and could not come. It appears that when they were on the point of starting, a bystander remarked, "What will the King say when he hears of your friendship with the English? Would he not say that you had gone out in their vessel in order to mature some plot against him?" The bare suspicion of such an idea being entertained was enough to inspire them with dread; but when the suggestion was expressed openly, they, very excusably, felt that to proceed further might expose them to the vengeance of their ruthless Sovereign.

We reached Dissee at 5 P.M., and anchored off the inhabited part of the island, on its western side. The chief was absent on the mainland, settling some dispute between his tribe and the Danâkil. Landing the following morning, we saw the so-called town—a miserable collection of tumble-down huts, with scarcely any life stirring, except what may have been in a few starved goats and fowls that strayed among them. We next visited the springs, situated between two hills about a mile from the hamlet, where we found a number of women trying to collect a little water by digging holes in the soil. These springs are generally very copious, but owing to scarcity of rain this year they were well-nigh dry, and what vegetation there was on the island was utterly parched. Lord Valentia thought fit to call Dissee by his own name, which, as might be expected, is quite unknown to the natives. The island was claimed by the French a few years ago, in virtue of its having been presented to them by the great Tigrê rebel, Agów-Negûsê; but the sagacious policy of Purtoo Effendi secured its continuance under the sovereignty of the Sublime Porte.

10*th.*—In fulfilment of a previous engagement, Dr. Blanc and I started from Massowah to visit Mohammed-bin-'Abd-ur-Rahîm, the Nâyib of Harkîko, accompanied by Ahmed Aráy, the chief of the Dánkali coast between Massowah and Raheita. The breeze being light, it took us two hours to cross the intervening four miles to the mainland. On the beach we were met by Mohammed Âdam, the cousin and presumptive successor to the Nâyib, and other local notables. We rode on mules provided for our accommodation, and on reaching the door of his residence were received very cordially by the Nâyib in person. The inclosure had been watered and a number of sofas placed outside the house for our greater comfort against the heat. Soon after our arrival we were visited by Idrîs Hásan, the rival Nâyib. I give him this title because the Turkish authorities, in furtherance of their policy, have divided the family into two factions, so that when dissatisfied with one party they can always rely on the other. In like manner, the respective representatives of England and France are said to have had each his favourite Nâyib for some time past; hence, it appears that our host was known as the "friend of the English," in con-

tradistinction to his kinsman, the "ally of the French." As
far as I was concerned, both vied in their attentions, and
the courtesy was reciprocated on my part. We all dined
together in the Turkish style called *kaldur-koy*, (literally,
take up, put down), in accordance with which the dishes—
there were fifteen on this occasion—are placed successively
on the table one by one, and removed after the guests have
partaken of each.

We spent part of the following day very pleasantly with
our host, and after returning the ex-Nâyib's visit, and
sipping a cup of coffee with him, mounted our mules and
ambled off towards Massowah by the landward route, a
distance of about six miles. The Mudîr Ahmed Aráy and
Mohammed Âdam, who accompanied us to the pier, expressing a wish to see the inside of a steamer, I took them on
board, and Lieut. Morland was kind enough to satisfy their
curiosity. What excited their surprise more than anything
else was the fact that the vessel was constructed entirely of
iron. "There is no god but the God, and Mohammed is His
apostle!", exclaimed one of them. "What wonderful
people these English are, who can cause even iron to float!"

While staying with the Nâyib, I could not help contrasting our circumstances with those of Bruce a century ago.
He describes the Nâyib of his time as a bigoted fanatic and
bitter enemy of Christianity, who did all in his power to
prevent the intrepid traveller from proceeding into the
interior; whereas his descendant and successor deems it an
honour to entertain our Mission, and does his best to assist
us in prosecuting our journey.

The Nâyib Mohammed was a great admirer of the Abyssinian Sovereign, despite some rather rough treatment which
he had received at his hands. This occurred at the time of

the disgrace of M. Lejean, the French agent who visited Theodore in 1863. At that period Purtoo Effendi, judging that the establishment of friendly relations with the King would materially facilitate his rule over the districts on the north-eastern border of Abyssinia subject to Massowah, and that he could not select a more acceptable agent than the Nâyib Mohammed, who was already personally known to his Majesty, dispatched him to Góndar with suitable presents, after obtaining a safe-conduct for him. The King received him very well and treated him with every distinction, but it was not in him to suffer a visitor to depart in peace. The Governor had limited the stay of his agent to a few days; but, under one pretext or another, he had already been detained six weeks at the royal Court. Becoming somewhat impatient, he begged the King to allow him to leave; but his Majesty was not so inclined, and said that he was anxious to enjoy his guest's society a little longer. The Nâyib, in reply, expressed regret that he could not prolong his stay, inasmuch as he was a subordinate of the Governor of Massowah, who had expressly ordered him not to prolong his sojourn in Abyssinia. Whereupon the King flew into a violent rage, saying, "How dare you admit that the Turks are your masters? Are they not my slaves, and the slaves of my forefathers? Seize the fellow who calls himself a Turk, and I shall see if his masters will venture to come and release him." After an incarceration of forty-one days he was liberated and brought before his Majesty, who forthwith apologised for his recent conduct, and begged to be forgiven. The Nâyib told me that he narrowly escaped a remand for attempting to remonstrate against the injustice with which he had been treated. Fortunately, some friends whispered to him to forbear, and he held his tongue. Next day the

my arrival I dispatched a letter to you by two messengers, named severally Mohammed Abawâs and Mohammed Sa'îd; but up to this time I have received no answer thereto. I hope that the cause is propitious.

"Different reports reach me daily regarding this delay, and a rumour has been current that the messengers did not succeed in reaching you, owing to some people on the road having intimidated them against approaching you. It is also suggested that perhaps the letter was handed to some individual who failed to deliver it to you. For this reason, I now write to you again, and enclose herewith a copy of my former communication, which may not have reached you, in order that you may learn its purport.

"As the Nâyib Mohammed-bin-'Abd-ur-Rahîm has proved himself to be a faithful adherent of mine, and also a sincere friend of your Majesty, I send this letter through him, he having, on account of the regard which he entertains towards our great English Government, as well as towards yourself, undertaken to forward it to you safely and speedily.

"I beg you to honour me with an answer soon, and to let me know what are your intentions regarding the duty on which I have been sent by our English Government. Thereby I shall be greatly obliged to your Majesty."

After the dispatch of the foregoing letter, conflicting rumours were again rife respecting my messengers and the King's proceedings, to detail which would be an endless task; but I must mention a circumstance that occurred about this time, which has been somewhat distorted. Two messengers, who alleged that they had formerly been in Consul Cameron's service, came to me within a few days of each other, representing themselves as bearers of messages from their late master. One stated that he was commissioned to request me to send Cameron some money and sugar; and the other that, in the event of my being sent to obtain the release of the captives, I was to write civilly to the King. They both decamped before I could give them an answer, and it was consequently supposed at the time that they were spies sent down by Theodore. I found out subsequently, however, that these two men had been in the Consul's employ, and that their sudden disappearance was due to the interpreter, who, instead of desiring them to wait, as I had directed him, told them that they were to wait, until I had made some inquiries about them. Fearing, it appears, that my inquiries might lead to their punishment for having left the Consul's service, they thought it best to place themselves beyond my reach. Not long after this, I had to employ Wald-Máryam, the first-named, through Mr. Munzinger, to convey supplies to the captives; and although he turned out to be a most troublesome scamp, nevertheless he was the first messenger who succeeded in communicating with the captives, and in bringing notes from them. He proved so dangerous eventually, that I was compelled to have him detained at Aden, on our starting for the interior, in order to keep him out of mischief. It appeared also that the other messenger, who was a native of Tigrê, and had proceeded to Aden and India, really did intend to give advice as to the style in which we ought to address the King. He declares, however, that he did not represent himself as having been sent by the Consul, and that if the interpreter had said so, he must have misunderstood him. I trust that the foregoing account will dispose of the question about these spies, and the mysterious errand on which it was fancied they were engaged.

21st.—There was a severe shock of an earthquake at 8·45 this morning. The vibration was so strong that Blanc and I rushed out of the house, fearing that it might fall upon us. The weather was bearable now: it begins to get cool at Massowah from the middle of October, when the nights especially are tolerably pleasant, the mercury falling about ten degrees lower than during the hot season. Nevertheless, the sun in this region seems to be equally powerful all the year round.

25th.—News reached Massowah to-day that the Muslims of Barca, the hereditary enemies of the Christian Abyssinians, had attacked the district of Bogôs and carried off several herds of cattle and about 120 boys and girls as slaves, after killing many men, women and children. These raids are of frequent occurrence, the Mohammedans and Christians assuming the offensive by turns; the latter, I was sorry to learn, being as ready to engage in them as the former. Foreign interference, instead of quenching the old enmity between these rival tribes, has only embittered it, and their annual conflicts are reported to be more bloody and merciless. As the Barca people are subject to Egypt, the Viceroy's Government might easily put an end to the practice of obtaining slaves in this way by severely punishing any tribe found guilty of carrying off the persons of their Christian neighbours.

Nov. 5th.—The 'Dalhousie' started this morning for Aden for provisions, as, now that the north-west monsoon has set in, no native boat will venture beyond the straits of Bâb-ul-Mandeb. Dr. Blanc proceeded in her for change of air, having suffered a long time from general debility, brought on by the climate.

11th.—A report reached Massowah that a "French General"—a "Count du Bisson"—had arrived on the northern border of Abyssinia with a large body of followers, intending to establish themselves in Hamasên, an Abyssinian district to the north of Tigrê. It was further stated that the governors of those districts were preparing troops to attack the adventurers, and had dispatched messengers to apprise the King of the movements of the " Franks."

It appears that this Count du Bisson had come into the same neighbourhood some fifteen months before, with about forty Europeans, picked up in Egypt and elsewhere, to assist him in forming a colony. Meeting with strong opposition from the natives, he abandoned the scheme and returned to Egypt, leaving his followers, who were utterly destitute, to find their way back as best they could. Some of the Count's letters at this period, about Theodore and Abyssinian affairs generally, which appeared in a French journal, and alleged to be founded on information received from strange officers of high rank in that country, afforded us a fund of amusement, owing to the stupid and barefaced inventions which formed the staple of the correspondence. The "General" must be a simple man indeed, and one easily hoaxed, if he himself really credited the fictions which he was induced to publish. Be that as it may, the report that he had come back into the neighbourhood of Hamasên afforded Theodore a good excuse at the time, as we subsequently heard, for retracting the promise which he had made to his European artisans at Gáffat to release Consul Cameron and the Missionaries. As it is morally certain, moreover, that his Majesty never intended to keep his word, the intelligence of the Count's movements came opportunely to prevent the Gáffat people from falling into disgrace by interceding in behalf of his " enemies," the captives.

16th.—The ' Dalhousie ' returned from Aden in the evening, bringing back Lieutenant Morland and Dr. Blanc, who had both benefited by the trip. Mrs. Blanc also accompanied her husband, and intended to remain with him until we started for Góndar. The addition of a lady is an acquisition to any society; in the present case it was especially so, owing to the monotony of the place, which Mrs. Blanc's genial frankness and kindly disposition did much to alleviate.

Dr. Blanc and I accompanied Lieut. Morland to the mainland to try a two-horse waggonnette which the latter had brought from Aden. There being no made roads in this country, I leave the reader to fancy what a tossing about we had, in danger every moment of being precipitated from our seats. The natives looked on and wondered, never having seen such an equipage before; while the water-girls seemed struck with awe, believing the "large chair" to be the mystical conveyance in which they are to be transported to Paradise after their worldly toil is ended. Some were so terrified that no arguments or entreaties would induce them to stand and watch the vehicle.

20th.—Dr. and Mrs. Blanc accompanied me on a visit to the Commissioner of Customs, the only Turkish official then on the Island. Our host being a strict Mussulman, the gentlemen, of course, were not admitted into the Harîm; but we were treated to coffee and sherbet, and Mrs. Blanc was similarly entertained by the lady, a native of Damascus. On our return to the shore, we were nearly run down by a large sailing-boat which was crossing to the mainland, windward of us. The Kâyim-Makâm ordered the whole of the crew to be imprisoned, in spite of their plea that the accident was to be attributed to the agency of Providence. He released them the next day at our solicitation.

The ex-Nâyib Idrîs having invited Dr. and Mrs. Blanc and me to spend a day or two at his house at Harkîko, we sailed thither in the afternoon. Every necessary preparation had been made for carrying the lady from the boat to the shore, and on landing we were met by a troop of elders and attendants to escort us, with mules for our use. Our kind host welcomed us outside his residence, and on entering the house we noticed that several changes had been made in its internal arrangements for our greater comfort and accommodation. Mrs. Blanc was at first received by the Harîm, but as there was no one to interpret between her and the ladies—about fifty in number—who were huddled together within a confined space most effectually hemmed in against intruders from without, she preferred joining us, and was at once accommodated with a seat by the courteous ex-Nâyib, who also provided her with a separate room. In the evening he gave us a sumptuous dinner in the *kaldur-koy* style, at which the *de facto* Nâyib, Mohammed-bin-'Abd-ur-Rahîm, was present. Although both Nâyibs are regarded as rigid Mussulmans, they made no scruple about dining with a lady, and merely remarked that Franks held the fair sex in high esteem and treated them as equals —an example which they feared might tend to spoil their own wives.

The night we spent at Harkîko was quite cold, and the awning under which we slept was wet through with dew in the morning. In the afternoon the Harîm of both Nâyibs called on Mrs. Blanc—another inroad upon the social customs of Islâm which I was hardly prepared to witness in these regions. After this interchange of civilities, we started on our return journey, both Nâyibs riding with us part of the way, and leaving their brothers to accompany us to the pier.

On the 23rd Dr. Blanc and I took up our residence at Moncûlu; he and Mrs. Blanc occupying the French Consulate, which had been lent to them by Padre Delmonte, while I located myself in Mr. Munzinger's house on a hill opposite, which the owner had kindly placed at my disposal for a time.   The day following, Wald-Máryam, whom I had sent up to communicate with the captives, returned to say that he had accomplished that object—a statement which proved afterwards to be utterly false.   He reported that he found the Consul in chains, and had been directed by him to request me to send him some rice and sugar, and that I was not to attempt making my way to Góndar until he wrote to me on the subject; that the Consul was afraid to write to me in English, but that he had got an Abyssinian to write in Amharic to Mr. Munzinger; and that the messenger, finding on his arrival at Bogôs that Mr. Munzinger was absent at Massowah, had left the letter at his house.

Although this information was by no means satisfactory, I decided to act upon it, especially as no trustworthy messenger was willing to venture up to Góndar.   I accordingly dispatched the man again with a sum of money and other supplies, and promised him a handsome present if he succeeded in bringing back a few lines from the captives.   I also gave him a slip of paper to sew up in his trowsers, as his credentials to the Consul that he was sent by me.

Dec. 3rd.—The transport steamer 'Victoria,' commanded by Lieut. Carpendale of the late Indian Navy, arrived this morning to relieve the 'Dalhousie,' which was required at Bombay.   As Lieut. Morland intended to start on the 5th, he invited us to spend the evening and the following day with him.   The party was increased by a couple of old Aden acquaintances, who had come up for a trip in the 'Victoria,' and after a most pleasant visit we took a final leave of our hospitable host.

12th.—On my way back from Blanc's house, at about ten o'clock in the evening, I saw droves of hyænas hurrying impetuously on all sides in the direction of Hittimlo. On inquiring of a passer-by what these animals were about, he told me that their agent among the *jinn* (or spirits) had probably informed them of the death of some domestic quadruped, on which they were going to feast. He demurred at first to guide me to the spot, alleging that it was dangerous to approach those "imps of Satan," who, if not satisfied with the carcass provided, might finish their meal by devouring us; however, he ultimately consented to accompany me. The moon was at the full, and we could see objects very distinctly. He led me straight to the spot, and a sight more horrible can hardly be conceived; for some time I fancied that we must be in the infernal regions. An unfortunate horse had strayed into a ravine beyond the village, where the hyænas had attacked him, and where they were now, upwards of a hundred in number, fighting over the prey. Their ferocious looks, lit up by the light of the moon, their diabolical yells, their savage snapping and snarling, the wild cries of fresh competitors hastening from all directions to the repast, formed together a scene of surpassing hideousness. I had some fear at first that they would attack us, for on our approach they retired from the carcass and eyed us with fierce malignity. Had they done so, I should have rushed at them, which is said to be the most effectual way of driving them off. These brutes abound in the plain around Massowah, and are so strong that a couple will move the body of a mule or horse with the greatest ease. About the time of which I am writing, there had been a great mortality among the riding-animals of the place, from ten to fifteen dying daily; nevertheless, nothing but the bare skeletons were left by the hyænas the following morning. They are so numerous and ravenous in the neighbourhood, that the inhabitants are obliged to secure their cattle within a strong fence, and even that precaution does not always ward off their attacks. Children also have been seized by them when found unprotected. During my sojourn, two mules belonging to the Nâyib were attacked inside a stable, and one of them—a gift from Theodore—had to forfeit a part of her hind-quarter before she could get rid of the beast, with the assistance of her keeper.

These hyænas are very sagacious, and have a regular code of howling signals, when abroad during the night. They have one cry when hungry and looking for prey; another, when they scent a feast awaiting them ; and a third, not unlike the human laugh, when they are satisfied. I have tested this characteristic, both at Massowah and at Matámma, and am fully convinced that the above statement is correct.

15th.—Another European attached to the Roman Catholic Mission died to-day. It rained heavily last night : this was the first shower which had fallen since our arrival at Massowah. The weather in consequence was much cooler.

18th.—The private messenger whom I had sent to Góndar, on the 28th of October, returned to day without having been able to communicate with the captives. He informed me that the King had gone to subdue a rebellion which had broken out in Shoa, and had placed Consul Cameron and the other European captives in a mountain fortress, called Mágdala; that he did not go there himself, because he had heard that there was no chance of his being allowed to hold any intercourse with the captives; but that he had seen a missionary, named Flad, who was living with the King's European artisans at Gaffat, who had told him that there was no hope of the release of the prisoners until his

Majesty received a reply to his letter from the Queen of England; that both batches of my messengers had reached safely, and had been well received by the King, who had made them over to an official, to be provided with food and lodgings; and that the captives were all well.

25th.—A dreary Christmas, although Mrs. Blanc did her best to enliven it by inviting the small European community to dinner. In the morning, a Mohammedan Abyssinian, a highly respectable merchant of Dhurita, about thirty miles S.S.E. of Góndar, called upon me, and gave me some information about the King and my messengers. He was present at the royal Court when the first party arrived and delivered my letter to his Majesty, who thereupon consigned them to one of his followers to be provided for. He had seen the European prisoners on several occasions, but had not spoken to them. Though chained, they all looked well. He spoke of Theodore as a man of very variable temperament: he might never reply to my letter or release the prisoners, or he might do both at any moment. In reply to a question whether there was any person at the Court, or in the country, who had any influence with his Majesty, or could assist us, he stated that the present Sovereign of Abyssinia never took any one into his confidence, and that none of his subjects would dare to tender him advice or solicit a favour at his hands, knowing that he would not listen to the one, and would certainly refuse the other. He assured me, that if I went to the King, he would treat me courteously, but he warned me against acting in opposition to his wishes; that his Majesty respected those who spoke the truth and were straightforward in their conduct, and that the reason he did not trust his own people was, that they were depraved and liars. This testimony from one who appeared well-acquainted with the King led me to hope that his Majesty's character was not quite as black as it had been generally described.

Theodore, it appears, had taken a great fancy to my visitor, in consequence of a clever answer of his to an order which his Majesty had given, directing that he and all his co-religionists at Dharîta should, under pain of death, receive Christian baptism. Though a conscientious Muslim, he had a strong objection to losing his head, and accordingly solicited permission to say a few words on the subject. That being accorded, he proceeded to observe, "How can your Majesty lay claim to being a great Sovereign, if you have only Christians for your subjects, while your neighbours, the Turks, have Mohammedans and Jews, as well as Christians? The Mohammedans of Dharîta comprise only a few families, and it is not of much consequence what religion they profess; but would you be able to say to your enemies, after making all your people of one faith, that you are as great a king as any of your predecessors, who had no less than four denominations under their sway, namely, Christians, Mohammedans, Jews, and Kamáwnts?" This ready reply so pleased Theodore, that he burst into a fit of laughter, and then said to the man, "You are a witty fellow, and may remain what you are; for I know there are many worse among my people, who call themselves Christians."

26th.—Having learnt that there were two gentlemen among the Europeans at Gáffat, Messrs. Flad and Schimper, who had befriended the captives, I wrote to them, asking them to let me know, if possible, the cause of the King's displeasure, his reason for not answering me, and what, in their opinion, would be the best way to obtain the release of the captives.

1st January, 1865.—The dullest New-Year's day in my life, despite the social gathering at Mrs. Blanc's hospitable house. The epidemic among the riding animals rages more fatally than ever. Lieut. Carpendale's horse, which he had sent into the mountains, died to-day in a mad 'fit, and many of the merchants, whose business calls them daily into Massowah, are greatly inconvenienced by the loss of their animals. There are only a few mules left in the place, most of them having been sent into the mountains to escape contagion.

From the 2nd to the 4th, while we were the guests of Lieut. Carpendale, the wife of the Commissioner of Customs, accompanied by several other native ladies, called on Mrs. Blanc and spent a day on board the ' Victoria.' They were shown over the steamer, which excited their admiring wonder; but some of them were dreadfully frightened when taken into the furnace-room.

On the 7th, Blanc, Carpendale and I set out on a visit to the hot-springs of Ailât, situated about thirty miles from Massowah. The Kâyim-Makâm, having heard of our intention of spending a few days there, ordered the Nâyib of Harkîko, and the Mudîr of the Danâkil to accompany us. They joined us in the afternoon with a large escort, as we were on the point of starting. After travelling about twelve· miles, we encamped for the night at a place called Sahâtee, near some puddles of water, which was neither agreeable to the smell or taste. At the Nâyib's suggestion, one of the puddles near a large boulder, in the dry bed of the torrent, was deepened, and to our delight an abundant supply of good water was obtained. There was a running stream hard by, but the water was brackish.

8th.—At daybreak this morning, the mercury fell to 68°,

but as soon as the sun was fairly up, it rose to 93° in the shade. We started from Sahâtee at 4·40 P.M., and reached Ailât at 7·25, when we halted to quench our thirst. Water was brought, and also milk; but we hesitated which to prefer, for the water was muddy and foul, and the milk sour and smoked. Continuing our journey for an hour, we reached the stream of Ailât, and ascending the valley as far as we could, pitched our tents on a level spot about a mile and a-half below the hot-springs.

The route during the latter part of the day's march was through a densely wooded country, and although very little rain had fallen hereabouts for the last two years, the trees were beautifully green. A stranger at Massowah could hardly believe such scenery to exist within fifteen miles of that arid spot; the only drawback is the intense heat of the climate. The wood teems with a great variety of game; but the thorny acacia, which abounds in all directions, is a serious hindrance to the sportsman. It is much to be regretted that the local authorities at Massowah take so little interest in promoting the welfare of the people in this quarter. With a little assistance, and adequate protection from the inroads of their beggarly neighbours, the peasantry here might soon convert this wilderness into a garden.

9th.—We went out for a little shooting in the afternoon; but although the game was abundant, consisting of antelopes of different species, hares, wild-boars, partridges, guineafowl, &c., we were very unsuccessful, mainly owing to the difficulty of forcing our way through the tangled bushes. But our old friend, the native sportsman, who was also with us on this occasion, came back laden up to the ears with game, among which was an enormous wild goose.

10th.—The Nâyib and the Mudîr accompanied me this

morning with a large body of followers on a shooting excursion in the direction of the highlands. After an hour's walk we reached another spring called Ikwâr. We had taken our mules with us, but the country was so thickly wooded that riding was out of the question; indeed, we found it a hard task to make our way on foot through the thorny forest. The route led through a pretty valley, and at Ikwâr we found a running stream in which numbers of diminutive fish were disporting, wherever the water was deep. The water itself was delicious, and the whole scene formed so striking a contrast to what I had experienced for years past, that I sat on a rock under the shade of overhanging trees, inhaling the fresh breeze which murmured through the glen, oblivious for the time of aught but present enjoyment. The ripple of the brook and the balmy air had nearly lulled me to sleep, when the guides aroused me, and on pursuing our journey over an adjoining hill we came upon a nomad encampment situated in another valley at its base. Grass grew luxuriantly all around, and the cattle were grazing close to the huts. The chief of the clan received us very civilly, and pressed us to spend the day with him, but we were obliged to decline his hospitality. I had just time to save the life of a beautiful little cow which was feeding with its companions, and which was on the point of being slaughtered for our entertainment. However, gallantry forbade my refusing to drink of the milk which some pretty half-clad damsels brought us in abundance. Here, as in Abyssinia, most of the drinking vessels used by the lower classes are made of straw, so closely interwoven as to be thoroughly water-tight. These baskets seldom spoil even by long disuse, and being little liable to break are admirably adapted to the domestic economy of the wandering population.

I may mention here, that all the nomad tribes in this part of Africa use moveable huts, of a circular shape, with domed roofs. The ribs consist of willow or cane, which are bent into shape while green. Each family carries these sticks, and, on encamping, the straight end is driven into the ground and the curves brought together and bound over-head, and are then covered with dry grass or matting. A hut of this description can be taken to pieces and re-erected in less than an hour; and one affording accommodation for a married couple with two children is borne by one bullock. Many of the soldiers of the late King Theodore adopted this kind of hut when on a war expedition.

We next proceeded to a thicket where we were told we should meet with wild boar. On nearing the spot, our old friend the sportsman shouted out, " Stand still! Be quiet!" intimating to us that he had espied a herd burrowing for roots. I jumped off my mule at once and went in pursuit on foot, and, coming suddenly on a different group, was about to fire, when the guide bawled out so loud that I was aiming in a wrong direction, that the wily brutes got scent of us and scampered off into the thick cover close by. During the excursion I only succeeded in bagging a guinea-fowl; but the sportsman had got so excited on seeing the larger game escape, that he would not return with me, swearing by the beard of the Prophet that he would lessen the number of the " unclean " by one at least, before he desisted. He was as good as his word; for towards sunset he brought in a wild sow on a camel, which he had hired from the wandering tribe. Our Mussulman friends eyed the trophy with disgust; not so their Christian companions, who looked forward with no small relish to a fresh pork-steak—a dainty we had not enjoyed for many a long day.

We found the temperature of the hot-spring to be 140°, and the water was so pure that we used it during our stay at Ailât for drinking, after leaving it to cool. In the evening a messenger came from Massowah to report the arrival of the 'Pantaloon,' and another from Mr. Munzinger apprising me that as he was about to return to Massowah he would require the use of the house which he had kindly lent me during his absence. He also enclosed me a French translation of the Amharic letter, which was brought to him while at Bogôs, purporting to have been sent by Consul Cameron, as already stated. We found out afterwards that this letter was forged at the instance of the messenger, who had hoped thereby to induce me to trust him with a large sum of money for the captives, which he intended to appropriate to his own use.

On the trip above described, Lieut. Carpendale took out with him an Abyssinian sportsman, who went by the name of " Karkîs," a corruption the native of " Guarghîs "— George. The man was accompanied by his son, Dasta, a lad about fourteen years old, who generally stationed himself under a tree near our tent, during the excursion, where I used to see him daily, busily engaged in cooking. His diligence and activity attracted my attention, and as he spoke Arabic well, I took an interest in him. On our way back to Massowah, I noticed that he carried all his father's and his own effects as well as the kitchen apparatus; yet with that load on his back he kept pace with the mules. I was anxious to take him into my employ, but hesitated to do so for fear of displeasing his father. A few days after our return to Massowah, I met him on the road to Moncûlu, carrying a bundle for a notorious Abyssinian woman, named Iskâl, who, I believe, had already changed her religion twice for the sake of a husband, and was now ready to embrace Judaism or even heathenism to secure another, although her first Christian lord and master had returned to regain, if he might, her forfeited affection, or, failing that, to bask in the light of her countenance. On learning from the lad that his father had made him over to Iskâl to assist her in entertaining Abyssinian travellers—she was then acting as innkeeper—I asked whether he would take service with me, as my personal muleteer. He was delighted with the proposal; and on my bidding him to get leave to come to me, he flared up and said, " Am I a slave that I must needs ask permission to serve you ? Thank God, I am a free-born Christian." However, I eventually obtained Iskâl's full consent to the arrangement. The lad entertained me on our way to Moncûlu, on that occasion, with stories about the mighty Theodore. On asking him whether the King's power was not on the decline, he replied: " Master, don't believe either our common enemies, the Mussulmans, or the depraved Abyssinians who would make you think so. Despite his dementation, he is a great sovereign, and I am sure you will like him when you see him. As to the report that his soldiers are deserting him, and that the rebels are getting the upperhand, rest assured that he has only to move against them and they will be scattered to the winds like this breath,"—breathing vehemently himself as he uttered the last word. Finding, after he had served me for a fortnight as muleteer, that he was fit for something better, I made him private interpreter. He knew four languages well: Arabic, Amharic, and Tigrêan both of the highlands and lowlands of Abyssinia—the first-named Tigrêan was his mother tongue, he being a native of Adwa; the latter is the dialect which prevails at Massowah and in the adjacent districts. He could also read and write Amharic, and after consorting with an Indian servant a few months he was able to speak Hindostanee. On our release from captivity, I asked him to accompany me to England, but his wise answer was, "Master, why should I go with you to that strange land, where I shall be of no use to you, but rather an incumbrance?" I cannot speak too highly of this lad's integrity and fidelity. I believe that had the King tortured him to death—and it was apprehended at one time by the Abyssinians that he would proceed to extremities with my servants to induce them to divulge what they knew of my transactions at Mágdala—he would not have betrayed his master. I enter into these minute particulars of the incidents which first led me to engage this young interpreter, because his name will frequently occur in the succeeding narrative. On our way down from Mágdala to Massowah, whilst conversing about the wretched existence which Theodore must have led during the last few months of his life, I remarked that, had he not made away with himself, he might have lived to be a better man. To this Dasta replied, with unusual warmth: "How can you say so, Master? Is not God merciful, and being so, how could He any longer spare a man whose career has been spent in shedding innocent blood; in bereaving thousands of parents of their children, and children of their parents; wives of their husbands, and husbands of their wives? Far be it from a merciful God to vouchsafe time for repentance to such a one, in order that he might escape punishment both in this world and the next!" As this appeal involved a nice theological question, I judged it best to drop the subject.

11th.—A new Kâyim-Makâm reached Massowah. On his arrival he immediately sent to inform the Nâyib and the

Mudîr that they were to remain with us until our return. On our way back, two days later, we were overtaken by a heavy shower after passing Sahâtee; but to our surprise not a drop of rain had fallen within four miles of Moncûlu, which looked more dry and dreary than ever.

14*th.*—After moving into the British Consulate at Moncûlu—which I had caused to be put in thorough repair—I went to Massowah to call upon Captain Purvis, who had been dispatched from Aden by Colonel Merewether to inquire whether any fresh news of the captives was forthcoming. On stepping into the boat I met 'Abdallah Effendi, the new Kâyim Makâm, returning from visiting an old man renowned for his sanctity among the Mussulmans of Massowah and its vicinity. 'Abdallah Effendi was a native of Kurdistan, and had been in the service of the Porte from childhood. He told me that he had seen Purtoo Effendi, who had strongly recommended the Mission to his best offices.

As the 'Victoria' was in need of supplies, and Captain Purvis consented to remain at Massowah, in the hope that some authentic intelligence might arrive respecting the captives, the former vessel left for Aden on the 25th. Wishing to consult Colonel Merewether about a selection of presents for King Theodore, I availed myself of the same opportunity and repaired thither, returning to Massowah in the 'Victoria' on the 4th of February. No fresh news had reached Captain Purvis since our departure; but Padre Delmonte informed me that a servant of one of the Europeans at Gáffat had arrived at the Island and reported that the King had taken all the prisoners with him to Shoa, obliging Consul Cameron, whom he treated very harshly, to accompany him on foot. I discredited the report at the time, attributing it to the lying craft of the messenger, who hoped thereby to ingratiate himself with the priest; for a common notion prevailed among the natives at this period that the Roman Catholics and Protestants cordially hated one another, and exulted in each other's misfortunes. Padre Delmonte was held to be one of our most inveterate enemies; nevertheless, I can truly say that during our stay at Massowah I experienced nothing but kindness at his hands.

8th.—The 'Pantaloon' returned to Aden this morning with nothing new respecting the captives beyond the report above mentioned, which, as I had anticipated, proved to be false.

I had taken advantage of a visit to the new Governor, soon after his arrival, to call his attention to the traffic in slaves, which was known to be surreptitiously carried on to a great extent by Arab boatmen visiting Massowah from the Hijâz and Yemen. He accordingly issued an order that all masters of native craft leaving the port should give security, under a heavy penalty, that no slave would be taken on board their vessels. The plan worked admirably until intelligence of its adoption reached the ears of the Governor-General of the Hijâz, who immediately ordered it to be discontinued. The discomfited Kâyim-Makâm was therefore obliged to proclaim through the town and country that his own order was rescinded, or, as he expressed himself to me, he had been made "to eat dirt."

CHAPTER III.

PRELIMINARY DIFFICULTIES.

16*th.*—THE messenger whom I had dispatched to Debra Tâbor returned with replies to my letters addressed to Messrs. Flad and Schimper. Both repeated the statement contained in Consul Cameron's first note after the imprisonment of the captives—that there would be no release until the arrival of a civil answer from the Queen to the King of Abyssinia. This stale announcement did not better my position in the least. The letter which was alleged to be necessary to secure the liberation of the captives had already been at Massowah upwards of six months, and the King had been aware of its existence since August, but had hitherto abstained from sending for it or answering my own letters to him on the subject. Dr. Schimper did, indeed, express his opinion that I might venture up, as the King, on ascending the throne (twelve years previously !) had caused it to be proclaimed that no one was prohibited from entering his territories. Therefore, " it can be accepted," he went on to say, " that you can simply come up;" adding, however, the important qualification, that " the instructions of his Imperial Majesty may change in time." Thus, while Mr. Schimper tacitly admitted that he himself was virtually a prisoner, he nevertheless recommended me to go up without a safe-conduct—which I afterwards found would have been impossible—omitting altogether to indicate how the attempt was to be made, independently of the royal assent and protection. Under these circumstances, I judged it best to wait and ascertain what account Consul Cameron and his captive companions would give of the cause of the King's displeasure against them, and his reason for not replying to my letters.

21st.—The messenger whom I had dispatched to Mágdala with stores, as far back as the 28th of November, returned with two notes to my address, one from Consul Cameron and the other from the Rev. Mr. Stern. Beyond the satisfaction of hearing that the captives were well, and that the stores had reached safely, these communications did not enlighten me in the least, as to my venturing up to the King. Indeed, the messenger told me that Consul Cameron had directed him to warn me against taking that step, unless the King first replied to my letter. But a new difficulty now presented itself, namely, how we were to make our way to the royal Court in any case, seeing that the whole country along the western bank of the Tăkkăzê was in open rebellion, and we could scarcely expect that the King would come in person to escort us through his revolted territories ?

On the 25th I dispatched the messenger again to Mágdala

with money and stores for Consul Cameron. On the 28th I also sent other messengers to Dabra Tâbor to collect information, requesting Mr. Flad at the same time to forward money to the captives and to draw on me for the amount, it having come to my knowledge that the European artisans had abundance of spare cash which they hesitated to send down to the coast, lest the bearers should be plundered on the way. On the 3rd of March I dispatched the 'Victoria' to Aden, with the latest particulars received from the interior, for the information of Her Majesty's Government and the relatives of the captives.

As the local authorities and mercantile community at Massowah had shown us much civility during our sojourn amongst them, I reciprocated the attention by inviting them to spend a day with me at Moncûlu. The Kâyim-Makâm, his predecessor the President of the Municipal Council, the Commissioner of Customs and the Commandant of the troops came to breakfast. At dinner, which was served in the *kaldur-koy* fashion, and on the ground, for want of a table sufficiently large, we were joined by the Kâdhi, the members of the Council, the Mufti, and a number of merchants. The dinner consisted of twenty dishes of meat and as many sweets. Of course, no wine or spirits were allowed in the presence of the learned Kâdhi and the other strict Mussulmans; nevertheless, the assistant Commissioner of Customs and the gallant Commandant—the former an Egyptian and the latter a Turk—could not resist quaffing several tumblers of the prohibited Christian drinks, as they styled them, behind the backs of their more abstemious brethren.

17th.—The 'Victoria' returned from Aden with a large budget of letters and newspapers. Earl Russell having judged that it might conduce to the success of the Mission if a British officer were associated with me, and her Majesty's Government having communicated with Colonel Merewether on the subject, the latter most kindly gave me the nomination, but I preferred leaving the selection to himself, knowing full well that it could not be confided to better hands. I was also apprised, at the same time, that his lordship had placed 500 English muskets at my disposal, to be presented to Theodore. As the option was left to me, I declined the suggested use of the proffered arms, fearing that the gift might be construed into a bribe. Moreover, such a present might lead the King's enemies to believe that we were aiding his Majesty against them, which would have had the effect of raising up a fresh obstacle to the further progress of the Mission..

22nd.—Wald-Máryam, whom I had dispatched on the 25th of February with money and stores for the captives, sent me a message from Hamasên stating that he had been plundered by the rebels in Tigrê, but had managed to save some of the effects, which he begged to return, together with the letter I had entrusted to him for the Consul; that he had retained the money left in his possession and would take it to Mágdala, excusing himself for not having done so already on account of the insecurity of the roads; adding, that it would be dangerous for him to convey a letter, as it might fall into unfriendly hands and bring himself and the captives into trouble. All this looked very suspicious, and decided me not to employ the fellow again, unless absolutely obliged. Fortunately, the messenger whom he had sent down with the remainder of the stores proved to be a trustworthy man, and being also the brother-in-law (by concubinage) of Dajjâj Miräad, an influential Tigrê chief, who was also a prisoner at Mágdala, I determined to employ him, and gave him a letter to convey to Consul Cameron. This man served us faithfully up to the date of our deliverance. He was slow, but he was sure.

29th.—The 'Victoria' returned from Aden, bringing Lieutenant Prideaux, third Assistant Resident, and for some time my colleague in the political department at Aden, to join me in the Mission to the King of Abyssinia. A better selection could not have been made: it was another proof of Colonel Merewether's personal friendship for me, and of the real interest which he felt in the success of the Mission.

I now began, however, to have serious misgivings about effecting a visit to the King, knowing for certain that he had received two letters from me, but had neither deigned to answer me nor to ameliorate the position of the captives. On the other hand, I had heard from various good authorities that his Majesty had not manifested any tokens of displeasure with regard to the Mission; on the contrary, our messengers had been well treated, which, as far as it went, was a favourable sign. After mature deliberation, I decided to address him a third time, and in the event of receiving no reply to relinquish the undertaking and return to Aden. At this juncture, I received a visit from two Mohammedans of the Shoho tribe—one named Ibrahîm, who described himself as a relative of Samuel, and the other as a country-man of the same. Having heard that this Samuel was the King's steward, and had great influence at Court and in the country generally, I availed myself of the offer of these two men, who promised to convey a letter direct to the afore-named functionary, and to prevail upon him to obtain an answer from his Majesty.

Ibrahîm said that he had come down to see me for the

sole purpose of informing me that the English had formidable enemies in Abyssinia, who did all in their power to poison the King's mind against us. On asking his opinion of the probable cause of his Majesty's delay in replying to my letters, he remarked that I had arrived at Massowah when rebellion had broken out in different parts of the interior, and that it was beyond the power of Theodore to ensure me a safe journey without furnishing me with a large escort, which in his actual position he could not well spare; that his Majesty was too proud to own his weakness in this respect; and, moreover, that he still remembered the calamity which overtook Consul Plowden, who had proceeded to the coast in spite of his warning and fell by the hands of the rebels near Góndar, and that he had been most careful ever since to avoid the recurrence of a similar catastrophe.

As this man informed me that the King had a number of people about him, both European and native, who understood English well, I addressed this, my third letter, to his Majesty in that language, and sent it by Ibrahîm and his companion on the 30th of March.

"Most Gracious Sovereign,

"I hope your Majesty will pardon the liberty which I am taking in addressing you this third time upon a matter which has given me much anxiety.

"More than eight months ago, I wrote and informed your Majesty that I had been sent here by the British Government as the bearer of a letter for you from our Queen. After having waited about three months for a reply, I was compelled to write to you again, through the Nâyib of Harkîko, as I feared that the first two messengers had not delivered my letter safely to you.

"Neither to the first nor to the second letter have I as yet received an answer, and the very thought of knowing that the two letters have reached you long since makes me the more anxious to learn the cause of your silence.

"I beg to inform your Majesty that the sole duty on which I have been sent is to convey to you our Queen's letter. I have nothing else to do but to deliver it to you, and to assure you of the sincere wishes which our Sovereign entertains for the welfare and prosperity of the great country which the Almighty has placed under your rule.

"It is rumoured that some evil-disposed persons, who do not wish to see England and Abyssinia on the best terms, have misrepresented the object of my mission to you. I can confidently assure you that the British Government takes a sincere interest in the welfare of your empire, and would greatly deplore any unfriendly feeling taking place between the two countries through a mere misunderstanding.

"The delay makes me feel this painful suspense the more, because I am at a loss what explanation to give to my Government as to its cause. Moreover, the rainy season is now fast approaching, and, if your Majesty will not honour me with an answer soon, I shall be obliged to return to my duties at Aden."

The messengers promised to return in forty days, if the King did not detain them long. I had decided that, if no reply reached me by the end of May, I would return to Aden with her Majesty's letter; but after their departure I heard that, owing to the spread of the rebellion in Tigrê, they were not able to effect a passage through that province before the end of April; consequently, it was not likely that they could reach the royal Court before the end of June.

31st.—In the course of the day I called upon the Kâyim-Makâm and was glad to learn that he had received counter-orders from the Hijâz authorities prohibiting the slave-trade. He accordingly directed the Nâyib of Harkîko and the Mudîr of the Danâkil to apprehend and bring before him any dealers in the traffic who might be found conveying slaves through the territory under their jurisdiction, and to liberate the slaves forthwith. This order, as I learnt subsequently, had a beneficial effect in checking the nefarious trade.

April 3rd.—The hot weather has fairly set in again, and the bare idea of spending another such season as the last in this place is unsupportable.   There was lightning and heavy thunder every afternoon from the 7th to the 11th, with dark clouds, which freely discharged their contents on the mountains to the west, but served to render the close atmosphere around us still more oppressive.   Much sickness was the result, and two of my servants were laid up with fever.   Dr. and Mrs. Blanc, who had both been suffering, the former from sore eyes, left on the 11th for Aden in the ' Victoria.'   Mr. Munzinger dined with us on Easter Sunday, prior to his departure for Cásala, where he had business to transact.   Notwithstanding my regard for him, I sincerely hoped never to meet him again at Massowah, otherwise than as a traveller passing through it.

26th.—An Abyssinian merchant, named Wald-Salassê Gobazê, called upon me.   He had been recommended to me by Mr. Munzinger as a man who might do me service at the Court of his Sovereign.   He spoke in bitter terms of the conduct of several Europeans, whom he accused of reviling " the Lord's Anointed."   In his estimation, Theodore was a pattern King, who had been driven by the course pursued by certain foreigners to treat them with severity.   He had come down to purchase lead and silks for his Majesty, and promised, on his return, to take the earliest opportunity of speaking about me to him.   He advised me to be patient, predicting that a reconciliation would be effected before long, and that thenceforward the King and the English would be fast friends.   This great admirer of Theodore had a narrow escape from being burnt alive by his liege lord for refusing to give up all his property. He saved himself by flight.

28th.—The thermometer rose to 107° in the coolest part of the Consulate at Moncûlu. I endeavoured to modify the heat by adopting tatties and keeping them well sprinkled with water. This lowered the temperature to 70°; but I soon found that the difference thus produced between the air inside and outside the house was not wholesome, for my health began to suffer in consequence.

30th.—Wald-Gobazê, the Abyssinian merchant, called to take leave of me to-day, and reiterated his promise of using his best endeavours to induce the King to reply to my letters. I gave him a few bottles of brandy by way of viaticum, knowing his strong partiality for " English 'Arak." To do him justice, however, I never saw him the worse for liquor; and a couple of wine-glasses of the stimulant, instead of loosening his tongue, made him very taciturn. On these occasions, any attempt to draw him out about the captives led him to place one hand over his mouth and to motion with the other that I was not to broach such subjects.

May 1st.—Lieutenant Prideaux and I started off this afternoon on an excursion into the interior, in the hope of finding an eligible locality, just below the high table-land, where we might escape the heat of Massowah until our plans were matured. Travelling in a westerly direction, we reached the valley of Gábza at 9 P.M. Here we found some muddy water in a hole at the foot of a precipitous rock, two hundred feet high, tenanted by baboons and monkeys. These hideous creatures made a great uproar on our approach, fearing that we were about to take possession of their cistern, and did not cease their clamour until we reached another puddle, half a mile farther on, called El-Agamât, where our cameleers advised us to halt for the night. Our rest was incessantly disturbed, however, by the shouts raised by our followers to ward off a number of leopards which prowled about the camp. One of these beasts carried off a sheep; though much mangled and torn, it was rescued by the cameleers, who at once appropriated it as their legitimate prize.

2nd.—Started from El-Agamât at 3·15 A.M., and after a march of three miles the road lay through difficult passes, when, owing to the darkness, we had to dismount and grope our way cautiously for fear of being precipitated down a deep ravine which was pointed out to us by our guides. At 5·40 we reached Asûs, but proceeded onward to the wells, situatèd at a place called Ab-hân, about two miles from the village, where we halted. It was deliciously cool this morning, the thermometer standing at 70°. The spot was well shaded by tamarisk and other trees, overhung with a thick-stalked creeper, very common in those parts. The water was muddy but abundant, and not disagreeable to the taste. Any quantity was procurable by digging holes in the sand. The villages hereabouts are invariably located at some distance from the wells. The reason assigned by the natives is, that it affords them some protection against the visits of Abyssinian marauding parties, who would otherwise not fail, when in want of water, to plunder their homes at the same time.

'Abd-ul-Kerîm, the Nâyib's brother, joined us at Ab-hân with a party of Irregulars who had been ordered by the Kâyim-Makâm to escort us during our stay in the interior. But for a nasty habit of indiscriminate expectoration, and a still more disgusting one of using any available article of furniture instead of a handkerchief, 'Abd-ul-Kerîm was very gentlemanly in his deportment.

3rd.—At sunrise, the thermometer was as low as 67°, and the water, which we kept in skins, almost too cold to drink. It was so hot, however, during the day, and the glare from the sand was so unpleasant, that we took 'Abd-ul-Kerîm's advice and marched to a place called Mâsir, in the valley of Dágree, about ten miles south-west of Asûs. We pitched our tents under huge tamarind and sycamore trees, with a clear stream of running water below us, and a copious spring within a hundred yards of our encampment. Two miles before reaching Mâsir we saw, for the first time, a corn-field belonging to the Abyssinians, who come down during our winter to cultivate the soil. They had just gathered in the harvest and returned to their villages in the highlands. A day's march from hence would have taken us into Bogôs, the nearest Abyssinian district on the table-land, where the climate is said to be very pleasant and salubrious. We repressed a strong desire to visit it, fearing that our object might be misapprehended by the King. The constant movement of the 'Victoria' had already been noised abroad through the country as indicating an impending resort to hostilities on the part of the English.

4th.—The only drawback to a residence at Dágree was the excessive heat, which became quite intolerable towards noon. On the other hand, the night was intensely cold, the thermometer standing at 64° shortly before sunrise. The next spot we tried was Mátrah-Maddai, situated in the valley of Shísharo, three hours' march from Dágree. Arriving there towards sundown, we fancied that we had at last found what we were in search of—a cool retreat within an easy distance of Massowah; but a very short experience effectually disabused us. At noon, the thermometer rose to 98° in the shade, whereas in the early morning it had stood at 54°. Notwithstanding the extreme heat, the whole country was clad in brilliant verdure. On the way, we passed several moving villages; and one that had just come to a halt supplied us with milk which, luckily, was not smoked. Water was plentiful in all directions, and sometimes we had to ride through running streams. Before reaching Shísharo we crossed a lofty mountain, one portion of which was so steep that we had to dismount, and our luggage was sent on by a different route.

Our guide now recommended us to try a more northerly direction; but finding that the farther we went the hotter the atmosphere became, we finally decided on an early return to Massowah. I may mention here that the Shísharo valley teems with game, and would be a capital resort for sportsmen, but for the extremes of heat and cold during the twenty-four hours, which render the climate most trying to foreign constitutions.

6th.—Wald-Máryam, one of my private messengers, who had gone up to Mágdala with money and stores towards the end of February, returned with two companions, servants of Dajjâj Miräad, an imprisoned Tigrê Chief, bringing letters from Consul Cameron and the Rev. Mr. Stern. Both concurred in the opinion that conciliatory measures would be of no avail with the King, and recommended the adoption of a stronger tone, as more likely to succeed with his Majesty. The former wrote as follows :—

" I speak advisedly, dear Rassam, and with the full consent and approval of our party — Mrs. Rosenthal and Mrs. Flad, who have not only their own lives, but those of their children at stake—when I say, that the only way of settling this matter is to write strongly, and act, if further writing is of no use. Of course, we have no wish to press the Government in saying this: the interests of England and the good of the country must be always the first consideration, and will be with us; but it may remove a difficulty to know what we all feel. If Government acts energetically, and it entails suffering on us, we are prepared, as it must come to that sooner or later. When the King refused to answer your second letter, requiring an answer in three days, he meant a defiance, as, not calculating on the defection of Shoa, he expected to return with 40,000 or 50,000 horsemen, who would give your people a hot reception if you wished to fight. Now things are changed. He would like matters settled, but does not see how. But, for God's sake, do not come up here; he will cage you as sure as a gun, as he thinks that while he has us in his hands he is safe from attack, and, of course, with a swell like yourself in addition, matters would only be better for him, according to his view."...

Consul Cameron was misinformed about the letter referred to. I had been most circumspect in my written communications to the King, and am persuaded that to have demanded a reply within three days would have exasperated rather than subdued him. Therefore, had I done so, I should have acted in direct opposition to explicit instructions, enjoining me to be "specially careful not to place myself in a position which may cause further embarrassment to her Majesty's Government."

The messengers reported that the King had returned from Shoa utterly vanquished, and that his army had been so decimated by hunger and death in the campaign against that country and the Wello-Gallas, as also by desertion, that he dared not return to Debra Tâbor; that Góndar, the capital, had been captured by T'issoo Gobazê, of Walkaït, whose power had been on the increase for the last eighteen months, and whose sway now extended over the whole country between Lake Dámbea and the Tăkkăzê; that the eastern provinces of Lasta, Agów and Tembên, up to the confines of Tigrê, were in the hands of the Wakshum Gobazê, another formidable rival and the hereditary enemy of Theodore; and it was fully anticipated that, within a few days, Tigrê itself must succumb to one or other of these powerful antagonists.

These startling reports increased my perplexity, as I now began to apprehend that the King might not be able, even if so disposed, to protect us on the journey. We might, indeed, by making friends of the insurgent chiefs, manage to traverse the intervening districts in safety; but knowing the jealous disposition of Theodore, I felt convinced that to do so would insure us but a very doubtful reception by him. As to sending him an ultimatum, as was suggested by the captives, such a step, besides being of questionable expediency, was one which I was wholly unauthorized to take.

Finding that the beautiful scenery of Mátrah-Maddai did not compensate for the excessive heat experienced during the day, we started on our return journey towards Massowah, and reached Moncûlu, thoroughly exhausted, the following evening. A private messenger had arrived with letters from Messrs. Flad and Schimper; also a note from Consul Cameron. The former gentlemen were of opinion that it would be dangerous for us to proceed into the interior without a safe-conduct from the King; but they advised me at the same time to forward the Queen's letter to his Majesty. Even this course, however, was not without its drawbacks, as Dr. Schimper himself pointed out in the concluding portion of his letter:—

"But I may not venture to express an opinion whether you should, under existing circumstances, yourself bring the letter or send it by messenger; partly for the valid reasons mentioned in my last letter [the King might detain me if I went up without his permission]; partly because the present perils of the road render it unadvisable to risk the future of this highly important document—a circumstance which, however, eventually must take place."

These undecided opinions from persons on the spot who, besides being personally interested in the success of our Mission, were known to possess considerable experience of the country and people, added to my perplexity. The King had been aware of the Queen's letter—which it was conceived would produce an entire change in his mind and tactics—for the last eight months, and yet he did not deign even to send for it! To force the royal epistle upon him, under such circumstances, appeared to me injudicious, as well as derogatory to the illustrious writer.

14*th.*—I received another letter from Consul Cameron to-day through Mr. Flad. As will be seen from the following extracts, he repeated his injunctions about my not going up to the King :—

"For God's sake, don't think of coming up here either with or without a safe-conduct.

"You will only get chains for your pains.

"Your person would be made use of, not to get terms—but concessions.

"All this business has been about the absence of an answer to the King's letter.

"If a simple answer had been sent, giving a courteous explanation of the delay, and begging that I and all the prisoners might be given a safe-conduct out of the country, the matter might have been settled after last winter.

"But your bringing up the letter yourself would have been a fearful risk.

"You might have got us out if you had been properly submissive and acquiesced in everything that had been done ; but the slightest movement of independence on your part would have got you into chains, or you might have been detained from mere caprice, or put amongst us as a sort of additional hostage ; after which a savage diplomacy would have been plied to get

Soudan and Sennaar, by working on the fears of the British Government. Things have changed here, however, and the country is on the eve of desolation.

" If, instead of your' third letter, the letter in your hands had been sent with a polite ultimatum accompanying it, it might have got us out, or brought matters to a crisis either one way or the other." . . . .

The foregoing letter increased my difficulties more than ever. Those on whose behalf I was ready to risk the journey protested against my going up to the King, either with or without a safe-conduct. With regard to the other alternative, there can be no doubt that the captives were sick at heart, and would gladly have encountered any dangers rather than endure further suspense ; nevertheless, knowing that I was not warranted in assuming so grave a responsibility, I decided to refer the matter to superior authority.

15*th.*—The ' Victoria ' arrived bringing Dr. Blanc to rejoin the Mission, and as I had important communications from the captives to forward to Aden and England, I sent her back to Aden the following morning with the latest intelligence from the interior. On the 18th and 25th I dispatched money, provisions and clothing to Consul Cameron and his companions in captivity, one-half through Mr. Flad at Gáffat, and the other direct to Mágdala. There was no lack of trustworthy messengers now. Wald-Máryam I contrived to employ in the vicinity of Massowah, for although he was not to be trusted in conveying letters or stores, I did not venture to dismiss him, lest he should do mischief.

Khoja Bedrôs, the Armenian merchant, informed me to-day that a Greek priest had arrived at Massowah with a letter from his Patriarch at Jerusalem to King Theodore, soliciting aid towards building a hospital in Palestine for foreign pilgrims. Bedrôs had strongly advised him to abandon the mad project, assuring him that, even if allowed to pass through Tigrê, he would get nothing better than chains on reaching his destination. As the priest had refused to listen to him, and boasted of the feats which he would perform mounted on a donkey he had just purchased, the Armenian begged me to interpose and arrest the further progress of the crazy adventurer before he got himself and others into mischief. I declined to meddle with the man in any way, telling my friend that I had no right to stop him, and that even if I had, I did not think that his mission would interfere with ours.

28*th*.—Letters were brought from Mágdala to-day by the servants of Consul Cameron, Mr. Stern, and Dajjâj Mirãad. Among these were accounts written by the Rev. Messrs. Stern and Rosenthal of their past sufferings, which were truly harrowing. On the 1st of June I sent the same messengers back with the letters which had been received for the captives. As I had been repeatedly asked by the latter to forward her Majesty's letter to Theodore, I wrote at this time to the Abûna, or Metropolitan, soliciting his good offices to insure its safe delivery to the King, in case he judged that the step would further the liberation of the prisoners. The worthy prelate, it appears, smiled at my credulity in making the proposition. He told me afterwards —for he never answered me—that he was on the point of writing to warn me against trusting the King, either with or without the royal letter, when he heard that we had started for Matámma.

June 2nd.—News arrived that no less than fifteen out of the thirty persons who had gone to Mecca from Massowah had been carried off by cholera, which had broken out among the Hajj. If the pilgrims generally suffered at the same rate, the mortality must have been fearful. There can be no doubt that the absolute want, up to a very recent period, of all sanitary regulations at Mecca, has been a fruitful source of this fell disease among the pilgrims, who have propagated it in all directions on their homeward journey.

There had been so many sand-storms of late at Moncûlu, and the heat was so intense there, that I removed to the Consulate at Massowah. Dr. Blanc and Lieut. Prideaux were living in tents on the mainland, on the Jarâr point, near the sea.

5th.—Sent a messenger to Matámma with a large sum of money, which I had been requested by Consul Cameron and Mr. Stern to forward to Mr. Eipperle on their account.

7th.—Padre Delmonte applied to me for some Amharic Bibles and Testaments belonging to the London Society for Promoting Christianity among the Jews, which were deposited at the Consulate. As his object was to take the books with him for the use of the Roman Catholic mission at Haibo, I gave him three copies of each, feeling confident that the Society would approve of the gift for such a purpose.

11th.—A report was current in Massowah that my third letter had reached Theodore, and that through the intervention of Samuel, the royal steward, his Majesty had released the prisoners on parole, on condition that Consul Cameron consented to remain at the Court until the King had communicated with the British agent at Massowah. This rumour was utterly groundless, as were many others to a similar effect which were circulated subsequently. I mention the fact to show how difficult it was to place any reliance on these local fabrications.

13th.—The 'Victoria' arrived with letters and papers. The delay of the Mission had been the subject of detracting comments in India and England:—the King had not deigned to reply to me because he thought me a Mohammedan, or, at best, a convert from that faith to Christianity, and, what was apparently deemed worse still, I was an Asiatic. As Theodore was known to hold Islamism in abhorrence, the malice of the first unfounded double reproach is apparent. With regard to the second, his Majesty would certainly have been at a loss to comprehend the implied demerit; nevertheless, the drift of some of the reported speeches and articles was obvious, and had they reached the King, through the medium of persons ill-disposed towards the English—and such were not lacking at his Court—they might undoubtedly have led him to construct a new grievance out of them, to the greater jeopardy of the captives. ' Fortunately, the Europeans at Massowah at this time—to their honour be it said—prevented the mischief by carefully suppressing the obnoxious publications.

We heard to-day that cholera was raging along the eastern coast of the Red Sea, and had extended to Egypt and Aden. At the same time, hundreds were dying from starvation in and around Massowah, as far as Adwa, in Tigrê. The locusts had been devastating the country for the last two years, and all supplies from the interior ceased. Moreover, scarcely any provisions were imported from the Arabian side, owing to the prevailing dearth in that quarter. The market of Massowah was denuded of all articles of food, and many of the natives were driven to subsist on boiled cow-hide and bones. Multitudes resorted to the beach in search of shell-fish to satisfy the cravings of hunger, and numbers are reported to have died suddenly after living on such food for several days. As the 'Victoria' had now been absent a month at Aden, my companions and I had to live on rice, of which we fortunately had enough for ourselves and servants.

16*th*.—News arrived that the Wakshum Gobazê had invaded Tigrê, and was shortly expected to enter the capital in triumph; and that Dajjâj Dakla Guargîs, on hearing of his approach, was preparing to retire, in accordance with the King's instructions not to risk an engagement with any of the rebel chiefs, because his Majesty wished them to "fatten" before he attacked them.   Orders couched in similar terms were issued by Theodore while we were at his Court, arising probably from his apprehension that, in the event of a defeat, his officers would surrender and join the insurgents.

17*th*.—My companions and I started in the 'Victoria' on a visit to Zoolla and other localities in the neighbourhood, partly for change of air, and partly in the hope of finding an eligible residence during the hot months, from whence also we might proceed direct to Mágdala, if sent for by the King. We steamed down Annesley Bay and anchored about a mile from the beach, and in the afternoon walked to the ruins of Adulis, a distance of four miles. Some scattered fragments of basaltic columns and heaps of rubbish were all that remained of this once famous emporium of ancient trade. The village in the vicinity was deserted, owing to a recent attack on its inhabitants by a ferocious Shoho chief, named Balâl-bin-'Abdallah, who had put some of the women to death in a most barbarous manner. This villain was eventually seized by the Massowah authorities, and I had the gratification of seeing him in chains in front of the Governor's house, awaiting his final sentence from Jiddah.

Our walk had been so fatiguing that we were ready to drop from thirst before reaching the beach. On asking the guide if he could not procure us a drink in the neighbourhood, he replied that it would be much easier for him to fetch it from the steamer. Even the villagers, it appears, had to go three miles for water when no rain fell in the lowlands. The following day we proceeded to Asfât, at the bottom of the bay, where we found a hot-spring not far from the beach. The temperature of the water, which was brackish and emitted a sulphureous odour, was 112°. Flights of partridges alighted at this spot towards the evening, and traces of elephants were visible in the sand, leading us to infer that no better water was accessible in the neighbour-hood. After spending a couple of days there, we returned to our old quarters at Massowah on the 20th.

22nd.—Mr. Munzinger, having arrived from Cásala yesterday, called upon me to-day. He had heard before leaving that place, that a Copt had passed through, who gave out that he had been sent by Her Majesty's Consul-General at Cairo to negotiate for the release of the captives. This fellow, it appears, had imposed upon the British authorities in Egypt by representing himself as having been entrusted with a message from the Abûna, to the effect that the latter would undertake to procure the liberation of the prisoners at the hands of the King, if a guarantee were given that her Majesty's Government would exact no reparation for the past. I discovered subsequently that the Abûna had no knowledge whatever of this impostor; and his opinion was, that if he had ever been in Abyssinia, it must have been in the suite of the Coptic Patriarch, who visited Theodore about nine years previously.

CHAPTER IV.

PRELIMINARY PROGRESS.

Despondency of the Captives — Hajj Adam on the Abyssinians — Excursion to the north-west of Massowah — The Samhâr — Mountain torrents — Lions and Leopards — Charming Scenery — The Hibâb tribe ; how converted to Islâm — Slaughter of animals by Christians and Mussulmans — The Chief " Sugar " — Scarcity of good water — Letter from Theodore — Reasons for and against accepting his invitation — Statements of the Messengers — Course decided on — Flying Fish — Ibrahim's marriage — Adjuration by the Death of Theodore — Mr. Gifford Palgrave — Reasons for proceeding to Egypt — Departure from Massowah — Jiddah — Purtoo Effendi — Arrival at Alexandria — Conference with, Colonel Stanton — Return to Massowah — Fresh Perplexities — Cholera — Preparations for journey inland — Reminiscences of Massowah — Start at last.

July 22nd.—More letters from the captives, all very desponding in tone, and without a gleam of light to indicate how their liberation could best be accomplished. My last messengers were now nearly two months over their promised time, and I began to conclude that my third letter had met the same fate as the preceding two—that the King, for some reason or other, had determined to prolong the sufferings of his prisoners, and therefore treated all our overtures with indifference. What more could be done was the uppermost thought in my mind. Hajj Âdam smiled at my perplexity; but, on perceiving that I was not in a mood to relish such levity, he remarked that had I listened to him at the outset I might have saved both money and paper. In his estimation, we had committed a great blunder in treating the Abyssinian as a human being; whereas, had we treated him as belonging to his proper species, the donkey, and employed the stick, we should have accomplished our object long ago. He hesitated to say that the lives of the captives would not have been risked by the process; but was of opinion that it must come to that at last. "Hah!" he exclaimed, "if I only had some of your money, would I not hurl that malefactor from his crazy throne, and send him to the grave of his ever-filthy progenitors for having begot such a serpent to torment God's creatures." After this outburst, I begged him to find me a trustworthy messenger to dispatch into the interior. Thinking, at first, that I intended to send again to the King, he declared that he would rather lose his head than co-operate in so thankless a service; but on learning that I wished to forward a letter to the captives at Mágdala, he procured a messenger forthwith. It is a remarkable fact that all the messengers which this man supplied proved faithful to their trust. Two of them were in my employ until the capture of Mágdala. Poor Hajj Âdam's subsequent history is melancholy. He went up to Abyssinia after we had started for the royal Court, and, on hearing of our imprisonment at Mágdala, sent to say that he was going to the Wakshum Gobazê with arms and ammunition, and hoped to accompany that chief and effect our rescue. He was plundered on the road by a petty rebel leader, and died afterwards of a broken heart.

24th.—My companions and I slept at Moncûlu, and started the following afternoon on another excursion. Taking a N.W. direction, we arrived at Ambâa after six hours' riding, and encamped on the side of a ravine where there was abundance of water, a torrent having come down from the interior the day before. We spent a day here, and found the heat greater than at Massowah, the thermometer marking 108° in a double-fly tent. Our old friend 'Abd-ul-Kerîm was again one of the party, having with him a number of Irregulars sent to escort us by order of the Kâyim-Makâm.

From Ambâa we proceeded to a spot called Kánfar, three miles distant, and passed the night on some sand-hills where water was attainable in any quantity on digging two feet below the surface of the soil. Here we replenished our water-skins on hearing that no such opportunity would offer between Kánfar and 'Ain, twenty-miles farther on. The route lay over a sandy district, called Shä'ab (literally, a reef), extending over thirty miles to the sea. This sandy plain is a famous refuge for the lowlanders when attacked by the neighbouring Abyssinians from the highlands. These inroads are of such frequent occurrence that the inhabitants of the Samhâr—the native designation of the lowlands on the north and north-west of Massowah—have spies constantly on the watch in Hamasên and Bogôs, to give early intimation of the impending foray. On these occasions the lowlanders retire in a body to the Shä'ab, with all their belongings, where they can defy their assailants, who, from want of water, and that indispensable animal in a sandy region—the camel—are unable to follow them. An inexhaustible supply of salt is also to be found in this plain, and hundreds of camels are yearly laden with it for the Abyssinian and Massowah markets.

Heavy rain had evidently fallen very recently in this district, and patches of grass were growing up here and there, in which we generally noticed a number of wild ducks and geese feeding. Halted for the night at a spot called Nûr Habibai, at the north-western extremity of the Shä'ab, and reached 'Ain the following morning in less than three hours.

Here we found a ruined village and an extensive burial-ground; a few sheep were grazing about under the care of a shepherd, from whom we procured a draught of milk. Half a mile farther we entered the valley of Lebka, through which a clear stream was flowing, and finally pitched our tents at a place called Kogât, on its northern bank.

29th.—A great rush of water had come down from the mountains during the night, rendering the bed of the torrent, through which our road lay, so slimy and slippery that the camels constantly stumbled. A ride of three hours and a half brought us to Gadarêt, where we breakfasted under a large tamarind tree overhanging the stream. Pursuing our journey we left the Lebka valley, and travelled in a north-westerly direction through another. The road was now up an acclivity, and at noon we reached the valley of Magamaya-tât, and encamped near a nomad village of the Hibâb, within a hundred yards of the wells; water being obtained here also by digging a little below the surface of the sand. Travelling had become most pleasant, as we attained the higher land, and the weather was deliciously cool—the thermometer marking 88° at noon, in the shade. Blanc and I ascended a lofty mountain in the vicinity, commanding an extensive prospect. The scenery around was magnificent, with here and there the most picturesque and romantic views.

30th.—We were unable to sleep last night, owing to the noise and hubbub raised by the villagers in driving off some lions and leopards from their sheep. Our camp was attacked twice, and a cameleer nearly lost his life in attempting to protect his camel from the onslaught of a lion. These wild beasts abound in this locality, and droves of elephants are said to frequent it from November to January—a statement confirmed by the droppings they had left behind them.

We left Magamayatât next morning, and in two hours reached Râro, where we halted for breakfast. The ride lay through a beautiful country, well-wooded, and alive with guinea-fowl. Proceeding onward we passed the huts of Ifabâd, and encamped under spreading acacias near the water-bed, which, as usual, was about two miles from the village. The spot had been so highly extolled, both on account of its climate and charming scenery, that we felt somewhat disappointed on reaching it. A few days' experience of this delightful district had made us over-nice, and an elevated plain 2,500 feet above the sea level, studded with trees, with patches of greensward here and there, hardly came up to our fastidious expectations. We had a refreshing shower during the day; but so much rain had fallen in the mountains that before sunset a tremendous flow came down, filling the torrent's bed in less than a minute. I had heard much of the sudden risings of these streams, but had no adequate idea of their force and velocity until to-day.

31st.—So cool was the night that I felt comfortable under a blanket. The Ifabâd villagers were churlish, and it was difficult to procure milk from them, even on purchase. The fact is, I had made a mistake in allowing 'Abd-ul-Kerîm to interfere; for, not having been used to receive payment from him, they very naturally inferred that I should follow his example. "Súkkar," or Sugar, the chief of the Atté-Máryam, called on me, and made many fair promises, all of which he forgot to fulfil.

The Hibâb, and more especially that section of the tribe styled Atté-Máryam—an Amharic phrase signifying "my sister Mary"—were Christians up to the end of the last century, and are said to have been inducted into Islamism through partaking of meat prepared for Mohammedans. The tradition is that they had been so much neglected by the then Abûna of Abyssinia, who thought more of his own temporal interests than of the spiritual welfare of this part of his flock, that they were eventually left without priests; and an invitation to a sumptuous repast, prepared for them by their Muslim neighbours, sufficed to seal their abjuration of Christianity. It is a curious fact, that in these regions this partaking by Christians of animal food slaughtered by Mussulmans is regarded by the latter as an outward and visible sign of conversion to their faith, and *vice versâ*. The reason appears to be this, that when Christians slaughter an animal they repeat the words, " In the name of the Father, of the Son, and of the Holy Ghost," on putting the knife to the victim's throat; whereas Mohammedans simply repeat the formula, " In the name of Almighty God." In the one case, there is a declaration of a belief in the Trinity, and in the other of the Unity of the Godhead. We found it expedient to bear this prejudice in mind during our subsequent sojourn in Abyssinia, taking care that none of our Mohammedan attendants slaughtered an animal destined for our use. Even if our Portuguese servants killed a fowl, without being heard by the Abyssinians to invoke the Trinity, we were stigmatized by the ignorant priests as a set of *Türkotsh*, Turks.

2nd.—I shot a fine bustard this morning near our encampment; it was so large that a couple of men had to carry it by turns. Two of the Hibâb kidnapped one of our sheep, and were taken in the act. 'Abd-ul-Kerîm sentenced them to receive a flogging, and to be bound to a tree in an erect posture until the following morning, which last punishment I induced him to revoke. Poor Sugar, however, came in for a load of abuse for not restraining the misconduct of his tribe, and especially for their niggardliness in the matter of milk. "Art thou not ashamed," exclaimed the irate Commandant, "to leave the English without milk, and yet permittest thy people to plunder them? By the life of the Prophet! were it not for thy grey hairs I would bind and drag thee by the beard as far as Massowah." The humiliated Chief called upon me afterwards, to complain of the treatment which he had received, begging me at the same time not to forget him in the matter of coffee and tobacco on our return to Massowah. A favourable reply seemed to efface all recollection of his recent rebuff, beyond a general denunciation of 'Abd-ul-Kerîm and his brothers as a set of tyrants. Highest range of the thermometer to-day 77°.

3rd.—There was heavy rain around last night, and again this afternoon, but only a few drops fell in our immediate vicinity. At about 3 P.M., however, a furious torrent came down from the hills, filling the ravine to overflowing, the water extending several feet as far as our tent. At one time it was deep enough to float a schooner, but it began to subside at half-past four, and by five it had dwindled to a streamlet. At that hour we started from Hozât on our return journey, taking a different route after passing Ifabâd, and reached the valley of Mâshlat in two hours, where we encamped on an eminence at a short distance from the bed of the river. Old Sugar honoured us with his company thus far, and, after seeing us safely located, took his leave, not however without reminding me of my promise about the coffee and tobacco; whereupon 'Abd-ul-Kerîm bade me beware of the old miser; "for," said he, "if you give him your horse, he will next ask for your wife." Sugar brought us the skeleton of a cow as a present while we were at Hozât, for which he would certainly have got a thrashing from 'Abd-ul-Kerîm if I had not interfered—the punctilious official deeming it an insult to his own dignity that an animal should be offered to the distinguished foreigners under his protection which could scarcely stand on its legs, and the flesh of which would be rejected by starving hyænas.

4th.—Left Máshlat at 6 P.M., and passing by Aidee and Magamayatât, reached Gadarêt after a ride of three hours. We had intended to encamp here; but, finding the place full of vermin, we resumed our journey at 2·50 the following morning, and at eight o'clock pitched our tents at 'Ain, in a grove of trees, on the southern bank of the stream. A heavy shower fell during the afternoon, which brought the thermometer down from 96° to 86°.

One great drawback to our excursion was the difficulty of procuring good drinking water. This may sound strange, after the foregoing description of torrents, rivers and streams encountered during our progress; but the fact is so, never-theless, and unless travellers remain sufficiently. long at a place to filter it, or to purify it in some other way, the water generally obtainable is undrinkable. The heavy tropical rains in the mountains, in their descent to the lowlands, sweep down an enormous quantity of alluvium, together with large masses of decayed vegetable matter, which have been accumulating during the eight or nine months of the hot season. These reach the plains in a liquefied state, rendering the water which holds them in solution not only thick and muddy but also feculent. It was most likely in order to avoid the diseases generated by the effluvia arising from this source that the forefathers of the Hibâb, and other tribes of the Samhâr, erected their villages at some distance from the beds of these torrents, and preferred using water which had been purified by filtration through the sand. At all events, such appears to me a more probable reason for the pecu-

liarity than that alleged by the natives themselves, as recorded
at p. 71.

Left 'Ain in the afternoon of the 7th, and on reaching the
Shä'ab found that the sand had become quite firm, owing to the
recent heavy rain. Small rivulets were running in every
direction, and some deep gullies were suddenly filled by a
rush of water from the mountains on our right. After wading
through streams and doubling well-filled pools for a mile
or more, we were obliged to diverge to the left of the high
road to Kánfar, for fear of being overtaken by a torrent, the
bed of which had been indicated to us by our guides. My
companions and self, with part of our servants and baggage,
had just crossed the water-course at midnight, when the
cameleers shouted out to us to look out for the flood. In less
than five minutes the flow and force of the water increased
to such an extent, that the remainder of our attendants were
obliged to spend the night on the opposite bank, while we,
roughed it as best we could where we were. Although there
was water enough in the ravine to float a good-sized ship, we
were unable to procure a drop to drink, so filthy and foul
was the stream.

8th.—Towards sunrise the torrent had subsided sufficiently
to permit our servants to join us. The heat was so intense
during the day that we wrapped our heads in wet towels to
alleviate its effects on the brain. During the afternoon
there was a mist of impalpable dust, so dense that objects
were almost invisible ten feet off. I call this dust-storm a
mist, because it came on without any wind, and seemed to
dissolve gradually in the atmosphere.

A little before noon, while seated in the tent, we heard
a voice exclaiming, *"el-Bashárah! el-Bashárah!"* (good
tidings!). On rising to see what it meant, I was accosted

by Ahmed, one of the Nâyib's nephews, who had ridden hard from Massowah to report that Consul Cameron had been released, and that Theodore had written to invite me to go up; that the letter had not actually arrived at Massowah, as the messengers, Ibrahîm and Mohámmed Sihâwy, were too tired to bring it on, but they had dispatched another man to announce the intelligence. I was so delighted with the news that I could have hugged Ahmed there and then, for the alleged release of the Consul was to me a most hopeful sign that all our difficulties with the King would be speedily and satisfactorily adjusted. If I enter somewhat into detail hereafter on this point, it is because some unwarranted remarks were made upon me at the time for transmitting to Government what proved afterwards to be an unfounded report.

We left Kánfar at 3.45 P.M.; Blanc and Prideaux pushing on in advance while I followed with 'Abd-ul-Kerîm. We found a considerable stream running through Ambâa as we passed it, owing to the recent heavy rain in the interior. Four hours' ride brought us to Dasait, and at ten we reached Moncûlu, where I found my two companions fast asleep from exhaustion.

9th.—Blanc and Prideaux took up their old encamping ground on the mainland, while I crossed over to the Island in quest of news. The famine was still raging and the bazaar empty. The starving multitudes had even exhausted the shell-fish on the beach for some distance on the north and south of Massowah.

12th.—While at dinner with Blanc and Prideaux the Nâyib sent to apprise me that my messengers had arrived with the King's letter, and were awaiting me at the Consulate. On going there, I found that the messengers who had carried up my two former communications had also been sent down; but the King's reply had been entrusted to Ibrahîm and Mohammed Sihâwy, who had taken up my third letter. These latter were extremely proud of the distinction, and standing up said that, in accordance with Abyssinian usage, their first duty was to deliver the message with which they had been commissioned by the King. It was as follows:—That his Majesty was angry with Consul Cameron for having gone to the country of the Egyptians, instead of doing as he had requested him, namely, taking his, the King's, letter to the English Queen to Massowah, and forwarding it from thence to England; to await an answer, and to bring it up to him. Thereupon they handed me the King's letter to my address, written in Amharic and Arabic. On opening it, I found, to my intense chagrin, that it was neither signed nor sealed by the writer, who justified rather than apologized for the discourteous omission on the score of the treatment which he had received from several individuals indicated in the epistle, of which the following is a translation :—

"In the name of the Father, and of the Son, and of the Holy Ghost, one God, to whom be praise for ever. Amen.

"The reason I do not write to you my name, because Abûna Salâma, the so-called Kokab [Stern], the Jew, and the one you called Consul, named Cameron (who was sent by you). I treated them with honour and friendship in my city. When I thus befriended them, on account of my anxiety to cultivate the friendship of the English Queen, they reviled me.

"Plowden and Yohanna [John Bell], who were called Englishmen, who were killed in my country, whose death, by the power of God, I avenged on those who killed them. On that account they [Abûna Salâma, the Rev. Mr. Stern and Captain Cameron] abused me and denounced me as a murderer.

"Cameron, who is called Consul, represented to me that he was a servant of the Queen. I invested him with a robe of honour of my country, and supplied him with provisions for the journey. I asked him to make me a friend of the Queen.

" When he was sent on this mission, he went and stayed some time with the Turks, and returned to me.

" I spoke to him about the letter I sent through him to the Queen. He said that up to that time he had not received any intelligence concerning it. 'What have I done,' said I, 'that they should hate me and treat me with animosity?' By the power of the Lord, my Creator, I kept silent.

" Be it known to Hormuzd Rassam that there exists just now a rebellion in Tigré. By the power of God, come round by way of Matámma. When you reach Matámma, send me a messenger, and, by the power of God, I will send people to receive you.

" Written on Wednesday, 29th of Sanné " (5th July, 1865).

This missive left me almost in the same position as before. True, I had received an answer from the King, but its tone was anything but encouraging, and there was not a sentence in it pledging me a safe-conduct. On the other hand, although several of the messengers had not seen Consul Cameron free, yet they all agreed that the King was well-disposed towards me, and that I should do well to go up. They expressed a conviction that the Mission would be successful, and to prove their sincerity they were all anxious to accompany me. The same course was recommended by two immediate attendants on his Majesty, namely, his Arabic scribe and head steward, who had written to their friends at Massowah to that effect. This advice, be it remembered, was in direct opposition to that of Consul Cameron received only a few days previously, who warned me against going up either with or without a safe-conduct. However, as the two messengers to whom the royal answer was confided affirmed that they had seen the Consul at liberty, I judged it not unlikely that such a favourable symptom on the King's part may have induced him to alter his opinion. It certainly surprised me that Cameron had not availed himself of the opportunity to send me a few lines; but then, again, all the messengers agreed that they had been hurried off without being allowed time to take leave of their friends. Moreover, I thought it highly probable that he may have hesitated to trust men, who had been in communication with the King, with any message of importance to me.

Puzzled how to act under these circumstances, I resolved to refer the whole case to superior authority, and to be guided by their decision. Prideaux and I accordingly took down the statements made by the different messengers which I forwarded to Government. The two following are the most important:—

"*Statement of* IBRAHÎM WALAD-SHÛM *and* MOHAMMED SIHÂWY, *who carried the third Letter to* KING THEODORE, *on the 30th of March*, 1865.

"On leaving you we went up to the King of Abyssinia through Tigrê, Tembên, and Lasta, and it took us nearly a month to reach the latter place, on account of the disturbances on the road. Frequently, we could only travel at night, and sometimes we had to conceal ourselves for a day or two through fear of the rebels. At Sokôta we had to remain a month, as the road was very unsafe just then between it and Debra Tâbor.

" We wished to deliver the letter through Samuel, the King's steward, and when we arrived at Sokôta, and learned that he was just then at Debra Tâbor, we sent to inform him of our duty, and craved his assistance.

" He sent us an answer to the effect that we were welcome, and so we repaired straight to him at Debra Tâbor, which we reached in twelve days. We found him busily engaged in packing up all the King's arms, guns and ammunition, to take to Mágdala; and after we had stayed there ten days, Samuel went on before us to Mágdala, and left us to come with the things which he had got ready for the King.

" We reached Mágdala in nine days, on the morning of Tuesday the 4th of July. Samuel had promised on leaving

Debra Tâbor that he would speak to the King about the letter which was in our possession, and no sooner had we arrived at Samuel's house at Mágdala, than a messenger came to tell us that the King wanted to see us immediately, and so we repaired to him at once.

"Before we delivered the letter to his Majesty, he asked who had sent us up. We answered that you had done so. Then he said, 'How did you manage to pass through the rebellious country?' We replied that, through his favour, and the favour of the British Government, we were enabled to do so. He asked us then if we had a letter from you, and in what language it was written? We said one was written in Arabic and the other in English.

"After he took the letter he asked us if we had any message to deliver? We asked his Majesty to read the letter, and we would tell him afterwards what we had to say. He said, 'Never mind, I will read the letters afterwards; let me know what you have to say.' Wo answered, 'The English Agent told us to give you his best salâms, and to say that he was afraid that his former letters had not been properly understood, and that he feared that there were some people who did not wish friendship between England and Abyssinia, and who misrepresented the objects of his Mission; that the best proof of the friendship of the English towards your Majesty is the letter which he bears from the Queen to you, and which he is very anxious to deliver into your hands.' He said, 'If he wanted to come, why did he not come with you?' We answered, 'How could he come without your Majesty's permission?' Then he laughed, and said, 'All right; I will send him that permission?' Then he told us to go back to our quarters, and after he had read the letter he would send for us.

"On our return to our quarters, he sent us abundance of his own food. After we had eaten, he sent for us, and on arriving in his presence he called for all your three letters, and ordered his scribe, Mu'állim Matta, to read them over again. He said that your second letter was better than the first, and the third better than the second, and that the last pleased him very much, and that he was much obliged to the writer. He said that formerly England and Abyssinia were always very friendly; but the Consul did not act properly between the two countries, but he hoped that on seeing you everything would be placed on a proper footing.

"He told us then to return to our quarters, and ordered Samuel to provide us with all necessaries. We replied, 'By your favour, O King, there is no lack of food, but the greatest favour you could confer upon us would be to send us back to Massowah with an answer.' He said to us that we had met with great difficulties on the road, and that as he intended to come down to Tigré himself after two months, we ought to wait, and that he would release the Consul. We said to him that we had promised you to be back in forty days, and then it was more than three months since we had left, and we did not like to prolong our absence much longer. He then said, smilingly to us, 'If the English Agent is really desirous to come up, how is he to pass through the rebellious country?' Samuel, who was then present, answered that there was a safe road *viâ* Matámma. The King immediately approved of that route, and told us to go back to our quarters, and come the next day for an answer.

"Early the next day, the 5th of July, the King sent for us, and for Samuel, and for his Arabic and Amharic scribes. The Arabic letter was written by Mu'állim Matta, and the Amharic by one of the Amharic scribes. He told us that he would have sent people to escort you up, but they would be of no use until you arrived at Matámma; consequently, he would send you the proper escort on your arrival there. He told us to ask you to write to him when you left Massowah, in order that he might write to his Deputy at Matámma to receive you.

"He then sent for all your former messengers, and told them to return with us to Massowah. He gave each of them five dollars; to us he gave nothing, but promised to reward us on our return with you. He told us that he had neither signed nor sealed the letter which he sent you, because he was very angry with the Consul, and he promised to release him after our departure. We told him, 'O King, we pray that you will fulfil your good intention before our departure that our hearts may be rejoiced, and that we could inform Mr. Rassam that we had seen the Consul released.' He said, 'Let it be; for the sake of Mr. Rassam and your trouble, you shall see the Consul liberated.'

"Then he ordered Samuel and Râs Íngădă, the General-in-Chief, to accompany us to the Consul, and have him released before us, and then we could inform you that we had seen him liberated.

"After the Consul was released before us, we wished to obtain a letter from him for you, but Samuel told us that it was impossible without an order from the King; and as we were directed by his Majesty to depart immediately the Consul was released, we were afraid to go back to ask this favour of him.

"We then commenced our journey, and arrived at Massowah on the 12th of this month, having been delayed by the insecurity of the roads."

"*Statement of* Mohammed Sa'íd, *who went up with the first Letter to* King Theodore, *on the* 24*th of July*, 1864.

"I and my companion, Mohammed Abawâso, went up to the King of Abyssinia in sixteen days, and delivered your letter into his hands immediately on our arrival at Góndar. Before he read the letter he asked us what kind of person the Bâsha [an Abyssinian title] was, who gave us the letter, and whether he had any troops with him? We said that he had none. Afterwards he sent for his Arabic scribe to read the letter, and he sent one of his men to provide us with food and quarters. The next morning he sent for us and asked us whether the person who gave us the letter wished to come up. We said to him ' Yes, he is very anxious to come up, and he told us that we must go down with an answer in forty days.' The King then told us to go and wait. Afterwards, we only got messages through Samuel, not to fear, but to wait; his Majesty would send us back with an answer. About two months after that the King went on to Debra Tábor, and all the Europeans went to pray him to release the Consul and his companions; he told them to come the next morning, but at night he sent to them not to appear before him, as he did not intend to do as they wished. Soon after that, we asked Samuel to take us before the King again, as we were anxious to return to Massowah—our business being only to bring the letter and take back its answer. We were taken the next morning to the King's tent, but before we were admitted into the presence of his Majesty, Samuel came out to say that the King had sent to tell us to wait a little longer. He intended to go to Shoa, and on arriving there he would dismiss us with an answer.

" While at Mágdala, the messengers sent by the Nâyib of Harkîko arrived, with another letter from you. The letter was received and read, and the messengers were sent to join us in our quarters. The King treated us always as he did his followers, and always provided us with the necessary provisions, except when he was on a war expedition, when every one in his camp was scantily supplied. Wald-Selassê Gobazê, a Góndar merchant, who had arrived from Massowah about the beginning of July, went and spoke to the King about us [the messengers] who had been so long detained. He told him that he had seen you, and that you had complained of having been kept so long for an answer. He said to him, that it was not at all proper for him to keep silence so long; he ought either to dismiss the messengers with an answer or without. My companion, Mohammed Abawâso, was present when this conversation took place, and it was said that the King had promised to send us back at once.

" On Tuesday, the 4th of July, Ibrahîm and Mohammed Sihâwy reached the King's camp with your third letter. The next day we were all called before the King, who was then in the fortress of Mágdala, and we were told to make preparations for leaving for Massowah. We saw at the time the King's Arabic and Amharic scribes: the former, Mu'állim Matta; the latter, Aläkâ Tecla, writing letters to you. The King asked us by what way we wished to return to Massowah. We said the Lasta route would be the safest. The letters were delivered to Samuel, and then we were told to come down and get ready. The letters were afterward delivered to Ibrahîm and Mohammed Sihâwy to give to you. About noon of the same day, we all left Mágdala on our way down to Massowah; after we left the King we heard that Consul Cameron had been released, and that Ibrahîm and Mohammed Sihâwy were present when the fetters were knocked off his legs. My companion and myself used to see the Consul very often, and once he sent us some money to buy clothes with. We had no time to see him after he was released, as we were hurried off on our journey to Massowah. The King's power has been on the decline ever since we reached his camp, and now he has not got half the force he had then, on account of desertion and deaths in his different engagements with the rebels. There was a rumour when we left Mágdala, that the King intended to come down against the chief rebel, Wakshum Gobazê, and on arriving at the river Tăkkăzê, we found the King's officers busily engaged in collecting sheep and cattle for their master's intended expedition.

"My companion, Mohammed Abawâso, left us at Fanara, near Tembên, to go and pay his family a visit at Godufelassee, in Serâwê, and he said he would join us in Massowah on our arrival."

The Nâyib's two messengers who took up my second letter to the King corroborated the foregoing, with respect to the release of Consul Cameron.

In writing to Government on the 15th of August, through the Resident at Aden, I remarked that his Majesty's letter "was neither courteous nor becoming, and that, contrary to all etiquette, the King had omitted to seal it and to affix his name thereto, on the plea of the breach existing between him and us." With regard to the royal invitation, I said :—

"This letter has placed me in a very difficult position, not only because I am asked to go up through Cásala and Matámma in the most unhealthy time of the year, but its tone seems to warrant in some measure the warning given to me by Captain Cameron in his notes of the 6th and 9th April about the base design of King Theodore. On the other hand, I anticipate deplorable results, in case I now retrace my steps by declining to go up, especially when the King has granted me permission to do so, in his own peculiar way, and has very properly released Captain Cameron before my proceeding thitherward.

"Unfortunately, all my messengers were hurried off to Massowah as soon as the King gave them the reply to me, and had no time to bring me a letter from Captain Cameron, which might have proved of some guidance to me. I have been in hopes that he would write and inform me of his liberation by a private messenger, and tell me what he thought of the King's object concerning his release. A note from him under the present circumstances will, no doubt, be of material assistance to me, and I yet hope that, before taking a decisive step, I shall hear from him upon the subject.

"If I go up to Abyssinia by way of Cásala and Matámma, I shall not be able to proceed on my journey before the middle of October, and I trust that before that time I shall be furnished with important communications from England and Abyssinia which may act as bases for my future proceedings."

The 'Victoria' was absent at Aden when the King's letter arrived, but deeming it necessary that I should proceed in her to Egypt as soon as she was available, in order to communicate all that had transpired to the Foreign Office, I prepared another dispatch, to send with the above, setting forth my reasons for taking that step:—

"I regret to say, that I cannot go by that route [by Cásala and Matámma] for the next two months, on account of the malignant fever which is said to infest the country between Cásala and Matámma during September and October. Even the natives of the country are afraid to travel about in that part of the Soodân during the unhealthy season.

"Moreover, if I go through the Egyptian territory, I require an order from the Viceroy of Egypt to enable me to travel with my companions through his dominions, without hindrance and with dignity. I also wish to obtain some suitable presents for the King, as I learn that her Majesty's Agent and Consul-General in Egypt had sent King Theodore, by a Coptic messenger, valuable presents, and it would be quite ruinous to my mission were I to approach his Majesty with scarcely anything worth presenting to him, while the Copt might make his appearance ultimately with the handsome presents he was entrusted with from Egypt. To meet this difficulty, I purpose, if found feasible, to go up to Suez on the return of her Majesty's steamer 'Victoria' from Aden, when I shall be able to obtain in Egypt what I require, and to communicate with Earl Russell by telegraph about the future policy her Majesty's Government wish me to pursue, after what Captain Cameron has written."

As regards the liberation of that officer, I merely reported, in these words, what had been told me:—"It appears, *from the statement of the messengers*, that on the receipt of my third letter his Majesty ordered the release of Captain Cameron." But my going up, or not, did not hinge on that simple announcement, whether true or false; what I wanted was an invitation from the King, and if I hesitated when the invitation did eventually come, it was not because the terms in which it was couched were discourteous, but because Consul Cameron himself had repeatedly warned me against going up at all. Placed, together with my companions, in this dilemma, I was assuredly justified in referring to superior authority for further instructions. In the mean time, as the King's letter had been nearly a month and a half on the way, we were in hourly expectation of hearing from Consul Cameron how matters were progressing at Mágdala.

When the arrival of the King's letter, inviting me to his Court, became generally known, all my Massowah acquaintances came to congratulate me on the termination of my suspense. Poor Hajj Âdam, however, did not concur in their felicitation; on the contrary, he prognosticated that our serious troubles were now about to commence. Nevertheless, he bade me God-speed, and hoped that before we reached Matámma the Walkaït rebel, T'issoo Gobazê would have closed the road between Debra Tâbor and Chálga, thereby preventing our ingress. Not so the lamented Khoja Bedrôs, who regarded all such wishes for the increase of strife among the Christians as the offspring of Mohammedan jealousy and fanaticism.

13th.—A supply of rice arrived from the Arabian coast, and the Kâyim-Makâm, fearing that the whole might be bought up by the wealthy, took possession of the entire stock and caused it to be distributed equally among rich and poor. Intelligence reached Massowah to-day that the Wakshum Gobazê had entered Adwa unopposed. When within a day's march of that place, Dakla Guargîs, the King's deputy, retired to his native district near the Tăkkăzê.

14th.—While out for a row to-day I was overtaken by a thick sand-storm, which obliged us to steer direct for the coast, to escape being dashed against the rocks in the harbour. About 7 P.M. there was a violent hurricane from the south-west—the first strong wind we had experienced from that quarter—which lasted four hours. At 9, it rained a little, and on my return to the Island, an hour later, sheet-lightning was so constant and vivid that night seemed turned into day in and around the harbour. In rowing across, a number of small fish shot into the boat. A similar incident was of frequent occurrence, especially when the trip was made in smart men-of-war gigs. On one occasion we picked up no less than eighty-seven fish, four inches long, in the gig of the 'Dalhousie.'

17th.—Ibrahîm, one of the messengers who brought the King's letter, called on me to announce that, in order to prove his gratitude " before the world," he intended to take unto himself a wife. (The fellow, I was told, had three wives already in his own country.) The damsel of his choice was the sister of his companion, Mohammed Sihâwy, aged twelve years; his own amounted to half a century. As being the master of her brother and guardian, I was applied to by both parties to undertake the delicate task of apprising the intended bride of her impending marriage. After some demur, I dispatched an interpreter to the young lady to inform her that she would gratify me by accepting the gallant warrior as her affianced husband.

Having thereby made myself in a measure responsible for the marriage, I was, of course, responsible for its accessories also—the expenses of the wedding, the bride's trousseau, &c. Ibrahîm was so elated with his position, that he took his seat on a bench at the gate of the Consulate, and began to dilate to the other messengers and a knot of bystanders on the successful issue of his errand, and the great attentions which had been lavished upon him by the King. At this juncture who should arrive but Wald-Máryam, the disgraced messenger, who seeing that "Muslim son of a dog" holding forth so majestically, was cut to the quick, and poured out upon him a volume of Abyssinian abuse, in which the epithet "liar" was repeated with many a foul supplementary adjective, winding up with a peremptory order that his rival should forthwith descend from the couch and squat on the floor. Ibrahîm refusing to obey, the other bawled out, "By the death of Theodore, you shall sit on the ground." No sooner were these words uttered than Ibrahîm made a sudden start and did as he was ordered; whereupon several of the bystanders rushed in to tell me that the great Ibrahîm had been forced by that scamp Wald-Máryam " to sit on the ground." As this was the first time I had heard of this singular form of adjuration, it took me some time to arrive at its import, and during my inquiries Ibrahîm did not venture to stir an inch. Among other things, I was told that, according to Abyssinian law, a third person was incompetent to remove the adjuration—that power resting alone with him who imposes it. I accordingly insisted on Wald-Máryam retracting his words, and then only did Ibrahîm deem it safe to move from his abject position.

23rd.—The ' Victoria ' arrived this afternoon, bringing me information that Mr. Gifford Palgrave had been appointed to open communications with King Theodore, while I was directed to return to Aden—retaining possession of her Majesty's letter—there to await further instructions. Had I been told that I was superseded, and ordered to hand over the royal letter to Mr. Palgrave, I should have done so on the earliest opportunity, and returned to my duties at Aden; but such not being the case, and the Abyssinian difficulty having just assumed an entirely new phase, I did not consider myself justified in ignominiously running away from it. Although the King's letter to me was neither encouraging nor polite, still it was an invitation for me to go up, and it can hardly be doubted that his Majesty expected to see me and not another acting in a similar capacity. Feeling convinced, moreover, that the primary object of her Majesty's Government was to obtain the release of the unfortunate captives, and that whether Mr. This or Mr. That was employed in the task was a matter of very secondary consideration to them, I judged it not merely expedient but incumbent upon me to transmit to the responsible Minister, with as little delay as possible, a full account of all that had recently transpired, leaving it with him to decide on ulterior proceedings. Wherefore, having ascertained from Lieut. Carpendale that the ' Victoria ' was available for the service, I requested him to hold her in readiness to convey the Mission to Suez, in accordance with a resolve which I had made more than a week before to proceed direct to Egypt, " if found practicable." My reasons for taking this step are set forth in detail in the subjoined dispatch, addressed to Lieut.-Colonel Merewether :—

" *Massowah, 24th August,* 1865.

"Sir,—My letter of the 15th instant will explain to Her Majesty's Government the turn the Abyssinian difficulty has assumed, consequent upon the release of Captain Cameron and the reply I received from King Theodore.

"The intelligence brought yesterday by the 'Victoria,' of the appointment by her Majesty's Government of Mr. Gifford Palgrave, for obtaining the release of our Consul and the Missionaries imprisoned by the King of Abyssinia, has more than ever necessitated my immediate departure for Egypt, in order that I might ascertain how far that gentleman has progressed with his mission, and, if possible, to prevent our respective duties coming to a clash; which event would most assuredly bring about ill consequences, which we are anxious to avoid.

"The non-arrival of any intelligence from Captain Cameron, subsequent to his release, has placed me in an awkward predicament, both as regards my answer to King Theodore and the future course I shall have to pursue.

"As the King might expect that I should leave Massowah for up-country soon after the receipt of his letter, I fear he would suspect that I had some covert reason for postponing my departure; consequently, I consider it necessary, for the safety of Captain Cameron and his yet imprisoned companions, that I should write to his Majesty at once, and explain the cause of the delay.

"In this letter, a copy of which I annex herewith for the information of Government, I have been careful to avoid using any expression which might give umbrage to the King, or bind Government to any ulterior policy.

"In the mean time I hope to hear from England, on my arrival in Egypt, as to the intention of her Majesty's Government regarding the obstacles set forth by Captain Cameron against my going up. That astounding revelation of his has placed no little impediment to the steps I intend to take.

"My greatest endeavours have ever been to avoid increasing the trouble and anxiety of Government; and with this object in view, I am now left to choose one of two alternatives—either to disregard *in toto* Captain Cameron's warning, and act as I had formerly intended; or bring matters to a crisis by breaking my engagement with the King.

"I must confess I anticipate evil results in case I pursue the latter course, being aware how cruel and vindictive a man King Theodore is; but with all the risk attendant on the former action, I deem it the most prudent to follow."

My letter to the King, referred to in the above, was as follows :—

" *Massowah, August* 24, 1865.

" Most Gracious Sovereign,

"I have the honour to acknowledge the receipt of your letter dated the 29th of the month of Sannê, and beg to inform your Majesty that, in consequence of the prevailing sickness at Cásala and the neighbourhood, I dare not for the present come up to you *viâ* Matámma, as you have directed.

"Moreover, I am informed by the people of the country that, after the rains, the road between Cásala and Matámma is most unhealthy, on account of the malignant fever which infests the land for the next two months. Even the natives of the country avoid the journey through those districts at this season.

"I have furthermore to obtain an order from the Viceroy of Egypt for passing with my party through his dominions, with the necessary protection, because, when I was sent here by my Government, I was unprepared with the needful papers, they not having anticipated that I should be obliged to come to you by the Egyptian route. I shall, however, take the earliest opportunity to acquaint your Majesty of the day I intend to depart for Cásala and Matámma."

As these letters clearly set forth the principles and motives which actuated my official conduct at this period in the history of the Abyssinian Mission, I shall pass it over without further comment.

We were ready to start on the day the 'Victoria' arrived; but I was most anxious before leaving to obtain a reply from the Nâyib to a letter which he had received from King Theodore, simultaneously with his Majesty's answer to me. Unfortunately, the Nâyib was absent, attending the death-bed of a man of great sanctity in the Hibâb country. As he had not made his appearance up to the 25th, I determined to embark forthwith, leaving instructions with the messengers, whom I had instructed to convey my letter to the King, not to wait for him or his reply beyond one day longer. I was most solicitous that his Majesty should be made acquainted as early as possible with my reasons for visiting Egypt, lest some mischievous persons should have an opportunity of insinuating to him that I had gone thither to consult with his enemies, the Turks, for sinister purposes.

25th.—Left the harbour in the afternoon and anchored off Râs Harb—a run of eighteen miles—Lieut. Carpendale wishing to have the whole of the following day to clear the numerous reefs which lie off the coast to the north of Massowah. On the 26th there was a dead calm, and the atmosphere was most stifling. On the 27th, the wind blew a hurricane from the north-west—a bad look-out for us, as it impeded the progress of the steamer so much that Lieut. Carpendale eventually deemed it advisable to steer across the sea to replenish the coal-bunkers at Jiddah.

28th.—Sighted Jebel Tâyif, the paradise of the Hijâz, at sunrise, and came to an anchor a couple of miles westward of the town, at 12·45 P.M., having successfully threaded our way, with the aid of a skilful pilot, through a labyrinth of sunken rocks extending five miles beyond the anchorage. So intricate are the channels leading through this maze of reefs, that the wonder is how comparatively so few vessels, from among the seventy or eighty which frequent the port during the Hajj season, come to grief in making it. The late Consul Calvert was absent in Egypt; but hearing that my old Massowah friend, Purtoo Effendi, was on board a Turkish man-of-war in the harbour, on his way to Kunfudah, to take up his new appointment as secretary to 'Abdallah-bin-'Awn, the Sherîf of Mecca, on an expedition against the 'Aseir, a branch of the Wahhâby sect, who were always giving trouble to the Hijâz authorities, I went with the port-officer to call upon him. The kindly old man received me with open arms, and repeatedly embraced me after the Eastern fashion. On hearing that I had received an invitation from Theodore to go up to him *viá* Matámma, and that I actually entertained the idea of accepting it, he said, with a sudden start, "What! under the same delusion still?" He accompanied me to dinner on board the 'Victoria,' where he remained while my companions and I paid a formal visit to the French Consul, and then strolled through the bazaar. I was agreeably disappointed in the town, having looked for nothing better than a tumble-down collection of dwellings, such as one almost universally meets in this quarter. The houses of Jiddah, on the contrary, are well built, consisting of several stories, and many of them might fairly be styled mansions. We found Purtoo Effendi fast asleep on our return, and after he had spent a few hours more with us, I accompanied him to his vessel. Had circumstances permitted, I should have been delighted to accept his offer of introducing me to the Sherîf, though I was rather surprised to find that one so little partial to prayer or fasting as my good friend Purtoo Effendi, should hold so important an office with the Guardian of the holy places of Islâm, and stand so high in his favour.

29th.—Quite a gale blowing from the north-west. The town being so far removed from the anchorage, and the passage becoming full of shoals at low tide, we could not obtain all the coals we wanted to-day. Coaling is a very slow process at Jiddah. The sixty tons which we required would have been put on board at Aden in two hours, whereas the lazy Jiddâwis could not supply us with forty in an entire day.

30th.—Discovered this morning that the 'Victoria' was

hard and fast by the stern on a coral reef, the existence of
which seems to have been previously unknown to the pilot,
or to any one at Jiddah. The reef at low water was fifteen
feet below the surface, and its summit was less than four
yards round. It appears that the gale of the preceding day,
which had also lasted part of the night, had caused the
steamer to drift a few feet backwards. However, she floated
with the rise of the tide at 1 P.M., without having sustained
any damage. Still, this untoward accident prevented our
starting that day, as it is dangerous to leave the harbour
after 3 P.M., owing to the reflection of the sun's rays on the
water, which prevents the pilot from seeing the reefs clearly.
Everything connected with the Abyssinian difficulty seemed
to go wrong. The actual position of affairs demanded dispatch, and here were we, not only obliged to visit Jiddah,
but detained there three days.

31st.—Resumed our voyage at 8 A.M., but owing to strong
head-winds in the Gulf, did not make Suez till sunrise on the
5th of September. The order to " let go," and the rattling
of the cable, sounded like music to my ears. It took us
several hours to get through the quarantine formalities, after
which we were free to land. At Suez, I had the pleasure of
making the acquaintance of Mr. Phillips, then Inspector-
General of railways in Egypt, who did all in his power to
serve us during the few hours we were detained there.

Immediately on landing at Suez, I telegraphed to Colonel
Stanton, her Majesty's Consul-General, announcing the object
of my visit, and stating that I should proceed at once to
Alexandria, where he then was, to consult with him on
various matters connected with the Mission. Accordingly,
my companions and I, accompanied by Lieut. Carpendale and
Mr. Westbrook of the ' Victoria,' started by the 9·30 P.M.

train, and reached Cairo a little after midnight. We were met at the station by Mr. Consul Reade and Mr. Palgrave, who, having had notice of our arrival, came to learn the latest news from Abyssinia. After a stoppage of twenty minutes, the train moved on, and early the following morning we found ·ourselves at the Hôtel d'Europe, or Prince of Wales's Hotel, at Alexandria.

I lost no time in calling on Colonel Stanton, who received me with a courteous affability which soon removed all conventional and official restraint. After perusing the dispatches which I was forwarding to Earl Russell, he sent a telegram to the Foreign Office, requesting instructions as to future measures, consequent on the new turn which the Abyssinian complication had taken. To this he received a telegraphic reply, directing that I should proceed with the Queen's letter to the Court of Theodore, and that in the mean time Mr. Palgrave's further progress was to be suspended. Other communications had to be made about presents, without which I felt convinced that our Mission would not be well received by Theodore, who would unquestionably attribute the disregard of the custom, which has prevailed from time immemorial throughout the East, of approaching a sovereign with a suitable offering, as an implied insult to his dignity.

We started from Alexandria on the 16th of September, but were delayed two days at Cairo in securing the requisite letters from the local Government for our passage through the Egyptian territory. In this and in everything else connected with the furtherance of the Mission, Mr. Reade, her Majesty's Consul, afforded me his very valuable and ready assistance. Leaving Cairo in the morning of the 19th, I reached Suez in the afternoon, where Dr. Blanc and Lieut. Prideaux, who had preceded me the day before, awaited my arrival, and in the course of two or three hours we all found ourselves once more on board of the 'Victoria.' At 6·30 P.M. we left the anchorage and steamed down the bay with a fair wind and in smooth water—a happy omen, as I then hoped, that the tide of Abyssinian affairs had turned in our favour, and that henceforward all would be plain sailing.

As it was necessary that we should procure tents, arms, baggage-animals and money for our journey into Abyssinia, and that some arrangement should be made, in concert with Colonel Merewether, for appointing an agent to communicate with the captives after the departure of the Mission from Massowah, I had decided to visit Aden for a day or two for that purpose. But knowing that it would take some time to purchase mules and to collect camels at Massowah, I resolved to touch there first and make the necessary arrangements, so that everything might be ready for a start on our return from Aden.

We steamed into Massowah in the afternoon of the 25th, having had a very pleasant voyage from Suez. Here the most staggering news awaited us. It was reported that messengers had arrived, during our absence, with letters from Consul Cameron, warning me once more against going up to the King; that the report of his release was utterly false, and had been put into circulation by his Majesty's special order; that, on my third letter reaching Theodore, the captives were laden with additional chains; that the messengers who had brought this news to Massowah had been embarked, with all the letters they carried, on board a French gun-boat bound for Aden; that all the secrets which had been entrusted to the said messengers had been divulged and made public at Massowah; and it was seriously apprehended, in consequence, that Cameron's warning to me, after the

King's invitation, on becoming known to his Majesty, might cost him his life. A fresh crop of perplexities this, upsetting all my fond hopes that our greatest difficulties had disappeared. However, on learning from Padre Delmonte that letters had arrived from the captives which had been forwarded to Aden, I determined to proceed thither, in order to obtain authentic intelligence before ordering the mules and making other arrangements for the journey. It was further reported at Massowah that the mutiny in the Soodân had assumed a most serious aspect; that the native troops had massacred all their Turkish and Egyptian officers, not sparing their families; that the tribes between Suâkin and Cásala and the Massowah borders had rebelled and cut off all communication between the Turkish authorities at those places; and that T'issoo Gobazê had captured Debra Tâbor and seized all the King's European artisans, whom he had put to death for having been engaged in making powder and casting guns for the execrable Theodore.

These different rumours were not calculated to cheer me; nevertheless, I consoled myself with the reflection that if there were any grounds for them, the real truth had most probably been grossly exaggerated. Sincerely hoping to have some of our doubts set at rest at Aden, we left Massowah on the 27th and reached that station on the 29th, when I learnt, to my great satisfaction, on calling upon Colonel Merewether, that the report of Consul Cameron and the other captives having written to advise my not going up was utterly untrue; that, on the contrary, the former had expressed his conviction that unless I went up the lives of all the captives would be endangered.

During our short stay at Aden, General Raines, the Commandant of the garrison, received me as his guest, and from him and his estimable wife I experienced a renewal of the kindness which I had enjoyed under their hospitable roof on former occasions. Colonel Merewether also, with his wonted zeal and friendship, materially assisted in expediting our arrangements. These being all completed by the 5th of October, we steamed off to Massowah and arrived there in the afternoon of the 7th.

8th.—M. Munzinger, who had returned from Cásala, gave me a deplorable account of the Soodân and of the fiendish spirit of the mutineers. As it was our intention to start for Cásala about the middle of the month, I availed myself of the proffered services of the Nâyib of Harkîko to obtain for us the requisite number of camels to transport our baggage and the presents designed for the King.

10th.—The sickness brought on by the recent famine, and which had proved fatal to hundreds of starving creatures, has developed into cholera, and numbers of people in and around Massowah have fallen victims to it to-day, after a very short illness.

The resident Abyssinian merchants, finding that we were actually preparing for the journey, came to offer their services; some even asked me to allow them to travel with their goods under our protection. A Góndar merchant, named Fántu, who was going direct to Abyssinia, volunteered to undertake any employment for us. Wishing to send some supplies to the captives, fearing it might be long before we reached them ourselves, I requested him to take charge of the same, and to hand them over to Mr. Flad at Debra Tâbor, to be forwarded on to Mágdala. To my surprise, he immediately acquiesced, and on asking him how it was that, whereas he and other Abyssinians were formerly afraid of coming near us, they now not only wished to travel in our company, but he himself had agreed to convey stores for the use of the captives? He replied, that as long as the King kept silence it was their duty to fight shy of me; but since his Majesty had invited me to his Court they had nothing to fear.

I must here remark, that the fact of the King's letter to me not having had the royal Ethiopian sign-manual attached to it was unknown to any of the Massowah people, with the exception of the two messengers who brought it, and the Nâyib of Harkîko. Had they been aware of the omission, and of the uncourteous tenour of the letter itself, we should have had great difficulty in procuring native servants to accompany us from Massowah.

11th.—Sent a large quantity of stores by Lámma, Consul Cameron's servant, under the care of the Góndar merchant above mentioned. I also dispatched a private messenger to Mágdala, with money and medicines; also a note to Cameron, apprising him of our progress. On my recommendation, Colonel Merewether had authorised me to offer the appointment of British Consular Agent, on a·specified salary, to M. Munzinger, in order that he might superintend all communications with the captives, after our departure, and look after British interests generally. As he was not merely the only fit person available on the spot, but a gentleman in every way suited for the office, I was extremely delighted that he consented to undertake the duties in conjunction with those devolving on him as Vice-Consul for France. I introduced him to the Kâyim-Makâm in his new capacity, and received his Excellency's assurance that he would render him every assistance in his power.

13th.—Nothing but weeping and wailing around me this

morning. Scores of people on the Island had been attacked with cholera during the night, and many had died in the immediate vicinity of my residence. These lamentations were more harrowing than the dread of the disease itself; but I was obliged to remain on the spot to hurry forward the preparations for our impending departure. The epidemic was raging on all sides: on the Island, on board ship, and among the villages on the mainland. It was especially fatal at Moncûlu, whither my good friend Khoja Bedrôs, the Armenian merchant, had gone to escape the dread scourge which, at the outset, was most virulent on the Island. After assisting me this same day to pack up the presents for the King, he was attacked by cholera on his way back to Moncûlu, and died there the following day.

15*th*.—Cholera at its height in all directions, so that those who would otherwise have assisted me in our preparations are busily engaged either in ministering to their sick relatives or burying the dead. I had determined positively to make a start to-day. The camels arrived yesterday; but in lieu of proper ropes for securing the packages, they were merely provided with a few unserviceable grass-cords of native manufacture. Then, again, the cameleers refused to take us beyond the Hibâb tribe, on the road to Cásala. I did not deem it worth while to haggle with them on the latter point, as our main object now was to attain the highlands out of the reach of cholera; but what was to be done for rope? The bazaars were closed, the natives being wholly absorbed by their fears, or in tending the sick, the dying and the dead. Poor 'Abdallah Effendi was at his wit's end, but by dint of perseverance he managed before evening to secure every rope that was to be found in the bazaar. We had hoped to start that night and accomplish a few miles at least beyond the cholera-smitten district; but on reaching the mainland with my companions, I found, to my utter dismay, that there was little chance of it. There was the poor Nâyib Mohammed with all his available male relatives hard at work trying to steady the heavy packages on the backs of the camels; but the attempt was bootless, for so rotten were the cords that, as soon as the animals moved, down came the loads with a heart-rending crash. On hearing of our embarrassment, the Kâyim-Makâm most thoughtfully sent to importune us not to remain in that dangerous locality—several men had been attacked with cholera in our immediate vicinity, two of whom actually died a few yards from where we stood—but to go on to Moncûlu, promising at the same time that he would use his utmost exertions to collect what rope we required. He was as good as his word; for neither he nor the Nâyib retired for the night before they collected enough for all our luggage, and sent it under the charge of a party of soldiers to Moncûlu. Of course, we ourselves were obliged to spend the night in that hotbed of cholera, and were not a little thankful on finding, the following morning, that only one of our Abyssinian followers—a muleteer attached to Dr. Blanc—had been attacked. Under his master's skilful treatment the man had rallied before we left Moncûlu, and we heard subsequently that he entirely recovered a few days after.

It is impossible for me to speak too highly in praise of the Massowah authorities, both Ottoman and native. Though disapproving, as they did, of the risk which we undertook, they did all in their power to further the object of the Mission. I had come among them, nevertheless, without a line of recommendation either from the Porte or from the Egyptian Government, and they had only heard of me as an official connected with the Residency at Aden. They inter-

posed no obstacle to our landing whatever we required either
for our own private use or that of the Mission; on the contrary, they were ready themselves to supply our wants, and
would even have given me arms to present to the King of
Abyssinia, had I been in need of them. Further, by a rule
which had always been enforced at Massowah, no mason or
carpenter was allowed to serve the representative of a foreign
Power, or any European merchant, without the special sanction of the local authorities; but on our arrival at the Island,
and during our sojourn there, Purtoo Effendi and his suc-
cessors instructed all artificers to attend to my orders,
whenever I required their services, without referring to
them.

Massowah, at best, is a horrible place to live in; still,
I cannot look back upon it but with feelings of deep interest
and gratitude. From the chief local authorities and from
the resident Europeans, from the dignified Muslim and the
unassuming Banian—from all, I ever experienced prompt
assistance and cordial sympathy.

The Kâyim-Makâm, with his usual solicitude, provided us
with letters to the different Chiefs between Massowah and
the Egyptian frontier, and also sent our old friend 'Abd-ul-
Kerîm, the Nâyib's brother, with fifteen Irregulars, to escort
the Mission to the nearest Egyptian district—Massowah
being at that time subject to the Porte, and under the immediate jurisdiction of the Hijâz authorities.

On the day we left Massowah, I dispatched other messengers to the King, in fulfilment of my promise, advising him
of our departure for Matámma, and expressing the hope of
reaching that place in the course of a month—the shortest
time I could name for accomplishing the journey. With all
the unforeseen difficulties which we had to encounter in

obtaining camels both from the Atté-Máryam and at Cásala, we were only six days behindhand. Had I been able to secure the requisite supply of carriage without delay, we should have reached Matámma in just half the time that it takes an ordinary Kâfilah to make the trip.

CHAPTER V.

MASSOWAH TO CÁSALA.

Ravages of Locusts — Difficulty in procuring Camels — The River Ansába — Magnificent Scenery — Descent into the Barca Valley — Elephants — Climate — Lions — The Beni-'Âmir — The tribe of the Barríyah — Impure water — Etymology of the word "Barca" — The Haránrua tribe — Sabdarât — Arrival at Cásala — Reception of the Mission — Effects of the late Mutiny — Kuchúk 'Ali Bey, the Governor — His opinion of Theodore — An old Camelcer — The Shûkry tribe — Dust-storm.

We left Moncûlu at four o'clock in the afternoon of the 16th of October, not a little thankful to have got clear of Massowah, with our faces now turned towards the goal of our expedition. Signor Marcopoli, an Italian merchant and partner to Mr. Munzinger, who had some commercial busi-ness to transact at Matámma, joined our company. Pur-suing the same route we had taken in our excursion to Ifabâd three months before, we reached Ambâa at 9·30 P.M.

17th.—The weather had cooled down, but it was still too oppressive to risk travelling during the heat of the day. Leaving Ambâa at 4·15 P.M. we stopped at the watercòurse of Kánfar an hour afterwards, in order to count the camels in our equipage, which now for the first time were collected together. They numbered forty-six, riding and baggage animals included. At 8·40 we encamped in the plain of Shä'ab for the night.

18th.—Started again at 4·30 A.M., and reached 'Ain at nine. During this part of the journey we encountered myriads of locusts, in flights so dense that they threw a deep shadow on the ground beneath them. They had devoured every scrap of verdure in the vicinity of 'Ain, and scarcely a vestige of any edible plant was left for our camels and mules.

19th.—'Abd-ul-Kerîm had a slight attack of cholera during the night, but a few drops of Collis Browne's chlorodyne in a dose of brandy, administered by Dr. Blanc, soon set him all right. Resuming our route at 3 P.M. we reached Gadarêt at 6·45, where we found a native encampment. It was surprising to see their beasts of burden still alive, for there was nothing for them to feed upon—even the trees had been denuded of their leaves by the voracious locusts. Two months before, this valley was green and flourishing; deprived of all its gay foliage, it was now painful to look upon.

20th.—Our camels had found so little to eat since leaving Massowah, that a number of them were unable to carry their loads. Some, indeed, could only bear their pack-saddles, while two, after going a short distance, were unequal to carrying their own weight, and all the alternate cudgelling and coaxing of their owners failing to move them, they were abandoned to the hyænas. Left Gadarêt at 4·30 A.M. It was now cool enough to travel during the daytime, so continuing our journey through the valley of Lebka—not diverging to the right as on our previous excursion to Magamayatât—we reached the halting-place at Máhabar in a little under four hours. The Massowah cameleers had engaged to accompany us thus far, and here we expected to find other camels belonging to the Hibâb ready to take us on to Cásala. However, although the Náyib had taken the precaution of sending his nephew a week in advance to old "Sugar," the Chief of the Atté-Máryam, he was unable to secure the requisite number of animals, and could not prevail on a single man of the tribe to accompany us. The Hibâb thought us mad to think of going to Cásala while the whole country around was in a state of anarchy. They allowed that we were wise in escaping from the famine and cholera at Massowah; but, in their opinion, we should only be leaping out of the frying-pan into the fire by prosecuting the journey any farther. True, the Franks would undoubtedly pay for the hire of the camels, but of what consequence would a few dollars be, when they and their camels had perished in the land of Tâka? It was also objected, that the fever in the valley of the Barca, which lay before us, was so malignant that even the natives were prostrated by it. Accordingly, some of the Atté-Máryam had sent their camels out of the way, while others had hidden their pack-saddles. On the following day, Sugar was taken in charge by the guard as a hostage, for the fulfilment of his promise. He appealed to me against the injustice of the Nâyib's followers in insisting on his people going to certain death. On my reminding him that we should all be in the same predicament, he pleaded on behalf of the camels, that, as they were not accustomed to carry boxes, all our equipage should be made into small packages. That, I told him, was impossible, as some of the cases contained glass, which could not be treated like so much salt; to which he coolly replied that all such fragile articles might just as well be left behind. By this time 'Abd-ul-Kerîm was fairly exasperated, and, after bestowing upon the old Chief every abusive epithet he could think of, he begged me not to listen any further to his hypocritical twaddle, swearing " by the tomb of the Prophet " that he would have nothing more to do with one so utterly ignorant of the precepts of his religion, and would appoint his son Mohammed to act in his stead. On being called, the young Chief undertook to procure the required number of camels without much ado. After three days' hurry and bustle, the animals were brought, some without drivers and others even without owners, whom the report of the rebellion had scared away. These were made over to the keeping of the guard, and on my expostulating with 'Abd-ul-Kerîm on such summary proceedings, he replied that I must needs take one of two alternatives: I must either follow the usages of the country, or make up my mind to remain where we were for an indefinite period; adding, "You don't know, Sir, that the Hibâb are like donkeys, who won't stir unless driven with the stick." Not being in a position for initiating a new system of procedure, especially with so obstinate a tribe as the Hibâb for the first essay, I was obliged to submit. When the loading commenced, some of the she-camels proved so frisky that they upset their loads and decamped. Soon after we had started, the owners who had refused at first to come with their animals joined us. On my asking whether they were not afraid, an elder among them replied, "What have we to fear while in your company? Surely, we are not better than our camels, and if we lose them we shall be lost ourselves." Having left Máhabar at 4 P.M. of the 23rd, we reached Kalamât after a ride of two hours and a half. Rain had fallen here, and the ground was quite wet.

24*th*.—A lión came very near our camp last night, and for the first time in my life I distinctly heard its roar. Began loading this morning at five o'clock, but did not make a clear start before half-past seven, owing to the intractable-

and we were assured that if we remained there during the night we should certainly receive an unwelcome visit from the former. Of all the places in the vicinity of Massowah, I would certainly recommend this, as offering the best field for a lover of wild scenery and large game.

Left at 4·30 P.M., and after travelling three hours through the bed of the Ansába came to the wells of Hibûb. Both banks were thickly covered with verdure and noble trees, and but for the slow pace of the mules over the heavy sand, one might have fancied himself riding through a beautiful park. The camels seemed to enjoy the soft ground amazingly, and were able to accomplish three miles an hour. The village of Hibûb, situated at some distance from the wells, had been quite deserted, in consequence of the incursions in late years of the Arabs of the Barca into the luckless district of the Ansába. I was told that forty years ago this valley was thickly populated, and was considered one of the most fertile districts of northern Abyssinia, producing grain and honey in abundance; but, through the negligence of their rulers, and incessant conflicts with their neighbours the Beni-'Âmir, the inhabitants had gradually fled their homes and taken refuge in the highlands.

Spent the night of the 26th at Hibûb, in order to give our animals a little rest. The Collector of Customs of Bogôs called on me to-day, bringing a cow as a present. He expected that the Wakshum Gobazê would shortly take possession of Bogôs and Hamasên; but he told me, on the other hand, that the people of Tigrê hated the arch-rebel, and were looking out for the arrival of the King every day —his Majesty having written to say that he was coming to their assistance. "Only let the King move," said my visitor, "and all the rebels will disappear."

27th.—Left Hibâb at 7·20 A.M., and reached the pass of Gâbê-Lukûm in two hours. Here the northern limit of Abyssinia ends, and the valley of Barca, subject to the Egyptian Government, begins. The grass in this locality was knee-deep, and we were put on our guard against venomous snakes which infest it during the heat of the day. The descent into the Barca valley was described as so difficult and dangerous, that 'Abd-ul-Kerîm advised us to remain on the summit until all the baggage-animals reached the level ground. My companions and I accordingly sat down to breakfast under a tree, and the weather was so cool that at noon the thermometer had not risen above 78°. Hearing at that time that all the animals had reached the foot of the mountain in safety—it took them two hours to accomplish the task—we commenced the descent ourselves, and it was certainly surprising to me how they had managed to thread the intricate and perilous path without any accident. The declivity was not only precipitous but encumbered with large boulders; and unless I had witnessed it, I could hardly have believed that so awkward a beast as the camel could have surmounted so difficult a pass, for, with a few exceptions, the roads here were worse than any which we subsequently traversed in Abyssinia. Indeed, were it not for the climate, which is unsuited to its nature, the camel might be used as a beast of burden throughout the greater part of that country. Even my mule, which had been accustomed to the worst Abyssinian routes, seemed rather at a loss how to make her way through the rocky pass. Although we were told at noon that the baggage had attained the level ground, nevertheless we had to continue the descent through a rugged water-course, called Shä'alab, until 4·30 P.M., when we halted at Máhlab. A large stream runs down the valley, which here and there is lost in the sand. At Máhlab we found some wells, apparently just dug in the sand by elephants; and our guides advised us to use them in preference to the pools close by, as those sagacious animals were very nice and discriminating in the water they drank. I judge that we must have descended two thousand feet, and the heat in the valley was most oppressive. In addition to the fatigue of the journey, it served to knock up both man and beast. Our halts hereabouts were rendered somewhat disagreeable, owing to the long grass being furnished with sharp barbs, which adhere to the clothes and soon penetrate to the skin.

28*th.*—If the cameleers are to be believed, a couple of elephants were seen last night refreshing themselves at their own wells. Left Máhlab at 4 P.M., and reached Hámarai at 5·30., where we halted forty-minutes to allow the mules to graze and the camels to pass on in advance. Continued the route till eight, when we gave ourselves another forty minutes for supper. Travelled two hours longer through the sandy valley, and then diverging a little came upon high ground, covered with dry grass and thistles, which greatly incommoded those of us who were mounted, but inflicted real suffering on our pedestrian followers. Reached Bâat in the valley of Adárdi towards midnight.

29*th*—Left Bâat at 4·40 P.M., and arrived at Kar-Obêl in three hours, from whence, after staying forty-minutes for supper, we jogged onward for the same space and then halted in the valley for the night—our guides assuring us that it would be impossible to make way through the thorny bushes in the road before us while it was dark.

30*th.*—Resumed our journey at 5·20 A.M., and reached Jâgê at eight. The ground here was swampy, and in some parts of the valley the grass and weeds had grown so thick and high, that it was not easy to force a passage through the obstruction. We spent part of the day on a hill near a small lake, under the shade of a clump of trees—with which the country abounds—and dispensed with tents. I can well imagine that the valley of the Barca must be most unhealthy just before and after the rains, when the whole district becomes one vast swamp. The inhabitants generally retire to the hills at those periods, but being obliged to return before the ground is quite dry, in order to find food for their cattle, upwards of a fourth of them are attacked with fever. The disease, however, is not so fatal as in some valleys in Abyssinia, although I was told that in many instances the patients suffer for months together without seeming to grow better or worse. Left Jâgê at 4·30 P.M., and in four hours came to Solîb, where we halted for an hour and a half to see the camels pass on, and then went to a spot in the same valley, called Täerarait, which we reached at 9·15 P.M. The heat during the day has been very oppressive since our descent into the Barca, and for the last two days the water has been very indifferent and unwholesome.

31st.—Two Chiefs of the Barca paid me a visit this morning, and informed me that a large encampment of their tribe was close by, but, owing to the thick cover which overspreads the country, we could not discern their tents. Our guides soon obtained some cows from them, and also a sheep, which we greatly needed. In the afternoon, Sheikh Arai, chief of the El-Bakhît—a subdivision of the Beni-'Âmir— called upon me. The poor man had been a martyr to fever for several months. Our cameleers lost one of their camels to-day, and we had no little trouble to get them to distribute its load among the rest. At 5·40 P.M. we started again, but after proceeding about a mile through the same sandy watercourse, my companions and I, under the direction of 'Abd-ul-Kerîm and a guide from the El-Bakhît, diverged to a hard soil on the left, leaving the camels and followers to pursue the route through the valley. At 7·45 we reached Awhê, where we found an encampment of the El-Bakhît. A cousin of Sheikh Arai, named Mansûr, received us on dismounting. Here we expected to get a drink of fresh milk, but, as the cattle had not returned from pasture, we were obliged to wait for it till nine o'clock. We were amply repaid for the delay, as the milk was most delicious, and we had not met with any so rich and good since our departure from Aden. It being a beautiful moonlight night, we pursued our journey by the upper road leading to the headquarters of the Beni-'Âmir, who were then encamped at a place called Zâga. We did not halt till we re-entered the watercourse at a quarter to four the following morning, at a spot called Lákaba, not far from the village. Soon after leaving Awhai, we heard the roaring of lions in every direction, so distinctly that some of the beasts must have been within fifty yards of us. Dr. Blanc's dog became so excited at the sound, that nothing would keep him from bounding off in search of the cause, and we saw no more of him. On reaching Lákaba we found that our baggage had not arrived; but so dead tired were we that we stretched ourselves near the well and fell fast asleep, heedless of the lions which were prowling about in the vicinity. It is wonderful how a man gets accustomed to danger, and how little effect any disturbing cause has to prevent sweet slumber, when the body is worn out by fatigue. Signor Marcopoli, who ordinarily shrank from the bare idea of a lion being near him, went to sleep this morning like the rest of us, taking care, however, to ensconce himself as close as possible to Dr. Blanc. We heard on the following day that two men had been killed by these wild denizens of the forest. The cameleers made their appearance about seven o'clock, and by a little after eight our tents were pitched on a plateau between the camp at Zâga and the valley. Sheikh Hâmid, the Chief of the Beni-'Âmir, called on us shortly after. He was very courteous and promised his assistance in every way; but he frankly told me that he could not provide camels to take us to Cásala, as all the available beasts of burden had been sent to bring grain from Tâka. This, he said, was owing to the fact that the country had been so disturbed for the last few months, that people had been wholly taken up with measures for self-protection, and had altogether neglected to procure supplies from Cásala and the adjacent districts. The Beni-'Âmir are a purely pastoral tribe, and depend entirely upon Tâka for grain. 'Abd-ul-Kerîm and his guard, as also the Hibâb cameleers, had discharged their duty in having escorted us this far; it was now for Sheikh Hâmid, the first Chief under Cásala within Egyptian territory, to see that we were conveyed on to that place; but the question was, how he could do so without camels? He offered, if we consented to remain till the return of the animals, to supply us with as many as we required; but in that case we might have to wait a week or a fortnight, whereas I was most anxious to push forward to Matámma.

I was glad to learn from the Sheikh that the mutiny at Cásala and throughout the Soodân had been effectually crushed; the only fear now was that the Albanians, who had been engaged in quelling it, might prove as mischievous as the late mutineers, and, in fact, it was reported that they were already giving trouble to the inhabitants of Cásala. I spoke to Sheikh Hâmid about the disgraceful behaviour of his tribe towards the Abyssinian Christians, whom they not only plundered and massacred, but whose children they also carried away into slavery. He urged, in reply, that the Beni-'Âmir being a nomad tribe, his power over them was little more than nominal; and then went on to say how pleased he would be if the King of Abyssinia and the Egyptian Government were to come to some arrangement to arrest these outrages on the part of their respective subjects. He alleged that both parties were equally to blame, as the Christians, at different times, carried off as many slaves from their Mohammedan neighbours. He admitted that the Barrîyah tribe had dealt most iniquitously with the Abyssinians; but what power, he asked, could punish them? They were as wild as hyænas, and when in danger of being attacked retired into the recesses of their native desert, where want of water prevented their pursuers from following them. Even the Beni-'Âmir were obliged to brook many of their misdemeanours, owing to their inability to cope with such wily antagonists.

2nd November.—After a good deal of grumbling and haggling, our old friends, the Hibâb, agreed to go on with us to Cásala; 'Abd-ul-Kerîm, also, offered to attend us, with his men. He had been ordered by the Kâyim-Makâm to convoy us to the Chief of the Beni-'Âmir only, where a Turkish guard generally awaited travellers; but owing to the late mutiny in the Soodân all the Egyptian troops had been recalled, and 'Abd-ul-Kerîm, unwilling that we should proceed without an escort, volunteered to accompany us. Starting at 8·20 P.M., we travelled all night and reached the valley of Hawashêt at five the following morning, where we encamped near some wells dug in the sand between the mountains of Karkuê and Surûr. The water here is very disagreeable to the taste, being rather saline, and apparently holding in solution other extraneous impurities; in fact, we have seldom met with any good drinking-water since our descent into the Barca. Even that which we obtained fresh, by digging for ourselves, became foul after a short exposure to the atmosphere. Examining the sand, on several occasions, I found that it was less pure than in other localities, traces of decomposed vegetable matter being largely blended with it. This, I presume, is owing to the powerful action of the sun after the rains, whereby the water absorbed by the sand, under the heating process, becomes mingled with that distilled from the decayed rank grass which covers the ground throughout the entire valley.

A journey through the Barca is most fatiguing: the path lies either over rugged ground or a soft sandy soil, any divergence from which brings the traveller in contact with briars, and brambles and uprooted trees, to the certain risk of his apparel and person. If one rides a mule, the animal is soon exhausted by trudging hoof-deep in the yielding sand; if a camel, he must make up his mind to be shaken like a churn whenever the ground is rough and stony.

I have written this district " Barca," as the word is generally spelt, but there can be no doubt that the correct name is *El-Bírkah*, the Arabic for a place where water collects and stagnates—a very apt designation of the depressed locality, which was probably given to it by the Arabs who migrated into this part of Africa.

3rd.—Left Hawashêt at 4 P.M., and reached Aigai after a ride of three hours and a half. Here my companions and I halted about half an hour for a little refreshment, and then resuming the journey for two miles overtook our Kâfilah, and encamped for the night on open ground.

4th.—Started at 4·45 A.M., and after four hours' slow

march, including a halt, reached the watercourse of Idrîs-Dâr, where we put up for the day. We went some distance out of the way this morning to insure a supply of water; had we taken the ordinary high road to Câsala, we should have been obliged to carry that indispensable article with us for ourselves and followers, which we could not do, having no vessels for the purpose. There is a much shorter route between the pass of Gâbê-Lukûm and Sabdarât, which is frequented by travellers during the rains, but is abandoned by Kâfilahs during the dry season, owing to the scarcity of water. Besides this, I was told by the Chief of the El-Bakhît that the water on the upper road was formerly obtained from wells, some of which were fifty feet deep. These had been filled up by the wild Barrîyah, in order to place an obstacle in the way of their pursuers. They live in a desert to the south-west of Barca, and doubtless take their name from that circumstance—*Barrîyah* being an Arabic word denoting growing or living in a waste. The tribe is unquestionably of Arab descent; but, like the natives of the Barca, they have lost the original meaning of their present appellation.

At Idrîs-Dâr we fell in with the Haránrua tribe, nicknamed "the Robbers," encamped along the watercourse. Their usual abode is the country to the north of Barca, bordering on Suâkin. They had migrated thus far in order to get out of the way of a great Pasha, who, it was said, had arrived at the latter place with orders to punish all those who had given the authorities trouble during the mutiny of the Soodân troops. Knowing, I presume, that some awkward charges might be proved against them, they very wisely placed themselves as far as possible beyond the reach of justice.

An inexhaustible supply of wholesome water is procurable

at Idrîs-Dâr by digging a few feet in the sand. We left
the place at 4·15 P.M., and reached Sabdarât at 2 A.M. the
following morning, travelling all the while. During the
night we passed through a regular drove of lions, whose
presence served to keep us on the alert. Instead of barely
roaring at a distance, as their compeers had done on our
route hitherto, they ran to and fro in all directions, in
sight of the cameleers—so, at least, they affirmed—and on
two occasions crossed the path of our Kâfilah, creating no
small commotion among the camels. The brave Massowah
guard kept up a constant fire from their muskets; but they
confessed, on reaching Sabdarât, that they had never been in
such a fix before.

Sabdarât is a very considerable village, situated on the
slope of a rugged mountain, on two sides of a deep and
narrow ravine, the greater portion of the houses being built
on the right side, as you go to Cásala. Its natural position
entitles it to be called the Gate to Tâka. The houses are
circular, with thatched conical roofs, like all Abyssinian
dwellings. Good water is abundant, obtained partly from
wells dug in the sand at the bottom of the ravine, and partly
from wells in the gardens, a little below the town. Arriving
at a late hour, we slept on the soft sand near the lower
wells, and at sunrise moved into one of the gardens, which
was placed at our disposal by its owner, through the intervention of 'Abd-ul-Kerîm. The valley of Sabdarât marks the
extreme limit of Barca; beyond it, the district called Tâka
begins.

5th.—Started at 4·45 P.M. and halted an hour and a half
for supper at 8·15; after which, pursuing our journey for
another hour, we came up with the cameleers who were in
the act of unloading the baggage at a spot chosen by the

guides for our stay during the night, as Cásala being only
an hour's ride in advance we could easily reach it in the
early morning. On emerging from the valley of Sabdarât
we came upon a level and well-cultivated country, and on
looking back, the mountain of Sabdarât, with the connecting
ranges on its right and left, looked like a mighty artificial
wall separating the two provinces of Barca and Tâka.

'Abd-ul-Kerîm dispatched his nephew Ahmed, with the
escort which had been furnished us by the Chief of the Beni-
'Âmir, to report our arrival to the Governor, to whom I also
forwarded the letter of recommendation, to his address, from
the Viceroy of Egypt. I requested Ahmed at the same time
to call upon a Greek merchant, and ask him whether he
could conveniently accommodate my companions and myself
during our short stay at Cásala. I also enjoined him to
use his best endeavours, in conjunction with the aforesaid
merchant, to procure camels for our speedy departure to
Matámma.

6th.—When within two miles of the town, at about six
o'clock this morning, we espied a body of troops, and shortly
after an official accosted me with an apology from the
Governor, begging that I would excuse his not coming out to
meet me, which he was unable to do owing to an attack of
fever, but that he had given orders that I should be received
with all the respect due to the representative of the British
Government. At the same time, the troops were pointed
out to me as a guard of honour, consisting of an entire
regiment of Soodân infantry and a troop of about a hundred
and fifty Bashi-Buzûk cavalry. I was greatly taken aback
by this display; had I known of it in time, I should certainly
have begged the Governor to dispense with it. The infantry
halted at the gate and saluted as my companions and I

entered the town, but the cavalry escorted us to the house of our host the Greek merchant, Panagiotes Kozika, who had also come out to meet us, and now led the way to his residence. I was grieved to learn from him that there were no camels to be had, and, moreover, that we should probably have to wait some time to procure them, as, since the mutiny, a report had reached the cameleers that the Egyptian authorities were on the look-out to press them into their service, to escape which none of them ventured to enter Cásala.

We found the town in a most wretched and desolate plight, owing to the late mutiny and a fatal epidemic combined, which had decimated the population. Hundreds of families had fled the place, first to escape the mutineers, and then the Albanians, the latter having completed the wreck of the unfortunate surviving inhabitants by despoiling them of what little property the murderous and plundering Soodân troops had left them. This town, which a few months ago was in a most flourishing condition, is now little better than a heap of ruins, with nothing but a scanty supply of millet, on which all classes indiscriminately have to subsist. The veteran colonel of the Soodân regiment which had turned out for us called on me during the morning. He is himself a native of the Soodân, and is renowned for bravery. He had served with Ibrahîm Pasha in his campaigns in Syria and Arabia. In the afternoon, my companions went with me to call upon the Governor, Suleimân Bey. He received us most politely, and apologised for not having called on us, but indisposition had prevented him. No such spoken apology was necessary, for he really looked seriously ill. He remarked that he had had many difficulties to contend against during the previous five months, owing to the mutiny, sickness and scarcity of food. Five persons belonging to his establishment had been carried off by cholera and fever, and within the last two months he himself had been attacked by the latter malady, and during that period could obtain nothing but bread made of ground millet to eat, to which diet he attributed his present ailment. He kindly promised to render me every assistance in his power—which promise he certainly kept—but remarked that we had come to Cásala at a most unfortunate time, when the authorities themselves were in great want of carriage; "however," he went on to say, "you shall have the first that can be procured, as it will not do to detain you here." He then gave orders to the head of the cameleers to look out for camels, and to see that we were provided with the required number without delay.

The mutiny had been entirely crushed before our arrival, not, I am sorry to say, without much unnecessary bloodshed. Of the four regiments which had mutinied about eight hundred men had escaped with their lives. These had been imprisoned, together with their wives and children; but so badly cared for were they that numbers died during our sojourn at Cásala, and their corpses, instead of being decently interred, were cast into ditches outside the town to be devoured by hyænas. During a ride one afternoon in the suburbs, I saw no less than three bodies thus exposed. Besides the carnage and anarchy consequent upon the mutiny, cholera and a most fatal fever had carried off their victims by hundreds from July to October. Even while we were there, a tenth of the garrison was laid up with one disease or another.

Kuchúk 'Ali Bey, the Commandant of the Bashi-Buzúks, called upon me to apologise for not having come out with his troop to meet us—attending to the wants of the sick and other duties had prevented him. He inquired if it were really true that I was going to that "son of a dog, Kâsa." (I noticed that neither at Massowah nor here would the Mohammedans deign to call Theodore "King.") On replying to his question in the affirmative, he looked amazed and asked how I could venture to trust myself to a man who was treacherous as well as crazy, especially while he still held our Consul in chains. His opinion was that Kâsa deserved a two-edged sword instead of civil treatment, and volunteered his services, under the sanction of his own Government, to go up with his troop and bring back the miscreant's head. Even our host, the Greek, was quite at a loss to comprehend the object of our Mission. He judged that if we were going up merely to tell the King that he was a brute, and that unless he liberated the captives we should pound him well, we had better keep at a safe distance, and send him a statement of our views in writing, as he did not see why we should risk our lives for the sake of personally delivering a threatening message. On the other hand, if our object was to humour the man, we should find that a most difficult task, as his Abyssinian Majesty, he believed, was no longer susceptible of blandishment.

After a detention of four days, the requisite number of camels was found, and the head of the cameleers, an Arab of the Shûkry tribe, was brought to me to arrange about the hire, and to draw up a bond. Khoja Panagiotes Kozika kindly settled the bargain, but when next the subject of the bond was taken up, the Sheikh remarked, "Shame upon my beard, were I to ask you to give me a sealed paper guaranteeing my due payment! Only say the word that you agree to my terms and I want no more." When I ordered the amount to be paid, which it had been stipulated should be given in advance, he said, "Before I was brought into your presence I deemed it prudent to be punctilious, but now let the matter be one of honour between us; and, as for the money, it will be as safe in your keeping as mine." I tried every means to prevail upon this man to accompany us as far as Matámma, but without success. Nothing, he said, would induce him to diverge from the line of business handed down to him by his forefathers. His father before him had only hired his camels to pass between Cásala and Kedârif, and he being a dutiful, and, moreover, a "legitimate" son was bound to do the same. Those whose occupation it is to convey travellers between Kedârif and Matámma belong to another tribe. On my reminding him that I had been delayed a long time at Cásala, and might probably meet with still greater difficulty in securing camels at Kedârif, he assured me to the contrary, as there were no godless Turks at that place to press the camels of the poor into their service. "If you find that I have deceived you," he concluded, "you may shave off my beard."

The Shûkries are thorough Arabs in language, dress and manners. Even in complexion they are not so dark as the natives of Massowah, and in that respect approach nearer to the hue of the inhabitants of the lowlands of Yemen. The Arabs generally in this part of Africa are certainly a fine race, with well-built frames and handsome features, and, as compared with the Hibâb and other tribes in the neighbourhood of Massowah, highly civilized. A couple of them would do the work of four or even six lazy Hibâbs—such as lifting heavy cases and loading them on camels.

A severe dust-storm, with a few drops of rain, occurred before our departure from Cásala; the difference between which and those we had experienced at Massowah was this—that the latter consisted of fine pure sand, whereas the former was largely intermingled with various kinds of filthy rubbish.

CHAPTER VI.

CÁSALA TO MATÁMMA.

A hospitable Arab — The Khôr-ul-Gash — Hásan Effendi, a Greek convert to Islâm — The Plain of Tâka — Heavy rain — Slow progress — The Atbara river — Crocodiles — Prairie and Forest — Conflagrations — Scarcity of Water — Guinea - worm — Hállet - Wadabsin — Shûkry Cameleers — A Greek Publican — A restive Camel — 'Abd-ul-Melek, the Copt Impostor — A go-ahead Kâfilah Sheikh — The District of Gallabât — Takroories — Government — Origin of the Inhabitants — Etymology of "Gallabât" and "Matámma" — Hásan Effendi's diplomacy — Khôr Ithrib — Arrival at Matámma — The Mission quarters.

10*th.*—Left Cásala at 5·30 P.M., our Greek friends, accompanied by Signor Marcopolo, who was to follow afterwards, escorting us a short distance to see us off. 'Abd-ul-Kerîm had already left the town on his return to Massowah, and was encamping by a village called Khatmîa, near the road to our halting-place, the Sheikh of which, who was also an Arab, had promised to supply us with water-skins—an indispensable requisite, we were told, owing to the scarcity of water on the journey before us at this time of the year. Dr. Blanc then went on to the halting-stage, while Prideaux and I proceeded to the village to look after the skins, and to see the last of our old friend 'Abd-ul-Kerîm. On reaching Khatmîa we found that not a single skin was forthcoming, but the Sheikh, Mohammed-bin-Osmân, received us courteously and treated us to a quantity of milk. On observing our dejection at the non-appearance of the articles we had expected to find, he ordered his servants to produce all the skins belonging to his establishment, remarking that he could not allow a guest of his to leave him in low spirits. I begged him not to give himself any further concern in the matter, and protested strongly against depriving his household of such useful utensils; but he swore by the Prophet that he should feel much hurt if I did .not accept them, and, moreover, that he should incur the stigma of meanness if, through his want of care for his guests, any of our followers should suffer from thirst on the road. Not satisfied with my yielding on that point, he insisted on my accepting a couple of sheep, before he would permit us to leave his house. Bidding the hospitable Chief farewell, after spending half an hour under his roof, we set out towards our camp, 'Abd-ul-Kerîm accompanying us beyond the village, where, after a hearty God-speed from both sides, we separated.

We reached our encampment at 8·30 P.M., guided on the way by the vivid lightning, without which we should assuredly have gone astray, for the sky was hung with heavy clouds, and it was very dark. Our baggage had been unladen in the bed of the Gash, where the road to Matámma crosses it, at a spot called Khôr-ul-Gash. The Gash is a very large river, known in Abyssinia as the Mâreb, taking its rise in northern Tigrê from no less than eighteen different sources. The river dries up in the lowlands of Abyssinia immediately after the rains, when water is only obtainable by digging in its sandy bed. We had hardly dismounted when the rain came down in torrents; luckily, we were encamped on sandy soil, so that after the rain ceased we were not troubled with mud. We were told that rain in that locality, at this time of year, is unusual.

On our leaving Cásala, the authorities wished to send a large guard to escort us as far as Matámma, but I prevailed upon them to reduce the number to five men, knowing that more were quite unnecessary. But I took with me from thence a Kawâs, one Hásan Effendi, a Greek by birth, and formerly a Christian by profession, but who had since become a Mohammedan, not by purposely or inadvertently partaking of meat slaughtered by Mussulmans—he cared little who the butcher or what the meat was, for even pork would not have come amiss to him—but by simply taking a new name on his formal initiation into Islâm. The fellow was scarcely of any use on the road; but once in a town his energy and flourish came into play, and he certainly did good service on those occasions.

11*th.*—Drying our soaked equipage detained us at the Khôr-ul-Gash till 1 P.M. Our road now lay due south. Having been apprised that no water was obtainable for two days between the Gash and the Atbara, we had all our water-skins filled and laden on separate camels, and then committed to the special charge of a cameleer, who swore by the sacred Kâ'abah that he would not touch the water himself, nor allow any of his companions to taste it, without my express order. From what was told us before leaving Cásala, we expected to encounter a fierce lion or lioness every minute after quitting the Khôr-ul-Gash; in fact, I had purposed making a long stage from Cásala, but was warned against doing so, unless we were prepared to contest every inch of the way through the jungle with the lord of the forest. Not feeling so disposed, we abandoned the idea of a night march. It is quite true that we had to travel through dense woods during the afternoon, but we neither heard the roar of lions nor saw any traces of them.

.. On starting, we missed all the guard, owing, it appears, to the owners of the camels which they rode having decamped with their animals as soon as the order was given to load, thereby obliging the guard to return on foot to Cásala to complain. The corporal, however, managed to secure another camel, and overtook us soon after. Being a native of the country he was very useful on the road, but he and Hásan Effendi could not agree. The corporal was a strict Mussulman who prayed five times a-day, whereas the Kawâs generally fell asleep instead of joining in the devotions of his adopted co-religionists. All that the pious guard ventured to remark on this scandalous neglect of a solemn duty was, that Christians had not lost much by his secession, neither had the true believers gained much by his conversion. Owing to the heavy rain last night the poor Effendi had an attack of fever, as we entered the forest. Being mounted on a rough-paced camel, he did everything but bless the Arabs for not having an easier beast for travelling than a quadruped which, in his opinion, was only fit for carrying wood or bales of cotton— goods which could not be injured by shaking.

Passed the Milwîa ravine at 8 P.M., at the upper part of which we were told that water would be found, collected there from last night's rain; but some old cameleers questioned the statement, remarking that they never remembered any water being lodged there at that time of the year, though their hair had grown grey in journeying by this road.

Beyond the mountains near Cásala, the whole country to the southward and westward is a dead level. While at Sabdarât, I ascended the high mountain overhanging the village, and beheld one of the most extensive prospects I had ever seen. The flat plain of Tâka lay outstretched before me, looking more like sea than land, while the thick cover on its surface heightened the resemblance by imparting to it the dark blue colour of the ocean.

Half an hour after passing the Milwîa the clouds portended a downpour, and thunder with lightning commenced in the southward. We accordingly deemed it advisable to encamp at once, and no sooner were our camels unloaded than the rain came down in torrents. With great difficulty we managed to pitch one of the servants' tents, but the wind was so strong that it drove the water in upon us, drenching us to the skin. As for the poor servants and followers, they were in a most wretched plight, being obliged to spend the night on the ground, which the rain had liquefied into a puddle. In fact, the whole country around was converted into a morass.

12th.—Another bout of drying after last night's washing kept us stationary for some time on the muddy ground. It was reported to me this morning that two of our riding mules, one belonging to me and the other to Lieutenant Prideaux, were missing. We feared they had been stolen, but after examining the trail of the stragglers the cameleers gave it as their opinion, that they had gone in search of food, though they would not venture to guarantee their safety after the past stormy night, when the beasts of prey became ravenous and would " eat their own mothers," if they could find nothing better for supper. However, in the event of such a mishap having befallen them, they comforted us with the promise that their bones would be forthcoming. After a few minutes' further search, both mules were found, one standing and the other reclining under a large tree, from around which they had cropped all the grass. We discovered afterwards that, owing to their own discomfort, the muleteers had neglected to give them their regular feed.

Started at noon, but at a wretchedly slow pace, the smooth

soles of the camels endangering their equilibrium at every step over the slippery soil. Travellers are generally obliged either to coax or force a cameleer to move with his animals on a wet day, and on this occasion I had no small difficulty in getting my friend Mohammed, the head-cameleer, to budge. He met my importunities with the Arabic proverb, "Haste is devilish; patience is godly;" following up the argument in this style: "What is the use of hurrying when the camels cannot walk steadily? Should a couple of them break their legs, who is to carry your boxes? Not that we care about the camels—let them be your propitiation; but some of your cases may be smashed, and you will be left in the lurch for want of sufficient carriage to convey the remainder." On my reminding him, after appealing to his best qualities, that it was his duty to "trust in God and fear nothing," he replied with a smile, "There is no denying the propriety of the injunction;" and forthwith called upon his comrades to commence loading, remarking to them as he did so that Christians now-a-days were more observant of the Divine precepts than the heirs of Paradise.

About two miles from our halting-place we came upon a lake, formed by the rain which had fallen during the night, through which the camels and mules had great difficulty in making their way, often knee-deep, in the miry clay. During the transit, which occupied half an hour, I had a narrow escape of being precipitated into the pool, two of the cameleers opportunely leaving their camels and coming to my assistance. Noticing that I was somewhat put out at meeting with such an unlooked-for impediment in our journey, one of them said: "Curse the devil and bless God for this day's bounty! since neither we nor our forefathers ever saw such a profusion of the Divine goodness at this time of the year, when ever the birds desert the place for want of water." The rain, which caused us no little annoyance, was regarded as a great blessing by the country at large. At 4·30 P.M. my companions and I halted half an hour by the road-side for dinner, and then overtaking the camels continued the journey till 6 P.M., when we put up for the night, being told that it would be dangerous to cross the rugged ground leading to the Atbara while it was dark.

13th.—Started at 4·30 A.M., with the moon in her last quarter, and reached the water-course of Marmadayât at six. The ravine was dry when we crossed it, but from the fresh water-mark left on its sides the stream must have been at least four feet deep, showing how heavily it had rained in the neighbourhood during the last two nights. Reached the Atbara at nine, and halted on its eastern bank at a place called Khâshm-ul-Ghirbah—the Mouth of the inflated Sheep's-skin—from the shape which the river takes in that locality in its winding course towards Egypt. Here the Atbara is an assemblage of different rivers proceeding from the centre of Abyssinia, the most famous of which is the Tăkkăzê. The water of the Atbara is highly prized by the natives, and the Arabs call it Zíbdet-un-Nîl, the Cream of the Nile. It is certainly a noble river at Khâshm-ul-Ghirbah, where it is divided by an islet two miles in circumference, and then flows onward in one broad stream to Berber, about one hundred and fifty miles below Khartûm. My eyes had not looked upon such a glorious sight for many a year, and contrasting the clear broad sheet with the turbid pools, and puddles and foul water we had hitherto met with on our journey, I squatted down on the pebbly bank and was soon lost in abstraction. My reverie, however, was interrupted by the appearance of a number of crocodiles in mid-channel, which had a wonderful effect in dissipating my dreams, for I fancied they were making towards me, and therefore deemed it prudent to rejoin my companions, who had taken up their quarters under the large trees which abound on the river's banks, their outspreading branches, closely interwoven with a thick-leaved creeper, forming a delightful retreat against the broiling rays of the sun.   There was a difference of at least fifty degrees between the temperature under the shade and that in the sun, and as many as seventy-five between sunrise and noon in the open air.

Left the Atbara at 2·45 P.M., and in four hours reached a place above the river called Shajarât—the Arabic for Groves. The heat was so powerful this afternoon that the right sides of our faces were scorched by it, if not kept covered by our umbrellas. Our route lay between a bend in the river, and, as we arrived too late to cross it at the opposite point, we halted for the night on a small plateau about a mile from the bank, and a mile and a half from the ford.

With the exception of a few barren spots here and there, the whole country which we traversed since leaving Cásala was covered with coarse, parched grass and thick wood, which, once ignited, continue to burn until the rain arrests the destructive element. I was told that hundreds of miles of prairie and forest land are sometimes laid bare by these conflagrations, especially after a long dry season; indeed, we ourselves came now and then upon groves of blackened trunks and huge leafless branches, which a few days' rain— so our cameleers said—would soon re-clothe with foliage. On the journey between Cásala and Matámma, which occupied nearly a fortnight, we seldom saw less than three fires around us, and one night I counted as many as eleven on the horizon. What surprised me not a little in this plain of the Soodân—*Nigritia*—(whether the Arabic name was given to it on account of the colour of its soil, or of its inhabitants, or of both, I leave it to the more learned to decide)—was the number of shells to be met with on its surface. I picked up many specimens, hoping to bring them to England, but they were unfortunately lost some time after, at Debra Tâbor, together with other collections which I had made in the country.

14th.—Started for the ford at 5 A.M., and were detained there two hours unloading the baggage and distributing it on different camels, to save it from getting wet on the passage. My companions and I had to cross on camels guided by expert cameleers, for the ford is so near a deep basin into which the stream falls, that a divergence of a few feet would inevitably launch the straggler into the dangerous whirlpool. Resumed our journey from the opposite bank at 7·30 A.M., and halted at 10·10, at a place called Tártar, for refreshment, and to enable our followers to cook a meal. This was the hottest day we had experienced since leaving Massowah, and between eight and eleven o'clock the heat was absolutely suffocating. There was a difference of forty degrees in the temperature between sunrise and noon, the nights feeling intensely cold, owing to this great variation. The health of our Indian servants suffered much, and most of them were ailing. After crossing the river, the monotony of the route was broken by the number of Kâfilahs we met on their way to Cásala, laden with corn. Left Tártar at 3·45 P.M., and travelled till 9, when we reached Sheikh Hasb-Allah, situated about two miles westward of the Atbara. Being told that no water was procurable between that place and Kedârif, we halted there for the night, in order to have the water-skins replenished for a two days' supply.

15th.—Off again at 4 P.M., and travelled till we reached El-Gaidât, at one the following morning, all dead tired. I had dispatched Hásan Effendi to Kedârif, from Sheikh Hasb-Allah, to secure a relay of camels for us beforehand, in order to prevent our detention there beyond a few hours. As it was market-day, and he was well acquainted with the place, he promised to have the animals in readiness. Started at 6 A.M., and halted at 10·40 under a tree at El-'Ázăză, to refresh both man and beast. Here I had an equal ration of water served out to all. Resuming the route at 3 P.M., we came in the course of an hour and a half upon some culti-vated land belonging to Kedârif. Jowâri, millet—*Holcus sorghum*—is the only vegetable which can be grown in this district to advantage, and I certainly never saw it flourish so luxuriantly. Hásan Agha, the foreman of our fictitious guard, brought us some stalks, which are chewed like sugar-cane. On asking him whether it was not wrong in him to pluck them in the absence of the owner, and without his permission, he replied, "Are not these people our brothers? Instead of deeming it a crime, they would esteem it a blessing that strangers from a distant land had tasted of their produce." Villages now appeared on our right and left, and also in ad-vance of us, and as the cameleers did not consider it advisable or propitious to enter so large a place as Kedârif by night, we halted at eight o'clock near a cluster of wells, called Sáraf-ul-Bawâdra, which supply the town and all the adjacent villages. This district is very subject to guinea-worm, and I was told that after the rainy season one-eighth of the population suffered from it. The natives attribute its source to the muddy soil of the ponds from which the villagers draw water during the heavy rains, when it is inconvenient to resort to the wells. Drinking the water, they maintained, did not induce it, for when the ground became dry, and the inhabitants began to draw water from wells dug in similar soil near Hállet-Wadabein, all the old cases commenced healing, and no new ones appeared. If drinking the water had anything to do with bringing on the guinea-worm, then, they argued, all those who used the wells at Hállet-Wadabein would contract it, which was not the case. The water at Sáraf-ul-Bawâdra is very muddy and disagreeable to the taste. The wells are about five feet deep, dug in clay of a greenish colour.

17th.—My companions started with me at 5 A.M., and on reaching the large town of Hállet-Wadabsin, after a brisk ride of about an hour, we went straight to the fine house belonging to our Greek friend at Cásala, Khoja Panagiotes Kozika, which he had placed at our service during our stay. His resident agent, also a Greek, was unable to do much for us, as the poor fellow was suffering from fever and ophthalmia. Hásan Effendi, we found, had secured the required number of camels, but as the Arabs never trust an Albanian—and the Effendi looked very like one—the Shûkry cameleers refused to make any bargain with him, saying that they must see the loads and the size of the boxes, the dimensions of which report had highly exaggerated. The house where we were located possessed a spacious inclosure, ample enough to receive two hundred camels. Just as the Kedârif cameleers had been brought by Sheikh 'Abdallah-abu-Khumeir, the acting governor, our Cásala cameleers defiled in with the Kâfilah, which led to a discussion between the Sheikh and his Shûkries about the job on hand, they looking aghast all the while at the size of the cases containing the glass-ware intended for Theodore. At this juncture, our old friend Mohammed hailed them with the usual salutation, "Peace be unto

you !" and then proceeded to address them in these words :—
"O ye believers, thank God for sending you such a father. Do
not be frightened at the size of the boxes, for they are light,
very light; they only require care. But even if they were
heavy, what would that matter, compared with the kind treatment which you will receive? Just look at that meat dangling
from the camels' backs, and be satisfied. Be of good cheer,
I say." This address was not lost on the Kedárif cameleers,
who readily agreed to the proffered terms, and forthwith set
about receiving over the different loads and binding them in
suitable packages for the journey. Sheikh Abu-Sîn, the
Arab Chief of Kedárif, had been absent at Khartûm since
the outbreak of the mutiny, assisting the local Egyptian
authorities in transporting stores and ammunition to Cásala.
Sheikh 'Abdallah-abu-Khumeir, his *locum tenens*, however,
did everything in his power to expedite our departure. He
offered to send a guard with us, but I only accepted a guide
to accompany us to Matámma. He himself went with us as
far as Hállet-ul-Kanz, in order to aid us in obtaining a
supply of water for the onward journey; had he not done
so, we might have been obliged to remain there for days, as
there is but one well at the place, which is very deep.

Hállet-Wadabsin is built like an Abyssinian village, with
circular huts covered with a conical roof; the thatching,
however, is not so well finished. We found a Greek publican there, who was driving a brisk trade in a spirit compounded of alcohol, gum-mastic and muddy water; but
Albanians and Bashi-Buzûks are not very particular what
liquor they drink, if it serve to inspire them with temporary
kéf. In a climate like that of the Soodân, especially during
the hot months, such stimulants must act like poison.

Our new cameleers loaded this afternoon, and started off

without much ado; but one camel, bearing the kitchen utensils, which had not been well-packed, hearing the rattling of the saucepans in the box, gave a sudden start, which of course increased the clatter. This made the beast perfectly unmanageable, and nothing would pacify it until it had upset its load, smashing the case into atoms, and then decamping. On being brought back, no blandishments would induce it to be reloaded, whereupon the cameleer gravely assured me that the saucepans had spirited away the animal's sense. My companions and I did not set out till towards 5 p.m., reaching halting-place at Hállet-ul-Kanz a little before 8. I was much pleased with the cameleers on this trip: they managed the loads well, and drove their camels as if racing for a wager. Their sheikh, El-Bushîr, was a splendid fellow, and tried to make himself generally useful. On reaching this place, 'Abd-ul-Melek, the messenger who had been dispatched by Sir Robert Colquhoun, her Majesty's late Consul-General in Egypt, called to consult with me about his future proceedings. This man, it appears, who was a Copt by origin, had represented himself to the consular authorities as having been sent by the Metropolitan of Abyssinia, the Abûna Salâma, for the purpose of communicating with her Majesty's Consul-General for the release of the captives. His tale proved subsequently to be a fabrication throughout. When we met, he told me that he had tried his best to reach the Abûna, but in consequence of the Prelate's incarceration by Theodore, and the insecurity of the roads to Mágdala, he had failed in the effort. I accordingly advised him to return to Egypt with the presents with which he had been entrusted for the Abûna.

18*th.*—Wishing to give our followers a rest, we did not

start till 3 P.M., travelling then till midnight, when we halted a little out of the road for a few hours. El-Bushîr was for pushing on, his motto being that " the faster one travelled, the more rapidly the time is got over." Being the Sheikh of the Kâfilah, he had charge of the glass-ware, and as his camel was a fast walker, he was always a-head of the others. Towards ten o'clock, the cameleers began grumbling about the length of the stage, and begged the Sheikh to halt and give the camels a few hours' rest. To this he merely replied, " When my camel shows signs of fatigue, it will then be time enough to think of a halt. It is useless that you tire yourselves by talking, because"—he went on to say, on their renewed importunities—" I will not halt, were it to save your fathers from being burnt in Jehennam; and, by the death of my progenitors, I will not listen to you nor answer you again; so you had better shut your mouths." When the cameleers found that their solicitations were of no avail, they began to move forward slowly, first one and then another bawling out that his camel had strayed, or thrown its load. Fearing that these reports were true, I suggested to El-Bushîr the prudence of drawing up, lest the animals straying in the dark might be pounced upon by hyænas. " Don't give heed to those sons of burnt fathers," was his cool reply; " if their camels are missing they will soon find them, for they are of more value to them than the loads they carry are to you. Hold me responsible if they do not follow, and if they are not found all right when we halt. Only, don't pay any attention to their lies." At last, all the cameleers began abusing him, devoting him to the companionship of Satan, and reminding him that in the Day of Judgment " he who has not shown mercy can expect no mercy him-self." Poor El-Bushîr could not stand these imprecations any longer, and turning to me said, " Master, let us halt here near the road-side for a few hours, otherwise these sons of rebellious parents will devour me."

19*th.*—Left our camping-ground, which was called Basabîr, at 5·15 A.M., and went on till 10, when we reached Wald-ul-'Ammâs, and halted in a ravine below the village, by the side of a muddy stream, under a clump of trees. The tree under which my companions and I located ourselves was so large, that the villagers had scooped a chamber out of its trunk capable of seating six persons. One of my ailing servants was put into it for shelter during the halt. Three other of our followers were also very ill to-day with fever, and I had a touch of it myself, while resting here; nevertheless, we started again at 3·30 P.M. and pursued the journey till 1 A.M. the following day, when we halted at El-Madág. Riding for nearly ten hours continuously, suffering from fever and a racking headache all the time, was not pleasant, and one of my Indian servants, who was upset by the least indisposition, groaned most piteously all the way. During this night's journey a serious accident did occur to one of our camels, which obliged us·to distribute its load among the remainder. El-Bushîr ascribed its " fate " to the malevolent heart of the owner. The trees here were very lofty, and the place would have resembled a park but for the thick stubble which had been collecting on the ground for generations. The village was about two miles off, but we preferred being nearer the wells than the huts. The wells are numerous, dug in a greenish clayey soil, but the water is muddy. They are also very large at the mouth, but so covered with trunks of trees, that only a small space is left for the passage of a bucket. This, it appears, is a precaution against man or beast accidentally falling into them.

20th.—Left El-Madág at 3 P.M. and reached Jä'afara at nine. Hearing that we could easily reach Mátamma the following day, I yielded to the solicitations of the cameleers and remained there for the night. The district of Gallabât, of which Matámma is the capital, begins a mile or two to the north of Jä'afara, and is mostly inhabited by negroes, called Takroories, immigrants from Darfûr in the south. It is a curious fact that the whole of the northern coast of Africa, extending inland for four hundred miles, from west to east, and from its north-eastern extremity in a line running towards the south-east as far as Cape Gardafoon in the Indian Ocean, is inhabited by people who have migrated thither either from the centre of that continent or from Asia. The Takroories, who are pure negroes, have ousted the Arabs, who had in like manner supplanted the aborigines— most probably when the Mussulman power had overrun central Asia and southern Europe.

The government of Matámma—if such a name can be appropriately given to consecutive misrule—has been perpetuated through fraud and treachery. No man holding the sceptre has been safe from assassination. If Sheikh Jumä'ah, the existing ruler, were not in the habit of drowning his senses by large indulgence in prohibited drinks—which he does every night—he could not close his eyes in sleep, for fear of the cold steel being suddenly thrust into his vitals. As it is, and while he lies dreaming of rivers of arrack and liquid butter, on the banks of which his sensuous imagination sees throngs of beautiful houris, three hundred trusty followers keep watch around his chamber. These men being chosen from among the party at deadly feud with the rebels, their charge knows that he may give full swing to his nocturnal visions in comparative security.

Within the last century, Gallabât was still governed by Arab Sheikhs; but as these were at perpetual feud with those of Er-Rashîd—another district between Kedârif and Gallabât—they took into their employ a number of slaves as auxiliaries from the negro races of Kordofân and Darfûr, who, following the example of the Mamlûk in the time of Mohammed 'Ali, rebelled against and killed the so-called Arab Chief—who had more African than Arab blood in his veins, his forefathers having intermarried for centuries with the negro race—and elected one of their own number in his stead. The population by this time had become so mixed, and received such constant accessions from foreign sources, that their Arab neighbours gave the district the name of " Gallabât," a term indicating change or variation: from the root *Kálab*, to change, to alter—the *k* softened into *g*, as is usual with many Bedawîn tribes.* In like manner, I take it that the name " Takroory " designates the new settlers—from the Arabic root *Kárra*, to abide in a place, to establish one's self. The Arabs do not call the capital of Gallabât, Matámma, but " Sûk-ul-Gallabât "—the Market of Gallabat—the fair of the district being generally held there. The cameleers never use the word Matámma among themselves, and some would not even understand what was meant by it. The term itself is supposed to be derived from the Arabic *Mutámm*, the place of cutting, or termination—indicating the end or limit of the Mohammedan provinces. The inhabitants of the Gallabât district are mostly Arabs or half-castes, and Sheikh Jumä'ah's

---

* An intimate friend of mine, a good orientalist, suggests whether the name does not rather designate the principal locality from whence the *Jellâbs*, or slave-merchants, procured slaves for the Egyptian market— the soft Arabic *j* being changed into a hard *g*—a transmutation common throughout Egypt.

Matámma militia is composed of men of all races, from the adjacent territories.

21st.—Left El-Jä'afara at 4 A.M., and at daybreak Blanc, Prideaux and I pushed on to Khôr Ithrib, where we were advised by our guides to halt for a few hours before entering Matámma. On reaching the Khôr, at 8·40, I dispatched Hásan Effendi in advance to notify our arrival to the authorities, in order that a house might be provided for us in a healthy locality, until our departure for Abyssinia. Unfortunately, I had not been furnished with a letter to the ruler of the place by the Egyptian Government, and the Effendi was consequently rather taken aback when first asked for that customary warrant by the Regent—Sheikh Jumä'ah, the lord paramount, being absent in Abyssinia at the time. The Kawâs, however, had too much brass to be long ruffled by this insignificant contretemps; so, assuming an air of offended dignity, he proceeded to address the astonished deputy in this strain:—"How dare you ask for such rubbish, when a great man visits you? Do you know who it is who is about to honour your place? As you may not have heard of him, I shall enlighten you on the subject. Neither you nor your Darfûr forefathers ever saw so great a man; neither will you ever have the chance of seeing his equal as long as you live. So I advise you to give up your nonsense about the trumpery paper, and prepare to receive him as befits his exalted position." Then, in order to impress upon him more confidentially the importance of the Mission, in the presence of a large concourse of people who had assembled on the spot, he approached close enough to whisper in his ear— taking care, however, to speak so as to be heard by the bystanders—that I was an envoy from the great Queen of England to the King of Abyssinia, who was coming in person to meet me. The poor deputy looked aghast all the while, and told Hásan Effendi, when the latter had finished his harangue, that all my orders should be obeyed. The Kawâs having intimated that the first requisite was a house situated on an eminence, as living in the valley would be unhealthy, all the authorities began to bestir themselves, and after no end of palaver, a large shed on a hill, with three rooms within an inclosure, formerly used as a summer residence by Sheikh Jumä'ah, was selected for our accommodation.

There is excellent water at Khôr Ithrib, and both banks of the ravine are thickly wooded. Hordes of monkeys were frolicking in the trees, so tame that, on descending for a drink, several of them approached very near to us. Left the Khôr at 2·40 P.M., and as Blanc, Prideaux and I wished to avoid the sun as much as possible, we cantered on to Matámma, leaving the baggage to follow. On arriving there, at about 5 P.M., we were guided by a messenger sent for that purpose to the house which Hásan Effendi's effrontery and energy combined had secured for us. It was situated on the top of a high hill, not far from the road by which we had come, and overlooking the town, which consists of about one thousand huts, occupying the whole length of the valley below, and containing a population of about 3,000 souls. The view from the summit was very fine, the country as far as the eye could reach being covered with verdure. My companions preferred living in the shed, but I had my tent pitched and took up my quarters under canvass during our entire stay. I heard on arriving that the King of Abyssinia was within a few days' march of us, having come into the neighbourhood of Góndar, in pursuit of a rebel. This news was gratifying, inasmuch as I was led to hope that being so near, and having Sheikh Jumä'ah on a visit to him, the King might send for me at once, since I fully expected that the messengers I had dispatched from Massowah would have reached him by that time.

CHAPTER VII.

MATÁMMA.

Reception by local authorities — Dispatch of messengers to Theodore — Mr. Eipperle's opinion of the King — Return of Sheikh Jumä'ah, the Ruler of Matámma, from Abyssinia — His welcome home — Inebriety of the Takroories — Want of good water — Climate — Food — Produce — Weekly fair — A Takroory belle before a mirror — Slave-Trade — Horses and Cattle — Revenue — Militia — Letter from Consul Cameron — Review of Matámma troops — Native military enthusiasm — An excursion to the Atbara — Buffaloes — The Festival of the Drum — Sheikh Jumà'ah harangues his troops — Takroory dancing — An alarm — Letters from Theodore — Preparations ordered for the reception of the Mission on the frontier — Raid on an Abyssinian village — Parting visit to Sheikh Jumä'ah.

Soon after our arrival at Sûk-ul-Gallabât (or Matámma), Sheikh Jumä'ah's two deputies paid us a visit. 'Arafât had charge of the revenue and the management of all military affairs; 'Iz-ud-Dîn acted as civil commissioner and keeper of the autocrat's conscience, including the duty of superintending the royal female establishment. The latter dignitary was, of course, my man, as I had neither come to settle a blood-feud nor to meddle in the finances of the country, but with the sole object of "loving and being loved." The former, therefore, merely appointed a guard of honour to prevent any intrusion upon our privacy, "except on business," and then left us. I requested 'Iz-ud-Dîn to find messengers to convey a letter to King Theodore, which he did the following morning. In this, my sixth letter to his Majesty, I simply apprised him of my arrival at Matámma, in fulfilment of a promise to that effect, and begged him to send an escort to accompany us to his presence. As the King was reported to be in the vicinity of Lake Dámbĕa, the messengers hoped to reach him in five days; and if his Majesty gave them a reply at once, they engaged not to be absent longer than a fortnight, which interval was to include all ordinary delays. 'Iz-ud-Dîn deemed it probable that as Sheikh Jumä'ah had met the King in Dámbĕa, whither he had gone to pay the yearly tribute, his Majesty might charge him, on his return home, with instructions respecting my projected visit.

Mr. Eipperle, of the Jerusalem Mission, who with his wife had gone into Abyssinia for change of air, returned on the night of the 21st. He and Dr. Schwainfurth, a Russian naturalist, called on us in the afternoon of the 22nd. The latter had been at Matámma for some time, collecting plants and insects, but he had suffered so much from ill-health that he left for Khartûm the day after, on his homeward journey. Mr. Eipperle spoke very highly of the King, with whom he had recently travelled from Debra Tâbor, and had left him within five days' journey of Matámma. He told me that all the Europeans in Abyssinia fully expected that as soon as the Queen's letter reached the King, he would release the captives. He feared, however, that I should have some difficulty in settling matters satisfactorily, as his Majesty had of late taken a great dislike to all Europeans, whom he was now in the habit of styling "asses"—a most insulting epithet among the Abyssinians—with an unmentionable expletive prefixed. On inquiring of Mr. Eipperle whether I might not proceed on my visit without an escort from Theodore, he fairly laughed at the idea, and warned me against being misled on that point. He himself had not dared to venture into the country until his European friends at Debra

Tâbor had obtained a safe-conduct from his Majesty, and on his return he was obliged to be furnished with a passport.

23rd.—Sheikh Jumä'ah returned from Abyssinia to-day, and on coming home from a ride I found him waiting for me, attended by a guard of about two hundred Takroory horse. The old Chief, who is a thorough-bred negro, received me with open arms, embracing me almost too affectionately. He welcomed me most cordially to his country, and said that he could not go to his own house without first calling upon me and expressing his readiness to serve me in every way. He informed me that he had parted from the King only eight days previously, but that his Majesty had said nothing to him about me. He praised Theodore, whom he described as a great and "good-hearted" man. There was no end of rejoicing when the Chief left me. All the Takroories seemed frantic with joy: the cavalry were cantering right and left, up hill and down dale, through the town and beyond it. The pedestrians clapped their hands and jumped about like madmen, while the constant discharge of musketry added to the wildness of the scene. After the Sheikh was reported to have gained the bosom of his loving family, all the ministers of state and other functionaries retired to their respective domiciles, to indulge in their favourite *'Asîda,* and to wash it down with the still more highly-prized *Marîsa.* Millet is the principal ingredient in both these messes: in the former, it is first boiled and then left to soak in liquid butter (ghee); in the latter, to ferment into a nauseous beverage. That substantial part of the ceremony over, every drum in the Gallabât metropolis was brought into requisition, accompanied by the most dismal howlings and ejaculations, in which barbarous merriment most of the night was spent. The cries which sometimes proceeded from

the multitude were so much like those of the hyæna when
in search of prey, that I was momentarily at a loss to decide whether they were the utterances of men or beasts. On
that memorable occasion, these unearthly sounds proceeded
from about twenty different points in the town; but,
generally, during our sojourn at Matámma, there were at-
least four gangs who kept up the discordant jubilation
throughout the night, the indulgent Ruler patronizing the
custom, by allowing all the idlers and vagrants to join the
principal performers, within the precincts of the royal residence.

In the afternoon, my companions and I returned the
Sheikh's call, but it was some time before we obtained an
audience, and we had reason to suspect that he was "the
worse for liquor," in which he indulged much too freely.
The Takroories generally are much given to inebriating
drinks, and, for want of a better, partake largely of the
noxious *Marîsa*. How any human being can imbibe that
disgusting beverage was always a matter of wonder to me.
Just as we were leaving the Sheikh's presence, a slave girl
entered the room, crawling on her knees, with a large dish
of *'Asîda*, of which we were pressed to partake; but our
having already risen to depart was a good excuse for declining the unsavoury native dainty.

A considerable stream runs through Matámma, but as it
passes through marshy ground, and is, moreover, made the
receptacle of all kinds of filth, the water is very unwholesome, and, to avoid it, I engaged an Arab to bring us a
regular supply from the Atbara, which lies about three
miles to the southward. Matámma is, undoubtedly, a most
unhealthy place, and during the rainy season the prevailing
fever must be very fatal. Mr. Schwainfurth had been a

of these among the ordinary reflectors—she raises it in front of her face with a smile, but on perceiving how much her nose is flattened and her mouth enlarged, and how exaggerated are her features generally, off she rushes in trepidation, declaring that she will have nothing to do with the accursed spirit of evil. A number of traders from Arabia frequent the fair, and carry back musk, coffee, wax, gold, ivory and a few concubines—if the latter can be had at a cheap rate. The Gójjam Kâfilah had not arrived before we left Matámma; I am therefore unable to say what number of unfortunate slaves were conveyed that year from thence to this market. I was told, however, that as many as three thousand boys and girls from the Galla and Shánkĕ́á countries are imported annually for sale in the Soodân. Although this nefarious traffic is no longer carried on in the open market, it is still prosecuted in a retired locality, and bargains are often made in private houses. I was sorry to find, during our stay, that even Europeans did not scruple to foster the abominable trade, and that certain lay missionaries had purchased slaves in order to bring them up in the Christian religion. This course, I believe, was pursued under the plea that the laws on the Continent of Europe sanctioned the purchase, if made with the design of liberating the slaves. Be that as it may, there can be no doubt that such a system is much to be deprecated, for it stands to reason that the more purchasers there are, the more slaves will be imported into the market.

Thousands of horses and cattle are brought to Matámma for sale, and, when the prices are moderate, numbers are bought up for exportation into the different Soodân districts, as far as Cásala and Khartûm. The price of cattle and horses, in my time, averaged from three to five dollars per head for the former, and from ten to fifty for the latter. Mules and donkeys are scarce: the average price of a mule was from ten to thirty, and for a donkey from three to ten dollars. Cereals were not plentiful in the market, but millet—the common food of all classes in the country—largely predominated over every other grain. Although cereals generally were said to be rather dear, I purchased a camel-load of millet—weighing at least 600lbs.—for four dollars = eighteen shillings.

Sheikh Jumä'ah's revenue is derived mainly from taxes levied on live stock and goods brought to the Matámma fair. Out of this, he pays a yearly tribute of 3,000 dollars to Egypt, and a like sum to Abyssinia, and maintains a standing army of about five hundred Musketeers; the balance is applied to the maintenance of an extensive Harîm, a host of underlings, and the entertainment of guests; any surplus he inters against the day of reckoning. There is a regularly organized militia to protect the district against any attack from without. Most of these are mounted, and they are bound to meet for consultation at the capital on a summons from the Sheikh, who dares not undertake any warlike expedition without their unanimous concurrence. That, once given, is said to insure their unswerving adhesion and loyalty. The present Ruler has been most bravely defended by them, on two different occasions, against a very superior force from Abyssinia. The latter of these engagements took place within the last twenty years, and so fierce was the conflict that the vanquished Christians retired, leaving five hundred men dead on the field. During our stay at Matámma it was stated that the enemy was preparing to attack the place. No sooner was this report spread abroad, than as many as two thousand of the militia met in the plain of the capital, who declared that they would uphold the Sheikh and defend his Harîm and his dignity to the last drop of blood in their veins.

28th.—Received letters from the captives this morning, through Mr. Flad; among them was one from Consul Cameron, of which the following are extracts:—

"*Mágdala Prison, October* 10, 1865.

" MY DEAR RASSAM,—I write you a few lines to tell you I have received a letter from Gaffat, to the following effect:—' If Mr. Rassam does not come now, you will all be lost first, and then ourselves.'

" I am requested to let you know this.

" The King sent us a cow a-piece some time back—the first notice he has taken of us, with one exception, since the torturing. He has spoken rather kindly about us lately in public.

" But we are still chained hand and foot."

It was satisfactory to hear that, although still in chains, the unfortunate captives were somewhat better treated; but I was distressed to learn, from another of Cameron's letters, that they had among them "two born devils"—one an Irishman and the other a Frenchman—who had been trying their best to hatch mischief.

The Takroories are a most disobliging set, and very laggard to undertake long journeys. On my endeavouring to obtain messengers from among them to go to Massowah, some would say, "If we lose our way, who will guide us?" while others were afraid that if they fell sick on the road they would never see Matámma again. They are unquestionably a lazy, indolent race, and would never do a kindly action except under coercion.

5th December.—Other messengers reached me from Abyssinia to-day: two had come from Mágdala, but hearing on their way down to Massowah that we had left that place for

Matámma, they came on here. They brought letters from Cameron—of course, of an earlier date than those lately received—and reported that the King had gone to Agów-mĕdĕr, to the westward of the Lake, and about ten days' journey from Matámma; that the letters which I had sent to his Majesty had followed him thither, and that, consequently, I could hardly expect the messengers back before the middle of the month. They apprised me that public opinion in Abyssinia was divided as to the upshot of my Mission: some holding that I should encounter endless obstacles in obtaining the release of the captives; whereas others were of opinion that, as soon as the King was assured of our goodwill, he would be reconciled to us at once, and comply with all my requests. All agreed, however, that the King had decided on putting the prisoners on their trial before me, and asking me to pronounce judgment in their case. The messengers reported further, that as soon as the dreaded monarch began the descent between Debra Tâbor and the Lake of Dámbĕa, all the rebels fled from Góndar and the surrounding districts; and that T'issoo Gobazê was preparing to go to the lowlands with his family.

8th.—A grand review of all the Matámma troops, cavalry and infantry, took place this morning, headed by the gallant Sheikh Jumä'ah. The demonstration was occasioned by a report that the Fakih Ibrahîm, formerly one of the Sheikh's Galla slaves, was approaching with an overwhelming force to attack Matámma, and, if possible, kill his late master and reign in his stead. The parade over, the cavalry made a circuit of at least half a mile to defile before our house. This, we were told, was done in order to display their horsemanship before the " Franks."

9th.—We invited Mr. and Mrs. Eipperle and Mr. Mutchler—

another lay missionary—to accompany us on a pic-nic excursion to the Atbara, where we were led to expect some exciting sport among the crocodiles, hippopotami and wild buffaloes. Starting at six in the morning, we reached the river after an hour's brisk ride on our mules. Having been recommended to select the opposite bank, we tried what appeared a shallow passage, but the mules were unable to cross it, owing to the large pebbles in the bed of the stream. Blanc got a spill in making the essay, and, of course, a good ducking; but no crocodiles took advantage of the breakfast thus accidentally placed within their reach; in fact, none appeared either to divert or scare us, though we had been told, on leaving Matámma, that we should see them "in hundreds." I went with a party of Takroories to what is called the "Bed of the Crocodiles," where the river expands into a pool; but even there they would not rise to the surface, although I threw so many pebbles into the water that my native companions may have likened me to a pious Hajjy, casting stones at the Rajîm, in the Valley of Muna. Discovering a better ford, we crossed without any difficulty, and took up our quarters in a grove of magnificent trees. Sheikh Jumä'ah had promised, the day before, to join our party, with all the Matámma braves, in order to protect us against a sudden attack from his quondam slave Fakih Ibrahîm, who was said to be hovering about the river, and also to show us what expert huntsmen his followers were; but he did not come, and I was never able to learn the real cause, so different were the reasons alleged for his absence. Some said he had a headache, others affirmed that it was rheumatism. Some attributed his indisposition to his having taken a drop too much—of tea! but his faithful major-domo, 'Iz-ud-Dîn, whom he sent as his representative, excused his master on the ground of important affairs of state, especially

connected with that " robber-dog and son of a pig," Fakih
Ibrahîm, who, having secured the services of a few hundred
Abyssinian robbers, had threatened to burn Matámma and
put the Takroories to the sword. 'Iz-ud-Dîn came armed to
the teeth, with a retinue of two hundred mounted followers,
who, after saluting us, rode off to scour the forest and drive
all the wild buffaloes to our halting-place, in order that we
might shoot them at our ease! Twice we heard the rush of
the horned beasts through the thick cover, but they declined
coming near enough to be shot at. 'Iz-ud-Dîn, however, and
his body-guard managed to bring down three buffaloes with
their javelins, while mounted on horseback, two of which
they had consumed in the wood, and the flesh of the third
was to be divided between the royal household and their
" Franjy " friends—the latter to have also the horns and the
tail, as their share in the success of the hunt. On 'Iz-ud-Dîn's
departure, I accompanied two men he had left with us as a
guard in search of wild honey, which was said to abound in
the jungle on the banks of the Atbara. We had hardly
proceeded two hundred yards when one of the party called
out that he had found a hive in the trunk of a large tree.
The smoke of a fire, kindled for the purpose, soon drove the
insect inmates to an adjoining tree. There was not much
comb in the hive, but the honey was delicious. We returned
to Matámma at 5·30 P.M., and heard that Sheikh Jumä'ah had
been playing great havoc with the royal cattle, having caused
no less than forty head to be slaughtered to provide a feast
for his militia. As this day, the 20th of the current
Mohammedan month Rájab—corresponding with the 9th of
December—was the anniversary of his accession to the
Gallabât throne, he thereby, as some of his people said,
killed two birds with one stone.

13th.—I had made repeated unsuccessful efforts, since my arrival at Matámma, to obtain messengers to convey letters to Khartûm and Cásala, to be forwarded from thence to Egypt and Aden, notifying the progress of the Mission thus far. Ultimately, I decided to send Hásan Effendi, who had not had a day's health at Matámma, to Cásala, and an opportunity simultaneously offered enabling me to send dispatches to Khartûm, by a return courier who had come to Sheikh Jumä'ah on duty from the Egyptian Government. I wrote by the same messengers to Khoja Panagiotes at Cásala, and likewise to the Prussian Consul at Khartûm, who acted as British Agent also, requesting them to forward my letters to their respective destinations—the former, those addressed to Aden ; and the latter, those for Egypt.

15th.—Went out shooting, but only bagged a dove, an ibex and a crane. A walk of two miles in damp long grass, and exposure to the scorching sun after the cold early morning, brought on fever, which was not improved by the savage music and singing which the Takroories kept up throughout the night and during the following day, in commemoration of the *'Eid-un-Nakkára,* or Festival of the Drum, which falls on the 27th of the Mohammedan month Rájab, when all the State drums are covered with new skins and presented to the Ruler of Gallabât. From the holiday of the succession up to that day, there is an interregnum, during which interval the powers of the Ruler are in abeyance, and an individual styled the " Chief of the Drum "—a sort of president—assumes the reins of government. This extraordinary annual custom is said to prevail for two reasons : 1st, to allow time for fresh covering the drums ; and 2nd, to prove to the Sheikh that the Takroories are capable of self-government, and that, therefore, he will only be tolerated pending good behaviour on his part.   When the drums are ready, all the Gallabât militia assemble at the capital, and, after the formal presentation of the State instruments—which are allowed to stand by as mute witnesses of the ceremony—renew their vows of allegiance to the reigning potentate.   On the present occasion there were at least two thousand warriors assembled, who were all hospitably entertained by the Sheikh, many more cattle having been slaughtered to meet their wants.   At noon, the State drums were conveyed outside the town, and formally delivered over to the royal drummers. The old Chief himself remained in the field for nearly two hours, and in a spirited harangue to his troops reminded them of his former exploits, and the share they had borne in his successes.   He felt sure that he saw the same devoted followers before him—men who would outshine their former feats of daring intrepidity—and make that "son of a dog," the Fakih Ibrahîm, rue the day he ventured to face such a phalanx of heroes as were now before him.   He then consulted them whether, in their opinion, it would be better to stand on the defensive and await the impending attack, or whether they should follow the "two-legged hyæna" into his den, and close his mouth for ever against eating *'Asída*.   If they took the former course, the very women, he said, would spit at their beards, and they would be ashamed hereafter to look even an old woman in the face.   At the conclusion of this martial address, the assembled warriors exclaimed: "Let us go forthwith and break the slave's skull, that the end of his life may be worse than its beginning."   All the militia were then dispersed through the town, some putting up with their friends, whilst those who could not find quarters elsewhere betook themselves to different huts belonging to the Sheikh's extensive establishment.

In the afternoon I went to the residence of a Takroory magnate to witness some negro merry-making. There were three different dancing groups within the enclosure. The gyrations and evolutions of the young men were very amusing, and the dexterity with which they made feint attacks on each other with their large clubs—bringing these suddenly in such close proximity to each other's skull that I fully anticipated some serious mishap—was most surprising.

17th.—The Takroories kept up their war-songs through the livelong night, in consequence of the apprehension of a spy, who confessed to having been sent by the Fakih Ibrahîm to find out the strength of the Matámma garrison. He further informed Sheikh Jumä'ah that the runaway slave was not far distant. At 2 P.M. the alarm was sounded throughout the length and breadth of the place, and immediately every horseman and musketeer turned out, fully equipped for active service, and assembled in the field outside the town, and in the course of half an hour began to march towards the reported whereabouts of the rebel. Before leaving, Sheikh Jumä'ah sent his lieutenant, 'Iz-ud-Dîn, to apprise me of his intended departure on the expedition, promising not to be absent more than three days.

I purchased one of the best horses in Matámma to-day, belonging to the Collector of Customs, for fifty dollars. He proved to be a capital trotter, with the sole drawback, common to all Abyssinian horses, of. excessive capering when once his head was turned towards home.

18th.—Received a packet of letters for the Mission from Massowah, which the Governor of Cásala kindly forwarded to me from that place by two Bashi-Bozûks, no other trustworthy messengers being procurable there.

19th.—This being the fair day again, I hoped to receive

some news about the messengers whom I had sent to the King; but no one had heard anything about them, and his Majesty's movements were involved in mystery. A month had already elapsed since their departure, and even if they had fallen in with him at Agówmĕdĕr, where he was reported to be, they ought to have returned a week ago. I now began to fear that Theodore intended to keep me waiting at Matámma as he had done at Massowah, and the prospect was far from agreeable. I therefore made up my mind to address him once more in the beginning of January, asking what his intentions were with regard to the Mission— since it would be sheer madness for us to remain in that unhealthy locality during the autumn months; and that if he took no notice of my appeal, after a fixed time, my companions and I would return to the coast.

A report reached Matámma that on hearing of the overwhelming force which his late master was leading out against him, the Fakih Ibrahîm retreated in the direction of Kwâra, leaving Sheikh Jumä'ah to return to his capital without achieving the victory which he had fully reckoned upon. However, as the Matámma troops had taken more than a week's provisions with them, it was unanimously agreed upon by them and the Sheikh that they should proceed against a petty Abyssinian tribe, who occupied a village named Awâsa, on the border of T'issoo Gobazê's district, about two days' march north of Matámma, and capture as many horses and cattle as they could, in punishment of the alleged crime of having furnished aid to the Fakih Ibrahîm. As with this booty they might make a triumphant entry into the capital, the Gallabât force, intent on plunder, halted in their southern course and turned towards the north, in the direction of the ill-fated village.

25th.—Truly a most dismal Christmas to us! Here we
were in an outlandish and pestilential place, away from relatives and friends, and, what was still more disheartening,
apparently as far from attaining our desired object as ever.
Nevertheless, we did our best to make ourselves as cheerful
as possible under the circumstances, by inviting Mr. and
Mrs. Eipperle, Mr. Mutchler and Signor Marcopoli — the
latter just arrived from Cásala — to join us in the evening.
The necessary ingredients for a plum-pudding were not procurable; but our Indian servants managed to make some
mince-pies, and a bowl of punch at the conclusion served, for
the time at least, to make us forget the loneliness and irk-
someness of our position.

26th.—A more propitious day than the last, owing to the
arrival of all my messengers from the King, with the cheering
news that his Majesty had ordered three officers of rank to
proceed to the Abyssinian border with a large escort, to meet
the Mission and to conduct it up to him. Mohammed
Sihâwy, who had carried my letter of the 25th of August to
the King, wherein I informed him of my departure for Egypt,
and Hailo, who took up mine of the 15th of October, apprising
his Majesty of our departure for Matámma, were also sent
back with the Matámma messenger. Mohammed was the
man who had deceived me about Consul Cameron's release,
but my position was such that I did not venture to allude to
the matter, fearing that if he once began to suspect that I
distrusted him, he might do considerable mischief; besides
which, I had since seen good reason to believe that the King
himself had had something to do with the fabrication. The
messengers brought me two letters from his Majesty, couched
in most courteous terms, but one of these, like the first which
I received from him at Massowah, was neither signed nor

sealed; the other contained an apology for the previous omission, and was both signed and sealed. It appears that when the messengers whom I had sent up from Massowah, reporting my departure for Egypt, reached Theodore at Debra Tâbor, while on his way down to Dámbĕa, he took no notice of them whatever, beyond consigning them over to a Bâldărăbâ to attend to their wants, saying that he would give them an answer as soon as he received intimation of my movements. They were consequently obliged to accompany him to the south, and on the arrival of my Matámma messengers at Dâmôt, he ordered the Arabic scribe to write me the following letter, courteous in its tone, but still, as already stated, without either seal or signature:—

"In the name of the Father, of the Son, and of the Holy Ghost—one God. Praise be to Him for ever. Amen.

"To the beloved and noble Hormuzd Rassam. After offering to you salutations, and asking after your good health, I praise God abundantly that I am well and in the best of health. I inform you that I have received your note, dated the 22nd of November, and understood it to the letter, and I thanked the Creator for your friendship. Now, oh beloved, I explained to you that the omission of my name to this letter has been occasioned by the people whom I used to love, and who used to sit on my bed [i. e., at my board], [but who] had reviled me. This is the obstacle which I mentioned to you while you were at Massowah. Now seeing that God has brought you safely to these parts, I have sent peremptory orders to the governors in the neighbourhood of Chálga for receiving you and bringing you towards me.

"Regarding the servants [messengers] who came to me while you were at Massowah, they got sick, and I found one of them, named Mohammed, not indisposed; him I send to you, according to your desire.* I have ordered the said Mohammed, if

---

* I had asked the messenger who carried my letter to come back to me, when the escort was sent.

they [his companions] are recovered, to take them with him. May you remain preserved.

"The 1st of Tahsâss [A.H.], 1282." [The 8th of December, 1865.]

The messenger Mohammed, referred to in the above, had just started when Hailo from Massowah reached the King, with my letter of the 15th of October. What his Majesty could have seen in that communication to strike his fancy, no one knew; but no sooner was it read out to him than he remarked to the bystanders, "How can I continue to treat Rassam so badly, after his anxious efforts to cultivate my friendship? He even sends messengers to inform me of his departure from Massowah to Matámma. Call the writer," he continued, "in order that I may send him a proper letter." The following was accordingly penned and sealed, and delivered to Hailo, who was instructed to overtake the messengers who had left the day before, and to come on with them to me:—

"In the name of the Father, of the Son, and of the Holy Ghost —one God. Praise be to Him eternally.

"From the King of Kings of Abyssinia, King Theodorus, to the beloved and true friend, Hormuzd Rassam, first Governor of Aden. After offering you abundance of salutations and presenting you with compliments, [I offer] to the Most High God abundant thanks. What necessitated the writing this, oh dear one, is that I wrote to you formerly a number of letters, not containing the name and seal, on account of what had taken place on the part of insolent people, who outraged God, and [the one] whom he had made ruler, and I do not know, nor understand, whether these people are Jews or heathens, who do not know God. When I examined in this matter [five words obscure] I find it necessary to affix for you our name and seal; and I have placed the name and the royal seal, because, if these wicked men have reviled us, you, oh beloved, what evil have

you done to me? Now I send you my name and my seal
by your servants, in order that every time I might not act
amiss, as formerly. Salâm.

"Written on Monday, the 4th of Tahsâss [A.H.], 1282." [The
11th of December, 1865.]

(The foregoing two letters were written in Arabic).

It will be perceived that in none of his letters does the
King once allude to her Majesty's letter, which he knew to be
in my possession, or manifest any concern because his letter to
the Queen had not been answered. He never questioned any
of the messengers about the Queen's letter, but invariably
spoke to those around him about an Envoy, who was on
the way to seek his friendship, and before whom he intimated, on more than one occasion, that he would again
try the captives for having "reviled" him. This was to
me a most surprising fact, inasmuch as I had been constantly hearing, since my appointment to the Mission, that
the King's anger had been originally caused by the omission
of her Majesty's Government to reply to his letter; and,
moreover, that he was now most anxious to receive it.

In accordance with the intimation conveyed to me in his
foregoing letter, dated the 28th December, the King immediately summoned three Chiefs who preside over the Chálga
district, and who were then at Court on business, to proceed at
once to their respective posts, in order to superintend the
securing of provisions, and porters to carry our luggage. He
wrote a note at the same time to other Chiefs, to render every
assistance in their power, both as regards our being adequately
protected and provided for on the journey, and the transport
of our effects. He also caused a letter to be written to the
European artisans at Gáffat, and to the local authorities
there, to make every preparation to receive me as a distin-

guished guest—it having been his intention at that time to send us to Debra Tâbor, in order that we might be near his European employés, during our stay in Abyssinia. He promised, moreover, to meet me in person near the northern extremity of the Lake, when I left Chálga, as he wished to have a private talk with me regarding the object of my Mission; but the plunder of Dâmôt, and his projected attack on Gójjam, prevented him from leaving his post after we left Bálwaha. I was subsequently told at Wahné that his Majesty would meet us at Wandígê, on the western side of the Lake; but on reaching that district, the place of meeting was changed to Agówmĕdĕr, and when there that it was to be in Dâmôt, where the interview eventually took place. The King had also written to the Chief of Matámma to furnish us with carriage and other necessaries as far as Wahné, where the royal escort would be awaiting us. All the messengers concurred in raising my hopes as to the success of the Mission; and the munificent manner in which his Majesty had behaved to them was an additional ground for anticipating a favourable reception. He clothed them all in handsome Abyssinian suits, gave each a fine mule, and ordered that they should be supplied with provisions on the road.

27th.—Sheikh Jumä'ah returned this morning from the expedition against his Galla slave, but as the rebel had discreetly got out of the way, the old Chief had been foiled in his intention of making him lick the dust. However, he had vented his rage upon the helpless people of Awâsa, whose only real fault was that they inhabited that part of Abyssinia which lies nearest to the district of Gallabât. The gallant Tekroories came back to-day immensely elated at having succeeded in capturing about one thousand head of cattle and a few mules and donkeys. On approaching the capital the infantry capered like maniacs, and the cavalry, giving the rein to their steeds, rode about as if they had lost all control over them, then suddenly checking them brought them to a standstill, and then again lashed them most unmercifully, to set them off once more at full gallop. The old Chief called on me in the afternoon, bringing with him the letter which Theodore had addressed to him. The contents ran as follows :—" A beloved friend of mine, named Hormuzd Rassam, an Englishman, is at present with you at Matámma. You are to convey him safely to the district of Chálga, where he will be received by my people. You will attend to this, because he is my beloved friend, and you should honour him." On the strength of this, Sheikh Jumā'ah procured for us the requisite number of camels. Writing on the 28th of December to a friend in England, to whom I had regularly sent a diary for years, I thus expressed my feelings at this juncture :—

"As we shall be starting this afternoon for Abyssinia, I must close this journal to send by the special messenger whom I have engaged to carry letters to Khartûm. Next month will be one of great importance to me, and of no little anxiety ; for not only will the release of the prisoners depend upon my diplomacy and the temper of the King, but also my own safety and that of my companions. I must trust to our Heavenly Father, and act justly and honourably ; and I have no doubt that everything will yet terminate successfully."

28*th.*—In the afternoon my companions and I called to take farewell of Sheikh Jumā'ah. The old man was very absent and grumpy, scarcely uttering a word, until I inquired of him whether the courier, whom I had asked him to engage for me to convey dispatches to Khartûm, and who ought to have left early this morning, had actually started.

His cool reply was, that he should set out in two or three days. I was greatly annoyed at this, as I was anxious that the Government at home should be apprised as soon as possible of the departure of the Mission for Abyssinia; so I manifested my vexation, and requested him to return the letters, which I should endeavour to send through some other channel. As he did not like me to do that, for fear of incurring the displeasure of the Egyptian Government on the one hand, and that of Theodore on the other, he directed that the courier should be sent for, and ordered him in my presence to start betimes on the following morning. This little jar amicably adjusted, my companions and I sipped coffee with him, and then took our departure, wishing each other every prosperity. I discovered afterwards that the old Sheikh had got into a scrape by his imprudent attack on the unfortunate village of Awâsa. It was fully proved, after the seizure of the booty, that the villagers referred to had never swerved from their allegiance to Theodore by entering into any relations with the rebel Fakîh. The owners of the plundered cattle had consequently come to demand the restitution of their property, which the Takroories had refused to surrender. The dispute, it appears, was at its height when we called on the Sheikh, and that doubtless had originated the ill-humour in which we found him. As the dispute was still pending when we left, I am unable to say how it terminated.

CHAPTER VIII.

MATÁMMA TO THE PLAIN OF DÁMBĔA.

Gábra, our new Guide — The Gondâwa river — Features of the country — Wahné — Reception by the King's deputy — Troublesome cameleers — Uxoriousness of the Abyssinian followers — Male and female occupations — Start for Balwáha — Romantic scenery —'Abd-ur-Rahmân Bey, late Envoy to Theodore from the Viceroy of Egypt — Visit from two "Shûms"— Mohammed Sihâwy's apology for his falsehood — Visit from an Abyssinian lady — Native etiquette — Arrival of the escort sent by Theodore — The title of "Lij"— A feast on Brundo, or raw beef — Brundo, how eaten — Têj — The "Order of the Shirt"— Courtesy of the Chiefs — Letters from the Captives and Mr. Flad — Precautions against spies — Potatoes substituted for Letters — Intense cold —Hyænas make sport with our kettles — The Sar-Amba — The Plateau of Chálga — Magnificent scenery — A Kamánt village — Worship and Creed of the Kamánts — Their devotion to Theodore, and its reward — Honesty of Abyssinian porters — Abundant supplies — Acceptance of the royal hospitality compulsory — Hyænas again — Wäízero Dinkee — Dispatch of letters to the coast — Glimpse of Góndar.

WHEN our baggage was being laden we found that, through 'Iz-ud-Dîn's carelessness, several of the cameleers had bolted with their animals. These, it seems, had been pressed into the service, and on hearing that they would have to carry large cases, they judged it rather too hard that they should have to work for nothing, and, perchance, lose their camels into the bargain. However, by hook or by crook, 'Iz-ud-Dîn managed to procure substitutes, some of which belonged to himself, and some to the Sheikh, and I took special care to make the cameleers understand that I should pay their fare. We started at 4·45 P.M., and on reaching Máryam-Wáha— an Amharic word, signifying "the Water of Mary"—Messrs. Eipperle, Mutchler and Marcopoli, who had accompanied us thus far to see us off, bade us farewell and returned to Matámma. Three hours' onward march brought us to Dakn-ul-Fíl—Arabic for "the Elephant's Beard"—where we halted for the night. Sheikh Jumä'ah had intended to send a large escort with us, but as he found there was nothing to be apprehended on the road between Matámma and Wahné— the first Christian village on the Abyssinian border—and probably in consequence of the dissatisfaction of his subjects in the matter of the plundered cattle, he ultimately put us off with a one-eyed, pox-marked, puny-looking guide, the most repulsive specimen of humanity I ever set eyes on. He rejoiced in the name of Gábra, and was a convert from Christianity to Islamism. He was a native of Kwâra, the King's native district, and having been bred up from child-hood among the Takroories, had embraced their doctrines, re-taining his baptismal name. I was quite amazed on hearing that he had been appointed to conduct us to Theodore, especially after all I had been told of his Majesty's antipathy to Mussulmans in general, and could hardly believe that he would welcome with any degree of cordiality this envoy from the Ruler of Gallabât, who, though a countryman of his, had abjured the Christian religion, and become a pervert to the detested creed. On asking Gábra whether he was not afraid to go before the King, he grinned, and said that he was in the habit of visiting him four times a-year, and that his Majesty always joked him about the way in which he had changed his religion. Some having told him that he had been converted by a woman, the King had repeatedly promised to give him as many wives as he liked, provided he returned to the faith of his forefathers. This man was first cousin to one of the Chiefs of Mágdala. Though surpas-singly hideous, he succeeded, before we had been ten days in

Abyssinia, in gaining the affections of two damsels, and married both. I had given orders that no woman should be allowed in our camp, but this fellow managed to evade the injunction under the plea that he always took care to erect his hut for his own and his wives' accommodation beyond our camp limits. Before leaving Matámma I engaged an Abyssinian, named Wald-Gabríêl, as interpreter, in order that 'Omar 'Ali's services might be exclusively given to Dr. Blanc on the road. Wald-Gabríêl had been in Egypt, and could speak Arabic well. It is a noteworthy fact that wherever I met an Abyssinian who had left his native country for any time, I generally found him to be well versed in colloquial Arabic.

29th.—The cold almost prevented my sleeping last night, and at 2 A.M. the thermometer was as low as 42°. Left Dakn-ul-Fîl at 5 A.M., passed the Kokai stream at 6·45, and reached El-Maradîb, or Komâr—the former an Arabic and the latter an Amharic name—at eight. Starting from thence at 3 P.M., in five hours we came upon the Gondâwa, a large river separating the Abyssinian from the Gallabât and all the Egyptian territories. Next to the Atbara, this is the most considerable stream we had seen since leaving Massowah: the water reached the mules' knees. After crossing the river, we pursued the journey till midnight, when we halted at a place with another bilingual name, Khôr-ul-Lailah and Wâka—the former Arabic, the latter Amharic. It was intensely cold on the road.

30th.—Two blankets and as many carpets for a covering only kept me comfortably warm last night. Left Khôr-ul-Lailah at 6 A.M., Blanc, Prideaux and I pushing on towards Wahné under the guidance of the new interpreter, leaving the baggage to follow. There is no lack of water between

Matámma and Wahné, we having crossed at least thirty streams in the interval, some of which were very large. As for wood, the country is so densely covered with timber and bamboos that, with few exceptions, the rider has to make a path for himself. Before reaching Wahné, we passed a large jungle which had been fired by the villagers, in order, as Wald-Gabríêl said, to get rid of the lions which infested the forest. Reached Wahné at 9·30 A.M., and took up our quarters under a large tree. Here we had our first experience of the arbitrary proceedings common in Abyssinia. No sooner had our interpreter informed the local Chief of our arrival, than he had all the villagers who were reclining under the tree dislodged for our accommodation. A sick man among them, hearing that there was a doctor in our party, begged to be left where he was; whereupon Blanc kindly took him in hand.

At Wahné, we were received very well both by the Chief and the King's deputy, who offered to render us every assistance in their power. The Chiefs whom his Majesty had dispatched to escort us sent to inform me on our arrival, that, having heard that the rebels under T'issoo Gobazê intended to intercept us, they had gone in pursuit of them, but hoped to join us in the course of five or six days. They advised me at the same time not to remain at Wahné, but to go on to Balwáha, a place about three hours' journey on the way to Chálga, where we should find better camping-ground, be in a safer position, and have an abundance of good water. The King had ordered his subjects to supply us with provisions and carriage; but owing to the recent plunder of the Wahné district by T'issoo Gobazê's people, the villagers could only furnish us with bread and native beer—the latter made either from wheat, barley, millet or a black grain called *Dâgussa.* As the district had been nearly deserted since the raid just referred to, they could not well supply us with the necessary means of conveyance to Balwáha, which led the Chiefs to order our Matámma cameleers to proceed with us another stage. The road beyond Wahné being considered very rough and precipitous, the men absolutely refused to obey, declaring that they would rather die than accompany us any farther. I tried all I could by holding out promises of a reward and a plentiful supply of meat to induce them to comply, but they were inexorable. "Of what use," said they, "will a dollar of yours be to us when we may lose fifty, by the death of one of our camels?" Whereupon, uncording the boxes and packages, they went away, followed immediately by the Abyssinian officials and their followers, on seeing whom the cameleers left their animals and absconded. Among the number of the runaways was the Arab whom I had employed at Matámma to bring us water from the Atbara, who, together with a friend of his, had promised to go with me to Balwáha, even if his comrades refused. When they eventually returned, I asked them why they had deserted, after engaging to go with me "even unto death." They replied that their "cousins" had adjured them not to split, and they were, consequently, afraid of incurring their animosity—a plea of rattening, in fact—but protesting at the same time that they had only intended to laugh at their cousins' beards, by accompanying them a short distance and then returning to us; "for, surely," they went on to argue, "you didn't think we should have gone away altogether, leaving you in the lurch?" I accordingly sent to the Chiefs requesting them to restore these two men's camels, and, on hearing what had occurred, the other cameleers began to return one by one.

31st.—Notwithstanding that the fellows had agreed to take us to Balwáha, on my engaging to pay them for the extra trip, when the time for loading arrived they obstinately refused to move. I had taken so much pains to secure the compliance of these Arabs that, on seeing how recalcitrant they still were, the Abyssinian Chiefs murmured at my persistent endurance, declaring that the stick was the only reward they deserved. In fact, I was ultimately almost obliged to resort to coercion in order to get them to stir. Mohammed, the waterman, and his companion had arranged their packages early in the morning; but neither threats nor entreaties had any effect upon the rest. We found out afterwards that one of their number had frightened them into a belief that, once at Balwáha, they would be forced to go on to Chálga—a feat, as we subsequently proved, as impracticable as the ascent of the pyramids to a clumsy animal like the camel. However, on proceeding to load, the cameleers began to alter their demeanour, judging, no doubt, that they might as well resign themselves as pleasantly as possible to their " fate; " protesting, in the mean time, that their only objection to the trip to Balwáha was the fear of breaking our boxes; as to the camels, they devoted them unreservedly as a sacrifice in my service, and, for their own part, they were ready to accompany me to the utmost limit of Abyssinia.

A number of our Abyssinian followers came to me at Wahné asking permission to take from thence a few Abyssinian women, to assist in carrying our drinkables and to collect fire-wood—avocations which, in Abyssinia, it is considered a disgrace in men to pursue. It had come to my knowledge that, in accordance with a common practice in the country, these men had already wooed and been accepted by girls of the village, who had promised to marry them, provided I engaged their services as aforesaid; but as I had determined, on entering Abyssinia, to allow no females whatever, whether wife or servant, to enter our camp, I refused their request, telling them that such as wished to marry must remain behind. From the time we left the coast until then, we had employed Massowah men exclusively in providing us with wood and water. Under the influence of the prevailing prejudice, they now came to me in a body, representing that they would be disgraced for ever, if seen doing the work only fit for females, and that thenceforth no man in Abyssinia would associate with them. Two of them, great swells in their way, declared that their wives would spit upon them for following an effeminate occupation, and that thereafter they would not dare to show their faces at Massowah. I reminded them, on the other hand, that I had fully explained to them, on engaging their services, that the obnoxious tasks would form a part of their duty, and that if they now objected to them they were at full liberty to return to Massowah, and I would write to Sheikh Jumä'ah to forward them safely to Cásala. I further told them that, with us, it was no disgrace to carry water—certainly not more so than washing clothes, which, in Abyssinia, is left to the men to do. Moreover, that the fact of a certain work being usually done by women ought not to debar them from doing it; besides which, inasmuch as they—the Massowah men—were pious Mussulmans, it was a sin on their part to try and induce me to admit temptation within a bachelor's camp. This effectually silenced their importunities; but they had no idea then that before leaving Abyssinia they would have to become Christians — by having their heads shaved and partaking of "Christian meat"—for the sake of these very female carriers of wood and water. More on this subject anon. Although I was thus strict in not allowing any women to be employed in our establishment, I little thought at the time that, before many months were over, I should myself be driven to engage a band of them in my own service.

By half-past one in the afternoon all our differences with the cameleers were settled, and I sent them on in advance, under the protection of five mounted police, in order that, in the event of an accident, we might be behind to assist them. I'ngădă, their Chief, started with me and my companions forty minutes later, and although we made two halts on the road, occupying nearly an hour, we reached Balwáha at five—twenty minutes before the baggage. Notwithstanding all the fuss which had been made about the badness of the road, we found it much less difficult than that near Biräad, where we began the descent into the Barca, from Ansába. The former is by no means smooth or easy, but it is far less precipitous than the latter. There were only two spots where the cameleers were driven to invoke their patron saint, 'Abd-ul-Kâdir, to protect their animals against accidents. The scenery along this route is most romantic, and I can recall none in Abyssinia equal to it in beauty. The mountains and dales were so thickly covered with wood, that I wondered how the camels had cleared them without losing their loads.

On reaching the rivulet at Balwáha, a large clump of trees was pointed out to us as having been the spot where the unfortunate 'Abd-ur-Rahmân Bey, late envoy from the Viceroy of Egypt to the King of Abyssinia, had taken up his quarters, and we were recommended to occupy it until the arrival of our escort; but, as the ground looked black, owing to the recent firing of the grass upon it, I did not like the idea of halting there. However, my new interpreter, Wald-

Gabrîêl, soon intervened to put an end to any demur on my part by calling our guide a blockhead—"one unable to distinguish between Christians and Mohammedans"—and telling him that we were not going to walk in the footsteps of that Turk, who lived by plunder, but to enrich the natives of the country. Then, turning to me, he said, "Master, do not stop in this ill-omened spot which that Envoy occupied, and who never knew a happy day afterwards, and ultimately took poison to rid himself of a miserable existence." Wald-Gabrîêl had a very bad opinion of 'Abd-ur-Rahmân Bey, asserting that there was not a family in Góndar which had not suffered from the exactions of his servants. He himself—so he asserted—had had personal experience of their rapacity and outrageous behaviour, for they had forced an entry into his house in search of honey for making 'araky, although the King provided the Bey and his party with ample daily rations, including ten jars of honey. During our sojourn in Abyssinia, I never heard a native speak a word in favour of this unlucky Egyptian officer. The general belief in the country is that he poisoned himself; but my opinion is that he died of a virulent fever contracted in the Soodân.

However, as I did not choose to select the spot in question —not from any fear of moral infection or superstitious dread but simply because it was otherwise uninviting—we crossed the brook, which in some places was quite dry, and occupied a snug corner on the opposite bank, until we were joined by the King's deputies. The locality resembled a large crater surrounded by lofty mountains, and the water of the tiny stream was sweet and clear. Barring the heat of the vertical sun, the climate is very salubrious. Two "Shûms," as the local Chiefs are styled in Abyssinia, received us here to pay their respects, in accordance with the King's orders. In the evening they brought us a cow and abundance of bread for all our followers; also fowls, eggs, milk and a quantity of beer, called Bûza or Talla. Being very thirsty, I drank some of the latter, and did not dislike the taste. It was rather acid, but very clear, and, mixed with a few drops of brandy, forms a very refreshing beverage after a hot day's march. Knowing that the poor people of the district had to contribute gratuitously towards the rations supplied to the Mission by royal order, I offered to pay for what had been furnished on that day, but was told that such a proceeding would not only displease the King, but that the individuals who accepted the money might probably have to answer for it with their lives; so I forbore to press the matter further.

Mohammed Sihâwy, the messenger who had deceived me about the release of Consul Cameron, has proved very useful on the road since our entrance into Abyssinia. He and Hailo—the latter was the man who brought me the King's letter which was signed and sealed—had been appointed royal extra-purveyors by his Majesty, and orders were issued to all the Chiefs on our route, that although coming from servants of the English their instructions were to be carried out as if emanating directly from the King. I taxed the first-named scamp for the lie he had imposed upon me; his cool answer was, that he did it to please me, and that having heard that the King was about to release Cameron immediately, he thought he might as well be the first to announce the glad tidings. "Had the report been gloomy," he went on to say, "I would not have given utterance to it." Unfortunately, in a country like Abyssinia, where a bad man has great facilities of doing mischief, and especially with a delicate mission on hand like mine, we could not afford to make an enemy of one who was already in favour with the King. I was therefore constrained to put up with such characters, knowing that by dismissing them I should only incur their greater malignity.

1st January, 1866.—The new year seemed to open upon us auspiciously by a visit from the Shûm Mammu Hailo's wife—she might have been one of many consorts, for aught I knew to the contrary. I was constrained to receive her, having been told that my refusal would be taken in bad part by her husband; and, moreover, that I should be considered a hermit, if I held aloof from such interviews. She brought me, agreeably with Abyssinian usage, an offering of bread, eggs and beer. As she was a Shûm's wife, and therefore a lady of rank, I rose on her entering the tent. No sooner had I done so, however, than a chorus of voices bawled out, "Sit down!" it being thought degrading for a man in my position to rise before any female, no matter what her rank might be, and the poor lady herself looking quite disconcerted at the unexpected attitude which I had assumed towards her, I was obliged to explain that, in our country, ladies were ever preferred before men, and that, in accordance with that custom, I had wished to do her ladyship honour. This interview I had reason to believe was reported to Theodore before we reached him, and caused him no little amusement. On the lady's departure, I had to come to an understanding with my advisers as to mĹ future behaviour under similar circumstances. They maintained that it would be simply disgraceful if I rose up before a woman; whereas I contended that the disgrace would be mine, if I retained my seat when a lady visitor entered my tent. Ultimately, a compromise was agreed to, whereby, in effect, I was to imitate the conduct of those high Osmanli functionaries of the old school, who, feeling on the one hand that it would be derogatory on their part to rise before the Christian representative of a foreign power, and, on the other, that to omit the etiquette might bring them into trouble, generally managed to be standing when the visitor made his appearance, and feigned to be taken by surprise. The material difference, however, in the two cases was this: the Turk had recourse to the subterfuge from a feeling of superiority and religious bigotry; whereas I was compelled to adopt it in deference of the rules and prejudices of the country in which I was a stranger. I adhered to the unworthy dissimulation until our arrival at Mágdala, where I dispensed with it altogether, and reverted to the more civilized way of receiving lady visitors. The change was the theme of a nine days' wonder on the mountain, but it was scarcely ever noticed afterward, except by the visitors themselves, who generally met it with a reiterated, "Ba-Máryam! Ba-Egziăbĕhêr! Ba-Máryam!"—"By the [Virgin] Mary! for God's sake! for the sake of Mary!"—adjuring me, by implication, to sit down.

4th.—Spies were seized this morning prowling about our camp. These, it appears, had been sent by the rebels to discover what force we had with us, as they intended to attack the villages in the neighbourhood. In the afternoon our escort arrived, led by three superior and two lesser Chiefs. The names of the former were Lij Tasámma, Lij Sharo and Lij Tasho; of the latter, Wald-Máryam and Gójjamy Kâsa. The two last-named were specially appointed by the King to see that we were supplied with provisions on the road, and to superintend the transport of the baggage; the other three were charged with protecting us, and with forcing the peasants to furnish our viaticum. The Lijs Tasámma and

Sharo were brothers of Bitwáddad Hailo, one of the Chiefs of Mágdala; and Lij Tasho, a Kamánt—a sect which I shall notice presently—was the son of Bitwáddad Wâsí, another Mágdala Chief. Their collective duty was to guard the fortress of Sar-Amba, in Chálga, and to maintain order in the districts around it. As soon as they arrived, they put on their *Kamis*—Amharic as well as Arabic for Shirt— and came to pay their respects. Before doing so, however, they had to gird themselves, in token of their inferiority to their Sovereign's distinguished guest; (these and other formalities I shall describe more in detail in a future chapter). My Abyssinian tutors in the native etiquette having impressed upon me that I should demean myself in the eyes of all their countrymen if I rose before these subordinate officials, I was constrained, in order to avoid the assumption of what appeared to me most ridiculous pomposity, to take a middle course and receive them in an erect position. They were extremely civil, and conveyed to me, in most polite terms, the congratulations of their Sovereign on my safe arrival. They informed me that they had dispatched agents in every direction to collect men and cattle to transport our baggage to the royal Court, and hoped that, as soon as their Christmas was over, we should be able to move.

I may here mention, by the way, that the common meaning of the Amharic word "Lij" is Son, but when prefixed to a proper name it indicates a title of distinction, implying noble or genteel descent. In former times, it was the Emperor's exclusive prerogative to confer the title; even the ruling Sovereign could not raise a peasant to that rank, although he might make him a Duke. It approaches nearer the title of "Honourable," borne by sons of British peers, than any other to which I can liken it. The King very seldom addressed any as "Lij;" but there were hundreds of respectable men who used the word when speaking to or of each other. Theodore himself was called "Lij Kâsa" before he was created Dajazmâtsh by the puppet Emperor, Yuhannês, through Râs 'Ali.

6th.—This being Christmas-day with the Abyssinians, according to the old style still observed by all Oriental Churches, I had a couple of cows slaughtered for our Christian followers, who devoured the greater part of the meat quite raw. It was a disgusting sight—though somewhat amusing to us on account of its novelty—to see groups of Abyssinians seated round a heap of quivering flesh taken from a cow which an hour before had been quietly grazing, each wholly absorbed in gorging himself with large pieces cut off from the mass with a knife, or sword, or a split reed, the natural sharp edge of which did far more execution than the blunt metal instruments. The beef, in its raw state, is called "Brundo," and is eaten in three different shapes, according to the time available, and other attendant circumstances. 1st. *Pur et simple*, in morsels large enough to suit the longing mouth. 2ndly. In conjunction with a paste compounded of red pepper, salt and roasted onions, into which the morsels of *Brundo* are first dipped. 3rdly—which is the most respectable way—together with bread made of a small grain called "Têf," previously soaked in the paste just mentioned, which is liquefied into a suitable consistency by the addition of *têj* or mead. *Têj* is the drink most prized by the wealthier classes—the stronger the better—but as very few among them have either the means or the privilege of preparing it, they are obliged to be satisfied with the native beer. *Têj*-making is restricted to persons of rank, who have been invested with the Order of the Shirt, and to publicans who have obtained a special license to brew it. According to strict Abyssinian sumptuary law, no male above eight years of age, from the lowest-born subject to the son of a Râs—the highest dignitary in the State — can wear any covering resembling a shirt over his naked body from the waist upwards, unless that garment—which should always be of silk—is presented to him, in the first instance, by the Sovereign. Once invested with this distinguished "Order," the persons so honoured may wear a shirt made of any material, from the finest velvet or embroidered silk down to the commonest calico. The wives, also, of those who attained this rank were privileged to appear before the Emperor, in a judicial or other case, with their bosoms covered. But when Theodore came into power, he was determined to abolish all such savage, and, as he styled them, "childish customs," and he accordingly decreed that all Abyssinians might wear a cotton shirt, which, however, was not to descend below the knees. At the same time, he raised the Silk Shirt into an Order of distinction, retaining its investiture as a prerogative of the Sovereign, and decreed that all those on whom it had not been conferred, and who held offices under the State, were to wear their cotton shirts below the knees, to distinguish them from his other subjects. Hence, when he sent my messengers back to me at Matámma, he ordered them to wear the longer cotton shirts, to give them the guise of officials in the eyes of his people, and told them that after he had seen me, he would invest them with the superior " Order of the Shirt."

A number of children from the adjacent districts flocked to us to-day, on hearing that I was going to regale the Abyssinians attached to our camp. I had a swing rigged for their amusement, which they got to enjoy exceedingly, although at first the novelty scared a great many of them. Shortly after breakfast, the Chiefs of our escort went to Wahné to learn why the animals and porters had not been sent according to requisition. They returned in the course of the afternoon with a portion of them.

7th.—More carriers arrived this morning, and Lij Tasámma, the head Chief of the escort, judging that we had now enough to make a move, ordered the baggage to be distributed amongst them; but on finding, to his great chagrin, that he had miscalculated the extent of carriage required, and not wishing to disgrace the name of his King by keeping us waiting, he requested me to take my companions and proceed a short stage in advance, while he remained behind to make the necessary arrangements for transporting the whole of the baggage on the following day. We accordingly started at about 2 P.M., and reached the Súnkwáha in an hour's ride. After crossing that stream, our guide suggested a halt there for the night, to allow time for the remainder of our baggage being brought from Balwáha, which did not arrive until the following morning, as the carriers had to be sent back for the remainder, part of which was conveyed on the riding mules of the King's officers, who, consequently, were obliged to walk. Even the royal guard assisted in carrying some of the effects on their shoulders all the way. This self-denying courtesy on the part of the Chiefs, as well as their behaviour generally, was most gratifying, and it was obvious that our detention was as annoying to them as to ourselves. The magic name of "Theodore" had a mighty effect in instilling energy into the peasants, and in eliciting the ready obedience of the guards, who were as submissive to their superior officers as the best disciplined soldiers could possibly be. More carriers arrived from Chálga in the evening, but as these did not make the number sufficient to transport all our effects, we were constrained to wait at Sûnkwáha for an additional supply from the same place. Some of them having been found guilty of plundering a party of wayfarers of their provisions were adjudged to a sound flogging by the Chiefs.

8th.—Another batch of porters came to-day, but as I began to fear that at the present rate of progress we might be delayed a considerable time on our way to the Court— where I was most anxious to arrive in order to know the upshot of the Mission—I proposed to the Chiefs that my companions and I, with two or three servants, should push on in advance, leaving the heavy baggage and the other followers to come on after us. But Lij Tasámma would not listen to the arrangement, urging that such a course would be highly displeasing to the King. I then offered to send and either buy or hire a few animals, which I was told were procurable at Wahné and Chálga. The only reply I received to this proposal was the question, Who would dare to accept any money from me while I was the King's guest? It would be far better, he said, for those who undertook to negotiate such a bargain for us, and who ventured either to sell or hire any animals to us, to leave the country at once, or join the rebels, for if they remained within reach their hands would certainly be chopped off. Under these circumstances, I was obliged to give up all thought of hurrying forward. Just as I was retiring to bed, I was startled by an intimation from Dasta, that messengers had reached our camp with letters from the captives at Mágdala, and also from Mr. Flad—the faithful lad urging me at the same time to secure the letters at once, before they fell into the hands of the guard, who were already apprised of their arrival.

Luckily, Mr. Flad had sent me some potatoes; so Dasta ran back to Lij Tasámma, and told him that certain servants of mine, whom I had dispatched from Massowah to meet me on my entrance into Abyssinia, had just come, bringing me some foreign eatables from the Europeans at Gáffat. On hearing that the belated intruders were men in my employ, the guards immediately allowed them to join our other servants, and Dasta contrived, under cover of the night, to bring me all the letters which they carried. It was subsequently discovered that one of the messengers belonged to the Rev. Mr. Stern, and was the bearer of letters from that gentleman, addressed to Europe. As it was feared that he might be seized on the way to Matámma, after leaving our camp, Lij Tasámma was informed that he was one of my followers whom I wished to dispatch to Matámma on business. The man left early next morning, orders having been previously given to the Chief of the district to see that he was not molested on the road. Had the Abyssinians been but half as wary and mischievously inclined as they have been represented, the Mission would have been in imminent danger on this occasion of being seriously compromised, inasmuch as the letters entrusted to the aforesaid messenger contained matter of which a maliciously disposed translator might have readily availed himself to damage me in the King's estimation. Another of the messengers was the person who had been procured for me at Massowah by Hajj Âdam, one of the King's bitterest opponents, and Consul Cameron alluded to the circumstance in one of his two letters to me, of which the man was the bearer. Had that fact been divulged, the messenger would undoubtedly have lost his life, and I should have stood a very good chance of being charged with having dealings with the King's enemies. Mr. Flad's letter to me also had reference to my Mission and his own communications with the captives; and, lastly, Mr. Stern's servant was the bearer of a report describing the King's cruelty to the writer, the perusal of which, had it fallen into the despot's hands, would certainly have stirred him up to still greater outrage.

Mr. Flad's letter apprised me of a rumour that "the King had sent a friendly letter to the English prisoners in the fortress." Three days afterwards, however, I was informed by the same gentleman, greatly to my sorrow, that the report was unfounded; in fact, that it had "proved to be a gigantic lie." This last letter reached me also at a most critical moment, but as Dasta was always on the alert he contrived to smuggle in the messenger with another "supply of potatoes," without exciting any suspicion in the camp. As I feared there were spies about us, and that his Majesty would not fail to hear of the arrival of these messengers, I retained one of Mr. Flad's letters, which contained nothing but a notice of the dispatch of the potatoes, intending to hand it over to the King, in the event of any question being asked relative to my communications with that gentleman. Luckily, I was not driven to that expedient; but I now took the precaution of requesting the Chiefs not to allow their guards to interfere with our servants, and I further appointed the two interpreters, 'Omar 'Ali and Dasta, to be the medium of intercourse between me and them. There were only two in our establishment whom I hesitated to trust, namely, Wald-Gabriêl—the man whom I had recently engaged at Matámma, and whose fidelity I had not yet put to the test—and the great rogue, Mohammed Sihâwy, whom I could never venture to rely upon implicitly after his having so grossly deceived me about Consul Cameron's release. Moreover,

I regularly instructed the interpreters and messengers—seven in number—how to reply in the event of their being cross-questioned by the King with respect to the Mission and my proceedings in Abyssinia, having been given to understand that his Majesty was much addicted to prying into one's secrets—a charge which my subsequent experience failed to substantiate—and that he invariably employed spies to watch the conduct of all foreigners visiting his country. This might have been so, but I can only say that if the same course was followed in our case, the spies must either have been blockheads, or they preferred me to their master, by abstaining from divulging any of my secrets; for I am not aware of a single instance of betrayal, either by my own Abyssinian followers or by the King's "spies." One probable reason may be this: that throughout my residence in the country I never said anything about the King, in the presence of the natives—not even when in chains—which I would not have uttered before his Majesty in person. Still, there were other matters connected with my after-position as a political captive, and more especially the communications which I managed to maintain with the coast, which if revealed to the royal ears might have been attended with awkward consequences.

Although the Sûnkwáha river was generally shallow, scarcely covering the feet of our followers at the point where we. crossed it, yet here and there, where the stream runs between two hills, pools are formed from twelve to fifteen feet deep, harbouring a number of small fish.

9th.—Left Sûnkwáha at 8 A.M., my companions and I pushing on to the rivulet of Dwârkin, which we reached in three hours. Resting there till 3 P.M., when some of the baggage came up, we resumed the journey for an hour and a half, and halted for the night at a place called Gint. Our tents not having arrived in time to be pitched, we slept in the open air.

10th.—What with the intense cold and the hubbub of the carriers, I hardly closed my eyes all night. At sunrise the thermometer stood at 43°, and at noon it did not rise above 70°. The wretched porters, having been without food for two days, made as much noise as an equal number of hyænas on being supplied with four cows for supper. I got up twice to drive them away from slaughtering the cattle near our sleeping-ground, and yet on rising in the morning we discovered that one poor cow, which must have struggled hard against the blunt swords of the butchers, had been killed and devoured only a few feet from our beds. The hyænas joined in the horrible chorus around us. They were evidently hungry, and the scent of blood had attracted them to the spot. My Portuguese cook had gone to sleep without washing the saucepans, but had put them into a bag, intending to perform that operation next morning. A hyæna, scenting the dainty savour, carried the bag off bodily among his companions, who were prowling about ready to share in the booty. The sound of the saucepans rattling over the ground aroused our followers, who went in pursuit, joined by the cook. The bag was soon found torn to shreds, the saucepans and other utensils being scattered about in all directions, each beast having apparently taken possession of one, and decamped with it. The night was so dark that some of the kettles were not forthcoming, but after a careful search in the morning only one and the cover of a stewpan were missing. Some of the Abyssinians gave it as their opinion that the hyænas had devoured them, which, of course, was ridiculous; nevertheless, I can vouch for the fact that the rim of one of the smaller saucepans was gnawed—evidently by the steel-like teeth of these voracious animals.

The spot which we now occupied was one of the most romantic I have ever seen. We were encamped on a small plateau at the foot of a high mountain. Just before us was a wide chasm, shrouded in evergreens, on the opposite side of which was another plateau, with a gentle slope towards the gorge, dotted over here and there with straw huts belonging to the Kamánts. Beyond this rose the famous mountain of the Sar-Amba, so perpendicular in outline as to convey the idea of artificial scarping. The mountain is inaccessible on all sides, except by a narrow ridge which joins it to the plateaux of Chálga and the Abyssinian table-land. Towards Gint it presents an almost vertical surface of more than a thousand feet. Next to Gîshen, in the Wello-Galla country, only a few miles from Mágdala, this Amba is reckoned the strongest fortress in the kingdom. There is an ample water-supply on the summit for one thousand men and their families, and from all accounts, if properly defended, the place would be impregnable. Until within a year of our arrival in the country, it was used as the prison for all persons charged with political crimes; but when the King went to Mágdala, in 1864, he carried away all such who were detained there, and placed them, together with the European captives, on the top of that Amba. We left Gint at 6 A.M., pushing on in advance of the noisy carriers, accompanied by Lij Tasámma and his brother Sharo, Lij Tasho remaining to bring up the rear with our baggage. These young Chiefs acted as our guides, and nothing could exceed the civility and attention of the elder brother throughout the whole journey. On several occasions he actually stopped to break off with his own hands branches of the prickly acacias which impeded our way through the wood. Towards 10 o'clock we attained the plateau of Chálga—the commencement of the table-land of Abyssinia—and immediately felt a great change in the atmosphere; the altitude above Gint must have been at least five thousand feet. Although the nights were very cold in the lower ground, yet the heat was always oppressive, and the air during the day was sultry; but here we could breathe the fresh cool air without feeling incommoded by the sun. The ascent was by one of tho worst roads I have ever seen in Abyssinia, and there were two awkward turnings in it, which I hardly believed it possible for the mules to surmount; in fact, we were obliged to alight, and found some difficulty in making the animals face the danger. On attaining the summit of the plateau, we came upon level land covered with green vegetation, but scarcely any trees. Such an extraordinary prospect as now lay outstretched around me, as I sat on the verge of the table-land and gazed upon the features of the landscape one by one, I had never witnessed. Before me, extending nearly a hundred miles away towards the north and west, were ridges of lofty mountains, with deep ravines of varying slopes and hues, here seeming to run parallel with each other; there, to cross each other's lines; elsewhere, again, to have been first thrown together in a mass of utter confusion, then to have been sprinkled over with groves of towering trees and rich underwood. To the south-west lay the rocky fastnesses of Kwâra, with projecting peaks nearly ten thousand feet above the level of the sea, but diminishing to a third of that altitude as they descend towards Sennaar. On turning round, however, the spectator almost fancies that he has been abruptly woke out of a pleasant dream, to find himself placed upon a confined spot of the earth's surface, as devoid of any of those

gratulating me on my safe arrival in Abyssinia and on the reception which had hitherto been accorded me by orders from the King. In the course of the evening it was discovered that some of the baggage was missing, and on further inquiry it turned out that the mules and donkeys which had been pressed into the service at Wahné were not forthcoming. Lij Tasámma immediately dispatched a strong guard to look into the matter. On reaching the edge of the plateau, they found that the owners of the animals had deposited their loads on the plain and made off, taking the animals with them. This act of temerity in a country under the most absolute despotism rather surprised me ; nevertheless, I could not help admiring the honesty of these men, who had hitherto refrained from the least pilfering, and who, even in this case, had brought our property safely up to the plateau, instead of leaving it at the foot of the ascent, where it must have remained till the following morning, to our no small inconvenience. Thanks to Lij Tasámma's energy, everything was conveyed into our camp before we retired for the night.

At this place we were liberally provided with live stock, butter, eggs and honey ; and in Aógwmĕdĕr generally, more especially wherever the inhabitants had not suffered from the exactions of the King or the rebels, our supplies were most abundant. On two different occasions we had to leave a large quantity of meat, bread, eggs and butter on the ground, after feasting all our camp followers, the carriers included. It appears that the King, having heard that Europeans were very fond of fowls and eggs, had issued stringent orders to the different districts in our route to afford us an ample supply of those articles, under pain of his heavy displeasure. It was, doubtless, owing to this arbitrary edict that, in some instances, as many as 500 eggs, 40 fowls, 1,000 loaves of *téf* and *dâgussa* bread, 10 jars of honey, 20 jars of beer, 4 cows, 5 jars of mead, besides a large quantity of milk and butter, were brought for our consumption. I twice remonstrated with the Chiefs of our escort against this un-called-for profusion; their only reply was, that it might cost them their lives were they to direct the local Chiefs to curtail the supplies. However, although these latter had been ordered to provide the Mission gratuitously, I never lost an opportunity of paying for what we received, whenever it was safe to do so. My position was most awkward in this respect; for whereas I was decidedly against inflicting any fresh burden upon the already over-taxed peasantry, on the other hand it was of the utmost importance that I should be on good terms with the King, and to have refused being his guest whilst travelling through his country—in accordance with Abyssinian custom—would have been regarded as an insult by the Sove-reign host. I felt that the slightest mistake on my part, even in such apparently trivial matters as these, might have given offence to the punctilious semi-civilized Monarch, and thereby thwarted the object of the Mission. The hasty and perverse temper of Theodore was universally known, and I did not consider myself justified in risking his animosity by declining those marks of attention which he, as the supreme ruler of the country, had been pleased to accord to the Mission; more especially as similar civilities had been shown to other British representatives before me. My refusing to accept any of his favours might have been misconstrued into an affront to his dignity, and not a single Abyssinian would have sympathised with me, had I got into trouble on that account. Besides which, none of the King's subjects would have dared to supply us with the necessaries of life, on payment, after his Majesty's order to the contrary. A man like Theodore would have thought no more of sacking a village and putting its inhabitants to the sword, for an offence of this kind, than of crushing the life out of a fly. It is, therefore, preposterous to say, as has been said, that I ought to have declined the Sovereign's hospitality. My critics would hardly have acted otherwise than I did in this respect, had they occupied my position, and preferred the success of the Mission to their own personal feelings.

11th.—Early this morning it was discovered that a leathèrn bag belonging to Dr. Blanc's Indian servants was not forthcoming, and as it was said to contain between twenty and thirty sovereigns, besides wearing apparel, it was presumed that it had been stolen during the night. The report that the missing article had been " stolen " reaching Lij Tasámma, that officer became highly indignant, alleging that no one would dare to steal in the territories under Theodore, especially from one of his Majesty's guests. He attributed the blame to the servants in charge, who, instead of taking proper care of their effects, had left the bag in the open field, where the hyænas had probably picked it up. On leaving Balwáha, and after we had dispensed with the camels, we were obliged, for convenience sake, to pack most of our luggage in leathern bags, which are made in Abyssinia for the purpose, and we had been repeatedly cautioned against leaving the skins, which we spread in our tents, or any other article made of the same material, exposed where the hyænas could get at them, as they would certainly gnaw them to atoms and, if hungry, devour them piecemeal. Scouts were immediately dispatched in search, accompanied by some of our Indian and Abyssinian servants, who found the bag about half a mile from our camp, torn into shreds, and the contents scattered about in all directions. When the different articles were collected together, not one was found missing—not excluding the sovereigns.

A rumour having reached our camp during the day that a large party of marauders belonging to T'issoo Gobazê had been seen in the vicinity, our brave protectors forthwith mustered all the guard, and proceeded to reconnoitre. On attaining the spot, however, where the brigands were reported to be, they found nothing but the offal of some cows which had been slaughtered by the rebel band early the same morning.

Wäízero Denké (Wäízero is the Amharic for Lady), the mother of Tasámma and Sharo, joined us in the afternoon. She had been waiting for her sons at Sar-Amba, and now brought with her a number of carriers to assist in transporting the luggage. Lij Tasámma and the Kamánt young Chief, Lij Tasho, brought their wives in the third degree also, with about ten female attendants, all of whom lived apart from our camp. The old lady presented me with an offering of mead, honey, eggs, fowls, butter and bread, wishing me every happiness, especially success in my present undertaking.

12th.—The redistribution of the baggage detained us here another day. In the evening, I arranged with one of the messengers, named Dábterâ Dasta, a native of Góndar, to carry a packet of letters to the coast, reporting the favourable progress of the Mission thus far. As Dasta was a very intelligent man, and highly respected by the Abyssinians, I selected him in preference to any other, knowing that if he was plundered of the letters on the road, he would be able to convey their principal import verbally to Mr. Munzinger. I had to obtain a safe-conduct for him from Lij

Tasámma, through the district of Chálga, in the guise of a messenger going on private business to Góndar, as I was not yet in a position to make known that I was communicating with the coast.

13*th.*—After infinite disputing and jabbering between the carriers, the guards and the Chiefs, we made a fair start at 11·15 A.M., and reached the summit of Lîság in an hour. Here my companions and I halted for about forty minutes, taking shelter under some trees from the heat of the sun, which we felt most acutely all the way from our late camping-ground. As we expected to meet the King either on the western or southern side of the Lake of Dámbĕa, we left the town of Chálga to the north-east. From the top of Lîság we had a glimpse of Góndar, about twenty miles to the north-east, and also a good view of the Lake, which lay about fifteen miles distant towards the south-east, with the extensive grain-growing plains of Dámbĕa filling up the interval.

CHAPTER IX.

ONWARD TO THE ROYAL COURT.

Plain of Dámbĕa laid waste by Theodore — Village of Wanzígé — Church of Kedûs Mikäil — Interior arrangement of Abyssinian churches — Paintings — Luncheon with Wäízero Barîtu — Markets — Place of Skulls — Love in a hovel — The Chiefs of our escort fall out — An impending affray — Game — Lake fish — The Tábot — Fatal snake-bite — Procession of the Tábot — An ominous Prayer — Native etiquette at meals — Unsavoury screens — The Abyssinians not adverse to innovation — How Theodore disposed of an old love — Visit from Wald-Salasaé Gobazé — An intruder summarily ejected — A priestly procession — Native contempt for the Clergy — The Agóws — Agówmĕdĕr — One of Theodore's ex-wives — A flourishing district — Valley of I'njábara — Theodore and the rebel Tadla Gwâlu — A vast natural Shrubbery — Inhospitable females — Message from Theodore — In sight of the Royal Camp.

Our carriers had now increased to 1,200 men, exclusive of the escort, which was 200 strong. This number was perfectly absurd: more than half of them carried scarcely anything, and when we approached the locality where the King was, less than four hundred conveyed all the baggage into the royal camp. It was quite ludicrous to see a couple of powerful men supporting a small chair between them; others, again, made a load of a stick, two or three tent-pegs, or a mallet. Resuming our journey at 1 P.M., we began to descend into the plain of Dámbĕa, then almost a desert, owing to the King's continued oppression of the poor inhabitants. Eventually, the whole of the district was completely despoiled of everything which the rapacious soldiery could lay hands on. Many a soldier had to plunder his own house to please his liege lord, while some followed their example as an expedient to save their property from the grasp of strangers. I was told that, only two years before, this district was in a most flourishing condition, every foot of it was under cultivation, and a succession of villages dotted the length and breadth of the plain. But now only a field here and there appeared to be under tillage, and the villages —small groups of miserable huts—were few and far between, while the bulk of the inhabitants were said to have died either of hunger or disease—the latter brought on by scanty and unwholesome food.

Crossed the stream of Sar-Wáha at 2·20 P.M., and reached Tánkwal at 3 o'clock, where we encamped for the night. As we had descended upwards of 1,000 feet into the plain of Dámbĕa during the afternoon, there was a sensible change in the atmosphere, which was now very oppressive.

14*th.*—Left Tánkwal at 9·30 A.M., and reached the village of Wanzígê, in the district of Tâcussa, in four hours. About two miles this side of the village a party of priests came out into the road to meet us, bearing a number of ecclesiastical symbols. They invited us to inspect their church, which was close by, dedicated to "Kedûs Mikäil," Saint Michael— all angels are called saints in Abyssinia. On reaching the place of worship, Lij Tasámma, who acted as our guide, knelt down and reverently kissed the wooden threshold. The priests seemed surprised that we, as Christians, did not follow his example by paying similar homage to the house of God, but Wald-Gabriêl, who was never at a loss for an answer, told them that we performed our devotions inwardly, in the heart. Nearly all the Abyssinian churches are circular, with corresponding walls dividing the interior into two en- closures. The space within the inner wall forms the Sanc- tuary, or Holy of Holies, where the Eucharist is consecrated.

No layman, nor a priest with any blemish, is allowed access to this part of the sacred edifice. The outer enclosure is for the congregation generally, male and female, the former occupying the western portion and praying with their faces towards the east; the latter standing opposite to them and facing the west. The inner walls of the Sanctuary are

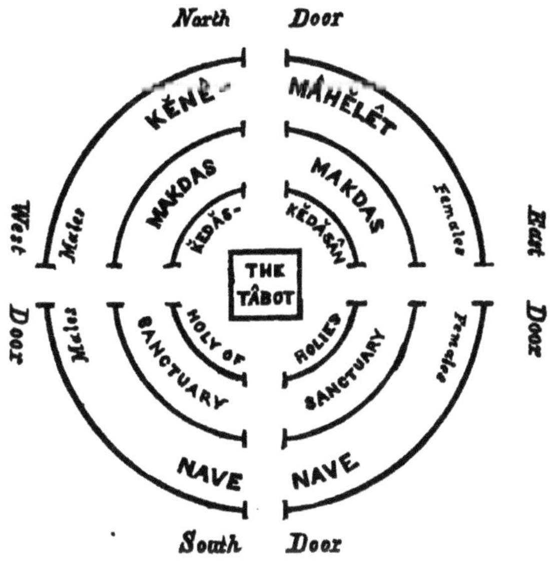

PLAN OF CHURCH.

usually decorated with a variety of pictures, representing the Trinity, Angels and Saints, the subjects being not unlike those found in other churches both in the East and West. The drawings which we saw to-day were extremely rude, and betrayed the artist's utter ignorance either of perspective or of the anatomy of the human frame, for the joints of the knees and the size and position of the feet were out of all harmony with the body which those members were made to support. It seems to have been a matter of perfect indifference to the native Rubens, whether the eyes of the saint he was depicting were larger than the mouth, or the thumb longer than the middle finger, so long as he did not forget to give his subject the proper number of eyes, fingers and hands. With the exception of Tecla Haimanôt and Waldt-Máryam, who were native Abyssinians and are represented with a dark skin, all saints and angels are painted white, while the arch-fiend, Satan, is uniformly represented in the deepest black. On leaving the church, the priests chaunted a psalm and offered up a prayer for our prosperity, the length of which, we were told, corresponded with the value of the gift which they expected from their foreign visitors.

At Wanzígê we were received by Wäízero Barîtu, the head of the village. As a reward for the distinguished bravery of her son, who held the rank of Bâsha in the army and had fought many a battle in the royal cause, Theodore had recently presented her with a thousand dollars, and permitted her to re-establish her old village, which had been laid waste, simultaneously with the plunder of Dámbĕa by his Majesty's order. Her energy, combined with a good reputation as proprietress, succeeded in inducing the scattered peasantry to return, and Wanzígê was now in a more flourishing condition than any other village within a circuit of thirty miles. As her own house was not over clean, she had caused a small hut to be erected for our special accommodation. We were no sooner located there than she brought us a native luncheon, serving us with. her own hands—a high honour in Abyssinia, where ladies generally superintend the entertainment provided, but very rarely take any active part in it themselves. The luncheon, which is called "fitfit"—like the Arabic *fatít,* signifying crumbs or morsels—consisted of curdled milk and pieces of *téf* bread mixed together into a porridge, to which a certain proportion of the red-pepper paste already described is then added and stirred into the mass with the hand, which seldom gets a cleaning by any other process. On the present occasion, no slave or other domestic servant was allowed to approach us, the affable hostess taking upon herself all the duties of waiting. Being very hungry, even this extraordinary mess—the first of the kind we had eaten—did not come amiss to us.   The taste, on being first put into the mouth, is refreshing, owing to the presence of the curdled milk; but the pungency of the combined condiment soon obliterates every other flavour.   The Wäizero not being sufficiently wealthy to brew *téj* in her own establishment brought us some good beer instead, after partaking of which we left her and retired to the hut. In accordance with orders to that effect from the King, she also provided our followers with a couple of cows and a large quantity of bread. Our carriers having had nothing to eat again for two days, I obtained the sanction of the Chiefs of the escort this morning to my presenting them with four cows, which they consumed during the night, partly raw and partly roasted, without salt, bread or sauce. Some of these poor fellows had been brought from Wahné on the understanding that they would be allowed to return from Chálga; yet they were still detained, and knew not how much farther they would be obliged to go with our party.

15th.—Wäizero Barîtu paid me a visit this morning, bringing a present of eggs in a handsome basket of her own making, followed by a female servant with half-a-dozen fowls. She, too, had received the royal mandate directing that our supposed predilection for those comestibles should be gratified.

Left Wanzígê at 9·45 A.M., and reached "Hamûs Gâbia" at 10·40, where we halted for one hour to let the baggage go on ahead. The name signifies the "Thursday Market"—*Hamûs*, like the Arabic *Khamîs*, Thursday; and *Gâbia*, the Amharic for a market. A *Gâbia* does not necessarily imply a village; on the contrary, the co-existence of the two is exceptional, as the peasantry dislike having such places of common resort, with their attendant turbulence and robbery, in close proximity to their dwellings. Traders in some parts of the country are obliged to travel for several days in search of a market for their wares, or for making purchases. As a general rule, a spot is selected in every district—a height is always preferred—within convenient distance of several villages, where a market is held one day in the week, Sunday excepted. No two markets, however, are held on the same day—say, within a circuit of five days' journey—thereby enabling those who wish to do so to sell in one and buy in another within those limits. The Hamûs Gâbia occupies an extensive eminence, one side of which was covered with human skulls and bones, the whitening remains of a band of rebels from the surrounding districts of Dámbĕa, Tâcussa, Wandígê, and Kwâra, who, according to Lij Tasámma's account, had risen up in arms against the King five years prior to our visit. After hemming in the insurgents on this spot, and cutting off all possibility of retreat, Theodore first got them to surrender their arms, and then had them all slaughtered in cold blood.

Resumed our journey at 11·40 A.M., and in passing the village of Aríko shortly afterwards were met by its Chief, Hailo I'ngădă, who invited us to put up with him until the baggage made its appearance. As the brothers Lij Tasámma and Lij Sharo were old acquaintances of the family—which included some sweethearts of theirs—they added their solicitations to that of the old Chief, promising us the luxury of a draught of fresh milk. We were accordingly ushered into a dirty circular hovel, about ten feet in diameter, where we found the mistress of the house busily engaged in cooking, and two strapping damsels, with brilliant eyes and plump cheeks, seated in a recess close by. My companions and I occupied a rude couch, made of crooked joints of wood, held together by strips of bark, which in Abyssinia often do duty for nails, as well as for twine and cord. After we had partaken of the promised milk, and the two Lijs had had enough of love-making, we resumed our journey, and at 2 P.M. reached the village of Gójja, just round the north-western extremity of Lake Dámbĕa, but at the recommendation of our conductors we went on two miles farther, and there encamped on a green spot, on the western side of the Lake. An intervening marsh prevented our getting access to the Lake itself, but we tasted its water for the first time, and found it tolerably good, though muddy. The locality seemed alive with game, flocks of ducks and geese and other aquatic birds appearing in every direction. We heard here that the King was so much taken up with suppressing the rebellion that he could not meet us in Wandígê.

16th.—Our carriers, who had been promised their discharge at Gójja, proved restive this morning on perceiving that no other peasants were forthcoming to relieve them. I had already noticed several indications of jealousy between Lij Tasámma and Lij Tasho, but there had been no very open manifestation of it until now. Lij Tasho, being a native of Chálga, and moreover a Kamánt, very naturally sided with the carriers, and accused his colleague, who was a native of Wandígê—then only a few miles distant from us—and the scion of a family claiming hereditary lordship over that district and Tâcussa combined, of oppressing his townsmen in order to spare his own. This altercation soon led to a regular row, whereupon Wäizero Denké, mounting her mule, called upon her party to separate themselves from the malcontents. The order was implicitly obeyed, all such as were neither Kamánts nor natives of Chálga joining her ladyship, headed by Gójjamy Kâsa. In the mean time Wald-Máryam, the other overseer, who was a Kamánt, drew his sword, and swore by the death of Theodore that all those who were not Kamánts were enemies to the King, and ought to have their heads broken. No sooner had he uttered these words than Gójjamy Kâsa, who was reputed to have killed at least two score of the "King's enemies"— whether in battle or otherwise I am unable to say—rushed at the Kamánt, with his spear pointed at the old man's breast, and called him a "son of the arch-rebel T'issoo Gobazê," threatening at the same time to denounce all the Kamánts to Theodore as being in league to overthrow his Majesty's authority. To this Wald-Máryam retorted by designating his assailant as "the son of Tadla Gwâlu"—another famous rebel in Gójjam—and declared that he would charge him before the King with being a spy. During these passages of angry words the old lady trotted about in all directions, in the greatest state of excitement, doing all she could to prevent the carriers from decamping or fighting, threatening that unless they accompanied her to her own district, Wandígê, and behaved themselves properly, she would herself report them to the King, warning them at the same time that if any part of the luggage belonging to his Majesty's guests was lost, the people of Chálga would have to answer for it with their lives. All this time the three Lijs were

vociferating and cursing at the top of their voices, and I
expected every moment that one or two broken skulls
would be the upshot. At length the local Chiefs of Wahné
and Chálga, who were in charge of the men of those districts
who had come with us, appealed to me to put a stop to the
contest, alleging that unless I did so they would be unable to
keep their subordinates in check, or prevent them from
leaving us in the lurch. Such a prospect was a great in-
centive to exertion, and accordingly I began with the lady,
begging that she would cease to give herself any concern
about our baggage. To her credit be it said, she desisted at
once, expressing herself quite satisfied now that I had taken up
the matter. I then parted the overseers, without succeeding,
however, in repressing a running fire of abuse which they
still kept up at a distance; but the Chiefs were far less
manageable. No sooner had I got one to listen to me, than
the other took advantage of his silence to throw in some
irritating remark, which set all three at loggerheads again.
Losing all patience at last, I turned to join my companions,
declaring that if they would not attend to me we should
proceed alone to the King, with what baggage we could
carry on our own mules, and leave them to vilify each other
as long as they pleased. The threat fell like a thunderbolt
among them, for no sooner was it uttered than each betook
himself to his respective duty, Lij Tasámma promising the
carriers that they should be relieved as soon as possible, and
that in the mean time they should be well supplied with
food. We started at 11·40 A.M., and having been told on the
road that the whole of the native party might get into
disgrace with the King, unless matters were made up
between the Chiefs, I called them and the two overseers
together and succeeded in reconciling them, all promising to

let bygones be bygones. I was glad to hear subsequently that they had kept their word and continued to act in concert until driven to surrender the fortress of the Sar-Amba to T'issoo Gobazê, in the beginning of 1868. We pursued the journey for a little more than five hours, and halted at 4·50 P.M., in a dried-up marsh, abutting on the Lake below the village of Bálas. The country through which we passed to-day swarmed with guinea-fowl, sometimes in groups of twenty or thirty brace, Dr. Blanc and I managing to bag a good number of them. Duck and geese were equally plentiful on the Lake, apparently so tame that one might approach near enough to knock them over with a stone. Dr. Blanc shot many, but we could not recover them, owing to the intervening swamp. Lij Tasámma got us some of the Lake fish to-day from one of the fishing villages; as a change of diet they were acceptable, otherwise we would hardly have eaten them, certainly not in preference to many other kinds of fish. They were full of diminutive bones, and had a very strong earthy taste; but Wäízero Denké cooked some for us in Wandígê in the native style, stewed in red-pepper paste and butter, and so dressed they were far more palatable. Although, as already remarked, I had set my face at the outset against any women being allowed into our camp as camp-followers, I discovered to my surprise this afternoon that it comprised no less than fifteen. Wald-Gabríêl's second-degree wife, with another female, had also joined him from Góndar. However, they all kept at a respectful distance from our tents. The mornings and evenings were intensely cold on this side of the Lake.

17th.—Left Bálas at 8·30 A.M., and reached Kânôha, within the district of Wandígê, at 1·10 P.M. Our route for the first two hours of the stage lay close to the border of the

Lake; we then diverged to the right. We saw a great many hippopotami basking in the sun close to the shore. Kânôha being the native place of Wäízero Denké and also of her two sons, the good old lady left us to encamp on the western side of the stream, opposite the village, which is situated on a hill, while she went home and dispatched us a plentiful supply of fowls, eggs, milk, butter, fish and *téj*. I never could overcome my dislike to this beverage, although many travellers get very partial to it. We had distanced the Lake so much that it now bore north-east from us. Next day being the great festival among the Abyssinians commemorative of Christ's baptism, the *Tâbot*—like the Arabic *Tâbût*, Ark—a symbol with them of the Ark of the Covenant, was brought out of the village church, which is dedicated to "Yasûs" (Jesus) to be baptized. The *Tâbot* is a square block of wood on which the emblem of the cross, with some appropriate passage of Scripture, is sometimes represented. No church can be consecrated without it, and in the church from which it has been removed the Lord's Supper cannot be celebrated. It is placed upon the altar in the centre of the Holy of Holies, and by the ignorant clergy is regarded with as much veneration as the consecrated elements. On the eve of the festival in question, the *Tâbot* is carried out of the church by the chief officiating priest, and left all night covered in a tent or hut erected for the purpose near a stream or pool. At daybreak the following morning, it is taken to the water, and after being sprinkled with a few drops is again enveloped in the church-cloth, and replaced under the tent until the time arrives for its formal restoration to the church—a grand religious ceremony, accompanied with singing of psalms and dancing. In this instance the *Tâbot* was deposited in a hut, in anticipation of the

baptism on the following day, the people of Wandígê
having been impoverished so much by the King's recent

THE TÂBOT.

exactions that they were unable to provide a tent. The
festival is of yearly occurrence.

18*th*.—Last night one of our carriers was bitten by a
snake, but instead of bringing the case to Dr. Blanc's notice
at once, his comrades left the poison to circulate in the poor
fellow's system until he was beyond medical treatment. He
died after a few hours of acute agony. According to native
report, all snakes near the Lake are very venomous, and very
few survive their bite.

As my companions and I wished to witness the ceremony
of taking the *Tâbot* back to the church, Lij Tasámma accom-

panied us to its temporary resting-place at 8·30 in the morning. When the priests were ready, we began to move, but it took a full hour to accomplish the march to the church, although the distance was not over a mile and a half. The priests led the way, bearing various sacred symbols, and chanting psalms all the while, followed by a train of about three hundred men and a score of damsels, all dancing, singing and screeching as they went. The Chiefs of our guards and others galloped about in front of the procession, enlivening the scene with their display of native horsemanship. When the *Tâbot* reached the church, as the priests were not certain that we were Christians—Europeans in Abyssinia being generally classed with Turks—they objected to our being admitted, whereupon Wäízero Denké, who was awaiting us in conjunction with Wald-Gabriêl, took upon herself to assure them that we were far better Christians than they, the priests, which at once removed the difficulty as regards ourselves; but Lij Tasho, being a Kamánt, was excluded. At the conclusion of the ceremony for restoring the Ark to its accustomed place, the priests sang a psalm and muttered the Lord's Prayer in our behalf, in which they were joined by the whole congregation, we being given to understand that the invocation was "for our safe exit from Abyssinia." Wald-Gabriêl and Dasta immediately turned to me, and said, "Do you hear what these priests say, sir? They have just prayed that you may leave our country in safety!" I certainly did think it strange that even the people themselves should thus openly express distrust of their Sovereign's sincerity; or perhaps it was a tradition among them that foreigners, when once in the country, generally encountered some difficulty in leaving it. Bruce, if I mistake not, says something to the same effect. Wäizero Denké then took leave of us to return home, in order to be in readiness to receive a visit which I had intimated our intention of paying her. We followed at a slow pace, accompanied by Lij Tasámma and other Abyssinian Chiefs. As it is not customary in Abyssinia for a lady to receive male guests, her children welcomed us in her stead. In the course of a few minutes a native breakfast was set before us, consisting of stewed fish, *téf* bread and sour milk, with mead and beer. The party were seated in different groups, in accordance with Abyssinian etiquette. My companions and I were left to eat alone, as there was no one present considered to be sufficiently high in rank to warrant his dipping fingers into the same dish with us. The Chiefs had a separate dish to themselves; next, the common soldiers and followers, who had been decorated; and, lastly, the servants and slaves, who formed the lowest group. The stew was not bad in itself, but the free admixture with it of the inevitable pungent red-pepper sauce kept our mouths watering all the time. Here, as was the case also at Massowah, it is considered unbecoming and vulgar for persons to eat in public—as at a pic-nic, for example, or in a tavern. When at home, they take their meals within a fence, so as not to be overlooked; and when on a journey, several of the attendants are made to hold up a cloth before them, with their backs turned to those who are eating. Where no servants are available, the members of a party sit round the dishes, throw a cloth over their heads, and proceed to eat as if afraid that some one was about to snatch the food from them. My companions and I had frequently to submit to this custom on our travels, after we had met the King. No sooner did our escort see us seated on one side of the road, than they directed some of the people to extend their

loose robes in order to screen us from passers-by, and those
who performed the task were always careful to turn their
faces away from us. As the generality of the garments thus
opened out for our seclusion had not been washed for months,
and probably not once since they were first worn, the reader's
imagination may be left to conceive the odour which surrounded us on these occasions. But even if they had been
washed no later than the previous day, the disagreeable smell
of rancid butter with which the natives besmear their heads
would suffice to render any such curtain almost intolerable.
On the other hand, this liniment has its advantages in a
country where hair-brushes and small-toothed combs are
unknown, especially as regards the female portion of the
population, who never cut their hair except when in mourn-
ing. Used as a *pomade* it acts as an insecticide, and serves
to check a disgusting plague common to all semi-barbarous
nations. To do the Abyssinians justice, however, I must
observe that they are by no means prejudiced against im-
provements of any kind; on the contrary, they seemed
rather disposed to imitate the habits and customs of those
more civilized than themselves. Unfortunately, their oppor-
tunities have been few, and the examples set before them
have not always been worthy of adoption. Poverty also has
stood in their way; but the greatest drawback of all has been
their subjection to successive despots, who regarded every
innovation, however beneficial, as a crime calling for the
severest punishment.

The family which entertained us at Kânôha boasts of
ranking with the oldest and noblest lineage in Abyssinia,
and of having possessed greater wealth than any of the
hereditary Chiefs in the Amhâra country. In former times
it exercised hereditary jurisdiction over the districts of

Wandígê and Tâcussa, and it was mainly owing to their wide-spread influence that Theodore gained his first successes over Râs 'Ali, every member of the family having fought on his side. Lij Tasámma had a very pretty sister, and when Theodore was still Lij Kâsa he thought he could not better cement the friendly relations existing between the two families than by marrying her; but as he had several wives already, he could only take her as a third-degree wife. Subsequently, however, on obtaining the hand of Râs 'Ali's daughter, to whom he was strongly attached, he judged it becoming to turn over a new leaf, and therefore dismissed his former wives, two of whom had borne him children, a son and a daughter. Râs 'Ali's daughter was made his wife in the first degree, by the two parties solemnly partaking of the Holy Communion together in the church. As the reformed husband could not well send Lij Tasámma's sister adrift, more especially as he still had some affection for her, he sent for a respectable merchant from Korâta, named Aito Wandé—of whom I shall have occasion to speak hereafter—and conferred on him, as a mark of distinguished honour, the damsel of his love. Of course, the poor girl herself had no choice in the matter, whether she would return to her former home or accept the proffered spouse: she was disposed of just as if she had been a bale of cotton goods, or a bundle of wax; besides, the will of the autocrat was a law which none dared to question. After residing with her new lord for a few years the unfortunate lady died, deeply lamented by the husband who had been forced to take her to wife—a regret which he continued to feel long after her death. These circumstances were the source of great grief to Wäizero Denké, which was subsequently aggravated by the plunder of Wandígê, by order of the

King, out of sheer wantonness, when not even the family from whom he had received such signal favours was spared. The only compensation they could obtain from the King was an empty promise that he would enrich them before he died. Instead, however, of making any arrangements to that end, he contrived by some means or other to despoil them successively of the wealth which, by their diligence and industry, they managed to accumulate. Before leaving Kânôha the kind old lady came to bid me farewell, invoking a blessing upon me, and praying that I might be vouchsafed a safe departure out of the country. The repetition of this prayer sounded like an omen in my ears; but I was unconscious then of what was awaiting me.

19th.—I had a visit this morning from Wald-Salassê Gobazê, the merchant who called upon me at Massowah, in April, 1865, and who had spoken to the King about replying to my third letter. He had come across the Lake with merchandise for the use of the royal household. He assured me that the reception which had hitherto been accorded to the Mission was regarded generally as a hopeful sign of my success. He warned me against saying or doing anything, either in the King's presence or behind his back, which might create distrust in his Majesty's mind. He bade me beware how far I trusted Aito Samuel, who, he said, was a bad man, and that if the King appointed him as my Bâldărăbâ, I should do well to decline his services and ask for another in his stead. With regard to interpreters, he advised me to employ Dasta exclusively in my intercourse with Theodore, saying at the same time that the new interpreter whom I had engaged at Matámma was not to be relied on, and that the sooner I dismissed him the better. Europeans, he remarked, had been brought into disgrace through having had bad people about them. As I had been told by several persons, both at Massowah and in Abyssinia, that this man was a spy, or at any rate that he repeated all he heard to the King, I was most guarded in my answers to him, especially as he gave me to understand that he would precede me to the royal Court. With respect to the Bâldărăbâ, I observed that it was not customary for the representatives of foreign Powers to dictate to the ruler to whom they were accredited the etiquette to be observed at his own Court; and that therefore it was no concern of mine whether the King allotted me a good or a bad man to act in that capacity. I should also leave it with his Majesty to select what interpreter was to be employed: Dasta, I thought, was too young and inexperienced to suit so exalted a sovereign as Theodore. The fact is, Dasta was already acting as interpreter, and I was afraid that promotion to the substantial office would spoil him; moreover, I considered him too juvenile to be trusted with matters requiring secrecy. However, before many months were past, I was compelled to employ him, the King having taken a great fancy to him after Samuel had introduced him to his Majesty as my domestic interpreter.

Our Chálga carriers were relieved this morning. The poor fellows were so delighted at the prospect of returning home, that they would not stay to receive a few loaves of bread which had been promised them for the journey.

Left Kânôha at 8·30 A.M., and reached the village of Dankôra, in the district of Acháffar, at 11·40, where we halted for the day, as the bearers were to be changed. As soon as my tent was pitched, I received a visit from Wald-Salassê Gobazê, the merchant who called on me yesterday. He was barely seated when Gójjamy Kâsa, one of the overseers, came in and asked him what business he had there. On receiving the reply that he had come to see me as a friend, Kâsa ordered him to leave the tent at once, telling him at the same time that if he intruded again he had better bring a warrant from the King, otherwise he would get a drubbing such as he had never experienced before. Poor Wald-Salassê Gobazê was quite dumbfoundered, and quietly skulked off, whispering however to Dasta as he left the tent that he would call on me again when he had seen the King. After Kâsa had escorted him beyond our camp, he returned to apologise for his rudeness in turning a guest out of my tent. "You are not aware, sir," he went on to say, "how troublesome these traders are, and Wald-Salassê Gobazê in particular is a bad man; there is no knowing what mischief he might hatch by loitering about here. Besides, he ought to have better manners than to intrude upon you immediately on your arrival, and without asking your permission. You might feel inclined to sleep, or to receive other visitors; in any case, you might not choose to be pestered with that fellow's presence all day long." On asking whether he was not afraid lest the man should complain of him to the King, he laughed and said that Wald-Gobazê was too astute to commit himself in that way, knowing that if he did he might safely reckon on a sound thrashing for venturing to call upon me without a Bâl-dărăbâ, contrary to the usages of the country; moreover, inasmuch as the King had ordered that I should be treated with the respect due to royalty, his Majesty undoubtedly expected that none of his subjects would present themselves before me, without having previously secured my permission through the proper officers whom he had appointed to escort me. The truth of the matter is, that Wald-Salassê Gobazê owed his summary ejection to Lij Tasámma and his colleagues, whose permission to visit me he had not asked on this occasion—which he certainly ought to have done—although he had sought and obtained it the day before. The man, however, had made himself so disagreeable by his disparaging remarks on other people, and engrossed so much of my time, that I was thankful to Gójjamy Kâsa for having rid me of his presence.

The trees surrounding the village were covered with large pigeons. I shot a number of them for dinner; we found them rather tough eating.

21st.—Left Dankôra at 9·15 A.M., and reached Yasmâla at 10·50. This was the largest village we had seen since our entry into Abyssinia, and, before the plunder of the Acháffar district by the King, was reckoned one of the most important in the Amhâra country, owing to its wealth and to the number of militia which it furnished to the Emperors in time of war. The church, which is dedicated to Yéldet-Guargîs, —Daughter of George—not having fallen under the royal displeasure, was in a better state of preservation than any other in the despoiled districts. After spending about half an hour on the church and village, we resumed our journey, travelling till 1·30 P.M., when we reached Nafâsa, another village situated on a hill, at the foot of which we encamped, after crossing a neighbouring stream. A host of priests followed us, singing and chanting, to this halting-place. They kept up the noisy din so long that Gójjamy Kâsa, losing all patience, ran after them and dispersed them with a liberal use of the cane, seemingly without any compunction. They were so terrified, that a number of them lost their turbans in trying to escape, and I was surprised to see the Abyssinians enjoying the fun, and laughing heartily at the expense of their own clergy. Formerly, the priests and other officers of the Church were regarded with respect and fear, but they had been so humbled and degraded by Theodore that few respected and fewer still feared them. On my asking Gójjamy Kâsa why he behaved so rudely to the clergy, he replied with a laugh, like an out-and-out Erastian, that they were bound to do honour to the King, and to abstain from annoying his guests with their noisy singing. "If they wish to pray for your welfare," he continued, "they ought to resort to the proper place—the church—for such exercises, and not come out into the open field, deafening you with their uproar. I like what the King likes, and as his Majesty objects to such demonstrations as these, they must not be imposed upon his guests."

22nd.—Left Nafâsa at 10·40 A.M., and reached Arûsa at noon. Here my companions and I halted for an hour to allow the bearers time to overtake us; then, resuming the journey, we reach the Kilté in half an hour's ride. This river separates the district of Acháffar from that of Agów-mědĕr. The country, after we had crossed the stream, bore the aspect of prosperity and affluence; the tyranny of Theodore had not yet been exercised over it, and the power of the Agóws had been their safeguard against the despotism of his predecessors. They had always paid the lawful taxes to the Emperors, and had never manifested any hostility to the reigning Sovereign, or withheld their legitimate contributions to the State. Nearly the whole of the district is flat, and is intersected by numerous streams, enabling the Agóws to irrigate the soil when rain is scanty. It is famous for breeding horses and mules, and when called upon by the Emperors the inhabitants were able to furnish them with a large contingent of mounted militia, fully equipped for active service. The Agóws, both of southern and eastern Abyssinia, are noted for their unity and bravery—two characteristics which have served to keep them from being trodden under foot by their unprincipled and ruthless sovereigns.

Passed a great many villages on our onward journey. After fording another river, called Lagásta, one of the local Chiefs came out to meet us, as our next halting-place was to be within his district. Passed the village of Zûgda, and at 2·10 P.M. reached the Branté river, which we crossed and then encamped on the opposite side. The stream was muddy, indicating that rain had fallen to the westward. It swarmed with three different species of ducks and geese, specimens of which were served up for our evening repast.

23rd.—It was so intensely cold this morning that I could scarcely handle my fowling-piece when out shooting at sunrise. The country was covered with hoar-frost, and the thermometer was down to 33°. Having to change carriers here, we did not start till 1 P.M. Our next halting-place was Kwâkŭra, which we reached in three hours, and encamped on the western bank of the river Trinka for the night. The whole country which we traversed this afternoon was under culture. The barley crops were still green, and the soil here and there was being irrigated by means of canals supplied by the Branté and other streams. It was quite exhilarating to look upon such evident tokens of industry and prosperity after a journey through the plundered and forlorn districts of Dámbĕa, Tâcussa, Wandígê and Acháffar. The provisions supplied to us by the well-to-do inhabitants were lavish, and far beyond our requirements.

In the course of the morning one of the King's pensioned ex-wives, who had borne him a child, came to pay me a visit. Luckily, she first applied to Lij Tasámma, who then came to beg me to give her an audience, as she was a "great lady," who resided in Agówmĕdĕr under his Majesty's auspices; that she had come a great distance to see me, and would be much gratified by my granting her an interview. As I objected to receive her, under the plea that, as she was one of the royal wives, it would not become me to do so before I had met his Majesty, he urged me to contrive to see her in his tent. However, I resisted all his solicitations in the matter, deeming it impolitic to hold any intercourse whatever with any of the King's family without his special sanction; but I promised the Lij that I would do my best to gratify his guest, and not leave her to regret the trouble she had taken. I accordingly sent Dasta to explain the reasons for my reserve at that time, holding out the prospect that I might be able to see her on some future occasion. Her polite answer was, that she appreciated my motives, and, after accepting a small token of my regard, she took her departure, wishing me health and prosperity.

24th.—Left the Trinka at 12·45 P.M., and reached the village of Sâbunja at 3·15, where we took up our quarters on the southern bank of the Mâswáha rivulet. The first part of the day's stage was through a beautiful and well-cultivated country, sections of which were under irrigation, and growing fine crops of green barley. Beyond this, the road lay through thickets of the wild rose and jessamine, here and there forming picturesque natural arbours, and spreading a delicious fragrance all around.

25th.—Another change of bearers again prevented our starting until noon, the change involving a close scrutiny by the Chiefs whether any articles were missing; besides which, it took some time for the new relay formally to receive over the different packages by a regular list. Since

King assured them that they had nothing to fear. In the mean time, however, they were surrounded by the royal troops, who, acting on a special command from his Majesty, began slaughtering them *en masse*. So utterly paralysed were these poor wretches—7,000 in number—that they suffered themselves to be butchered like sheep, without attempting the least resistance, although their arms were within reach. The victors, I was told, came off without a scratch.

Our afternoon ride from Sâbunja until we began the descent into the l'njábara valley still lay through groves of the wild rose and jessamine, which covered hill and dale with their flowered wreaths, and made the air redolent with sweet perfume. A variety of creepers also, with blossoms of different shapes and hues, added grace and beauty to these bowers of Nature's making. And as I recall the journey over that enchanted ground, I am reminded of the pains I took to gather specimens of the gay flora for presentation to lady friends in England; but these, alas! with many other collections, after-circumstances — unforeseen then — obliged me to abandon at Debra Tâbor.

Reached our next halting-place, Shállăka Shatûsh, at 3 P.M. The clouds had been threatening rain for the last three days, and now it came down heavily. Our tents not having arrived, we resorted to the village for shelter, the Chiefs of our escort trying to gain admission into the first house on the road; but no sooner were we espied by the female inmates, than they shut and bolted the door, and neither threats nor entreaties prevailed to make them open it again. The eaves of the hut would have protected us sufficiently, but the continued shrieks and screams of the women, and the buzzing of a swarm of bees whose hive we had disturbed, drove us to take refuge elsewhere. The Chiefs would have resorted to force had I not prevented them. We were more civilly received at the next house we came to, but we preferred standing in the verandah to entering the darksome dwelling, from whence we might have carried more animal life than we took in. The rain lasted for an hour, thoroughly drenching our poor servants who had to remain with the baggage, the tents not having arrived in time to be pitched. The smoke of the King's camp was visible about eight miles to the eastward, but the Chiefs having received instructions that we were not to move from this place until they got further orders, I began to fear that one of his Majesty's whims might detain us here some time.

26th.—I received a kind message from the King, and about noon orders were sent that we should move towards the royal camp; but as it was then too late to obtain bearers, all the peasants being out at work in the fields, we were unable to set off before noon of the following day. After my companions and I had ridden forward a couple of miles, we heard that some difficulty had arisen about the baggage, owing to a scarcity of bearers. By 2·30 P.M. everything was reported to be in order, when we resumed our route, and crossed a branch of the large river Fáttam at 3·15. As the escort judged that we could hardly reach the royal camp before dark, and not wishing to halt very near it, they advised that we should put up for the night at the village of Dangwé, a short distance from the eastern bank of the river. Another inducement was that the clouds portended heavy rain. On dismounting, I was taken by Lij Tasámma to see the royal camp from the foot of an adjacent hill. The King's white tent, pitched on an eminence, at a place called A'shfa, in Dâmôt, with thousands of huts and tents surrounding it on all sides, was distinctly visible. At five, the rain began to fall and lasted four hours. Immediately on our arrival here, I received a message from the King, announcing that he was looking forward with pleasure to meeting me. I reciprocated the greeting in my best style, but it came short of the redundancy of his. I was hardly a match, in that respect, for so finished an adept in courtly phraseology as the Sovereign of Abyssinia.

CHAPTER X.

THE MISSION REACHES THEODORE.

Hopes and Fears — Messages from the King — Equitation Etiquette — Guard of Honour — Letter of welcome from Theodore — His reception of the Mission — Complaints against the Captives and the Abûna — I'ngădă Wark — The King's opinion of his subjects — Reasons for the Author's reserve — Aito Samuel appointed Băldărăbă — Theodore prepares a reply to the Queen's letter — Râs I'ngădă, the Prime Minister, his character and career — Samuel, his biography and fidelity to the Mission — Second interview with the King — His letter to the Queen, promising to liberate the Captives — Theodore reverts to his grievances against the Captives — His acceptance of the presents brought by the Mission — The King's knowledge of Arabic — Duties of a Băldărăbă — Arrangements for the future.

This, the 28th of January, 1866, is one of the most memorable days in the history of the Abyssinian Mission. After dragging out a miserable existence for eighteen weary months, in an unhealthy climate and among semi-barbarous races—nearly worn out both in mind and body with worry and anxiety in vain efforts to reach the most impracticable man that ever swayed a sceptre, and who held in his hands the lives of several of her Majesty's subjects—here we were at last, about to obtain the long-desired audience. It would be in vain to attempt any description of the hopes and fears which the prospect now more than ever awakened within me. The feeling, however, which impressed me above all others was this—that the least want of resolution, or the least false move, on my part, might doom me and my companions to share the fate of the unfortunate captives whose liberation was the sole object contemplated by the Government in the dispatch of the Mission. Should success crown my efforts, the satisfaction of having overcome an awkward political complication, and restored the despairing captives to their friends and home, would be immense; but as failure seemed equally probable—despite every precaution—I must be prepared for the consequences.

We left Dangwé at 10·10 A.M., after having received no less than three congratulatory messages from the King, with inquiries after my health and that of my companions. We encountered similar courtesies every ten minutes of our progress, his Majesty having given orders to· all the Chiefs who were returning homeward, and to all officers dispatched on duty to different parts of the country, to make it a point to meet us and present his compliments to me. All so commissioned, without a single exception, wore the " Royal Shirt." About half an hour after we had started, the Chiefs of our escort received an intimation that the King had ordered Râs I'ngădă, the Prime Minister, and all the state officials to come out to meet us. We accordingly halted at 11·10, about two miles from the royal camp, in a tent which had been pitched for the purpose, where we dressed ourselves in uniform in order to receive the deputation with becoming respect. Resuming the journey in the course of twenty minutes, we crossed the large river Fáttam, which separates the district of Agówmĕdĕr from that of Dâmôt, and at 12·15 P.M. met the guard of honour, headed by Râs I'ngădă, who came forward on foot to greet me, accompanied by Aito Samuel as his interpreter. My companions and I immediately followed his example, and on approaching within speaking distance both parties halted. Râs I'ngădă, on behalf of his royal master, then inquired after our health, and welcomed us to

his Majesty's dominions. The King, he said, had been looking forward with pleasure for our arrival, and hoped that
the interview which had been so long delayed would be
propitious. He then presented me with a mule, equipped
with one of the King's saddles and covered with embroidered
cloth, which was sent for me to ride into the royal camp;
apologizing at the same time for the meanness of the gift,
which his Majesty, he said, would have disdained to tender
for my acceptance, were it not that he was on a campaign,
with nothing at hand really worth offering me; he hoped,
however, to be able in a few days to present me with a more
suitable equipage.

It may be a matter of surprise to some, why the King
did not furnish me with a horse instead of a mule whereon
to approach the royal presence. In other countries, where
the horse is regarded as the nobler animal in every respect,
that course would have undoubtedly been followed on a
formal occasion like this. But in Abyssinia, persons of re-
spectability only mount horses in battle, or when out on a
hunting expedition, or, in the case of gay cavaliers, to display their horsemanship. On entering a town or camp,
natives of rank who wish to appear sedate and dignified
should always ride a mule and have their horses led either
before or behind them. According to strict etiquette, the
horse should be led about twenty yards in advance, in order
to announce by its trappings the rank or station of the owner,
and prepare bystanders to receive him with proper respect.
Theodore, who hated all these punctilios, never allowed a
horse to be led before him; his steed was generally made
to follow, and he not unfrequently moved about without
any such ostentatious show. His gift, therefore, of a mule,
whereon I was to make my formal entrance into the royal

camp, was a mark of distinction; and, further, that the highest military honours should be accorded on the occasion, he ordered that no officers under the rank of A'mbal (corresponding to our Lieut.-Colonel) should ride before me on horseback.

After Râs I'ngădă and I had exchanged civilities, he mounted his horse and bade us follow. He was attended by about three hundred officers, comprising persons holding the undermentioned ranks:—

1. Râs,	4. Balambarâs,
2. Bitwáddad,	5. Bâsha,
3. Dajazmâtsh,	6. Ámbal,

while about 10,000 men, some on horses and mules and others on foot, brought up the rear. We rode at a quick pace, and at 12·30 reached the foot of the hill on which the King's tent was pitched. Here Râs I'ngădă requested us to dismount, and invited us to rest in a red cloth tent, which had been erected for the purpose, until our own tents were ready to receive us. After bidding us be seated, Râs I'ngădă retired, accompanied by Aito Samuel, to report our arrival to the King. Refreshments were then brought to us from the royal establishment; also ten cows, as many sheep, and fifteen jars of mead, one of which was so strong that a draught of it would have turned the head of an experienced toper, much less mine, unused as I had always been to intoxicating stimulants. The smell alone produced drowsiness, and sufficed to put us on our guard against indulging in the dangerous beverage; though, for civility's sake, and in order that it might not be reported to the King that we rejected his cheer, we ventured to taste it. I was subsequently informed that his Majesty invariably sent a jar of very strong mead to the representative of every foreign Power on his first arrival at the royal court. The object, it is said, was to test the sobriety of his visitor.

At 3 P.M. the following letter, written both in Amharic and Arabic, was handed to me:—

"In the name of the Father, Son, and Holy Ghost—one God. Amen.

"From the King of kings, Theodorus. By the power of God, may this reach my friend, who is wishing for my friendship, Hormuzd Rassam. It would have been better for you to have rested to-night, and to-morrow morning I should have had the meeting; but I have been staying long in this country, which has been devastated, awaiting your arrival, and the troops are in want of food; consequently, I have directed the interview to take place between you and me to-day. To-morrow morning we start on our journey. Now come to me."

A verbal communication was also sent with the above, to the effect that although it was Sunday his Majesty could not postpone our interview any longer; that having waited for me too long already, we must now see each other without further loss of time. Immediately on receiving this message my companions and I repaired to the royal presence.

On leaving our tent, Aito Samuel remarked to me that as it was not customary for the King to receive any foreigner wearing his sword, it would be better if my companions dispensed with theirs. I replied, that if such had been the rule hitherto observed by other Europeans, we should certainly conform to it; at the same time I gave him to understand that the uniform was incomplete without a sword. After a little reflection he said, "Never mind; let them come on as they are."

On ascending the hill we found two rows of musketeers drawn up on either side of the road leading to the King's pavilion, and as we entered between the two ranks the infantry commenced file-firing, which was kept up until we reached the royal tent. As we drew near, the King inquired after our health, through the officer in waiting, and after I had returned the salutation we were told to approach.

On entering the tent we found the King sitting on a sofa, with his feet resting on the ground; on his left stood all the Ministers of State. He was dressed in a *shámma*, the common robe of the country, with which he was muffled up to the eyes, according to the Abyssinian custom, but after a while he allowed it to drop from his face to enable him to make himself better heard.

I at once delivered to the King her Majesty's letter of the 26th of May, 1864, and deeming it advisable to say a few words befitting the occasion, I addressed him as follows:— "I have the honour to present to your Majesty this letter from my sovereign, her Most Gracious Majesty the Queen of England, wherein you will find expressions of friendly feeling and good-will towards you." He replied, "I receive it with pleasure, and I am glad to see you." He then took the royal letter, and, after placing it on the couch on his right, invited me, as also Dr. Blanc and Lieutenant Prideaux, to be seated on the same side. I then formally introduced my companions as two servants of our Queen who were associated with me, one as a medical officer and the other as an assistant. He replied that he was happy to see us all, and hoped that we were well after the fatigue of the long journey; and then, without more ado, he opened the subject of his grievances, attributing all the misunderstandings that had arisen between him and the English to the bad conduct of certain Europeans who had come to his country. He complained in bitter terms of the Abûna Salâma, the late Metropolitan of Abyssinia, Consul Cameron, and the Rev.

Mr. Stern. The former he denounced as a mischievous intriguer, who, instead of attending to spiritual matters, had meddled in the political affairs of the country; he called him a mere slave, whom he had purchased for money, (alluding to the impost exacted by the Egyptian Government from the rulers of Abyssinia for providing them with a bishop), and accused him of being the cause of all the anarchy and confusion which then prevailed in Abyssinia. The existing complications between himself and the British Government he ascribed to the conduct of Consul Cameron, who, he said, had neglected to fulfil his request of conveying a letter to our Queen, and bringing an answer to the same. Both Mr. Plowden and Mr. Cameron had told him that the English and their Queen had a great regard for him, which led him to judge that he could not do better than make them his permanent friends. He had accordingly written a friendly letter to the Queen, which he gave to Mr. Cameron to take to Massowah, and asked him to return with the reply; but instead of going to Massowah himself, he sent the letter by an Abyssinian, and went to Cásala, on a visit to his (the King's) enemies, the Turks, and caused him to be reviled before them.

The King's story was, that Consul Cameron had taken some Abyssinian servants with him to Cásala, who, at a party given to him by the Turkish authorities there, were told to imitate the war-dance of the royal troops; that some had refused to obey, but one was forced to do as he was ordered, and made the Turks laugh at his Majesty; that they had said sneeringly to the Abyssinians, "Is that the way the soldiers of your great King fight?" This story, it appears, was related to the King by I'ngădă Wark, who had been in the service of Consul Cameron when he was on the coast.

He hated his late master intensely, because he considered himself wronged, not having been paid his proper wages. This man, who was in my opinion at the bottom of all the misunderstanding which existed between the King and the European captives, and whom I shall have to refer to hereafter on more than one occasion, was killed by the King on the 9th of April last, together with 197 men that were massacred in cold blood, below Mágdala. I had hoped on gaining my liberty to have been able to obtain from this I'ngădă Wark important disclosures regarding the origin of the King's displeasure, and his subsequent conduct towards Consul Cameron and myself. His death deprived me of the opportunity which I might otherwise have had of acquiring information which would have explained much that must now remain a mystery.

With regard to the Rev. Mr. Stern, the King declared that he had treated him well all the time he was in the country, but that gentleman had behaved ungratefully to him, abusing his mother, and calling him a murderer; that on Mr. Stern's first visit to Abyssinia, he had told the King that his sole business was to convert the Jews to the Christian faith. This had pleased him very much, as he was an advocate for converting all the world to the religion of his forefathers. He had consequently treated Mr. Stern well, and allowed him to do as he pleased; but notwithstanding all his kindness Mr. Stern had listened to the stories of the Bishop about the origin of his (the King's) mother, and proclaimed to the world that she was a woman of low degree, who used to sell *kósso*—an Abyssinian vermifuge — on the common highways.

He then complained bitterly of the Abyssinians in general, whom he styled "a wicked people." He said that when he

was anointed King he had intended to govern the country
well, and to root out all the barbarous practices and evil habits
which then prevailed; that he had tried to establish good
order and wholesome rules, but the people preferred misrule;
that before his time Abyssinia used to be governed by different feudal chiefs, who, instead of benefiting the country, kept
up perpetual civil war, which had ruined the Christians, and
caused their enemies, the Mohammedans, to triumph; that
as soon as he became King he proclaimed a general amnesty,
and offered the Chiefs who held hereditary Governments
fixed stipends, deeming it better that Abyssinia should have
one ruler, than that the jurisdiction should be divided among
so many Chiefs.   He found out, however, before he had been
many years on the throne, that the Abyssinians were not
capable of appreciating good government: they preferred the
opposite, and therefore he had resolved to rule them henceforward according to their liking.   He remarked that I might
judge from the state of the country that what he stated was
correct.   He then concluded by saying, "If I go to the
south, my people rebel in the north; and when I go to
the west, they rebel in the east.   I have pardoned the rebels
over and over again; nevertheless, they persist in their dis-
obedience and defy me.   I am now determined to follow them
into every corner, and shall send their bodies to the grave
and their souls to hell."   The Mohammedans, he added, had
always tried to encroach on the rights of the Christians;
that before he ascended the throne the Gallas had overrun
the country of the Amhâras, and the Turks had unjustly
taken possession of Sennaar and the Soodân, which formerly
belonged to Abyssinia.   The former he had brought under
his yoke, and the latter he hoped to eject before his death.
He then stopped and waited for my answer.

The King's complaints were so various and contradictory, involving matters in no way connected with her Majesty's Government, that I deemed it prudent to avoid alluding to any subject which might entangle me in a political difficulty, or give rise to any misunderstanding which might lead him to mistrust me. I found, moreover, that the King mixed up the Bishop with his grievances against the English. Had I been placed in a different position, I should have disabused him at once of the error that the Bishop had any connexion with us, and have proved to him that the friendship between the Bishop and Messrs. Cameron and Stern was merely of a personal character, with which the British Government had no concern whatever. Moreover, the general impression in the country then was, that the King wished to constitute me a judge between himself and the European captives, in order that from my verdict he might infer whether I leaned to his side or theirs.

I have reproduced the charges alleged against the captives, without expressing any opinion of my own respecting them, although the reserve may lay me open to a reiteration of the reflections, that I was deceived by the King into recognising the validity of all his grievances, and regarded him as an ill-used man. Nothing that I have ever said or written can fairly warrant any such conclusion. In my letters to friends in England, I abstained from committing myself either in favour or against the parties concerned, for the simple reason that the differences between them had arisen out of antecedent circumstances of which I was utterly ignorant, and of which I was therefore unable to form a correct judgment. The case, indeed, was so difficult and complicated that, upon the same grounds, I preferred restricting myself, even in my official correspondence, to a simple statement of what fell under my own personal cognizance. The presumption, therefore, that I was duped by the King, to which this reserve on my part has given rise in some quarters, is wholly gratuitous; it is more, it is contrary to the fact. It did not require any great penetration to discover that Theodore was labouring under a variety of hallucinations which warranted the general belief that he was occasionally demented. I inferred as much after a short acquaintance with him, and subsequent experience abundantly confirmed the impression. I treated him accordingly; at the same time always taking every available precaution against his aberrations, to insure, if possible, the success of the Mission with which I was entrusted. But to return to my narrative:—

I had heard enough about his Majesty to know that it would be imprudent, and indeed most hazardous, to tell him at the outset that he had acted unjustly towards Consul Cameron and the Missionaries. On the other hand, had I even considered him the injured person, I could not show any sympathy with him, or give him to understand that I thought the European captives guilty, lest he might continue to ill-treat them, and quote my authority for so doing. I therefore gave him the following answer, without alluding to any of the subjects which he had raised :—" I beg to inform your Majesty that I have not been sent to you by my Queen to act as a judge, or give an opinion about the past. In your Majesty's position as a King, you ought not to be over-sensitive, but should bear and forbear. A private person has only to look after his own affairs; but monarchs have to attend to the affairs of millions, and in thousands of cases they have to forgive even those who have committed heinous crimes. Is not your Majesty, as a sovereign, a father? and ought not a good father to be patient with his children, and teach them to do what is right, instead of continually employing the rod? I trust that after your Majesty reads the letter of our Queen, and takes into consideration the friendly mission on which I have been sent, you will forget the past, and try to establish amicable relations with England, which I, as a humble servant of her Majesty, will use my best endeavours to forward." As soon as I had concluded, he smiled and said he was satisfied, but he reverted again to what he called the misconduct of those who had abused him.

While with the King I told him that I had two interpreters with me, but left it to his Majesty to employ either of them, or any other he chose. He said that he wished Aito Samuel to translate on that occasion. I then solicited a favour at his hands, namely, that as my companions and I were strangers, and did not know either the customs of the country or the etiquette of his Court, I trusted he would overlook any mistake which we might commit through ignorance, during our sojourn in his dominions. He laughed and said, "I'sh-shi,"—very well. On leaving, I also asked him to appoint me a Bâldărăbâ to act as an intermediary between us, as I understood that such an officer was indispensable, according to the usages of the country. He at once nominated Aito Samuel to that post.

We then left the King, Râs I'ngădă escorting us by his master's order as far as our tents, which we found had already been pitched for us. We had scarcely arrived before his Majesty summoned Aito Samuel, whom he sent back soon afterwards with the chief Amharic scribe, Alăkâ Ingădă, with the Queen's letter, which I was asked to translate. I replied that I had an Arabic translation, which could be easily rendered into Amharic by the Arabic scribe Mu'allim

Matta. The King, however, said that he could not trust the Copt, and begged that I would translate the original into Amharic, with the assistance of Aito Samuel and my own interpreters; and Alăkâ I'ngădă was ordered to write the translation in Amharic. On finding that the King was determined that I should translate it with the assistance described, I set about it at once.

After I had returned her Majesty's letter, with the translation, I was gratified to learn that the King was pleased with its contents, and that my first interview had left a good impression upon him. He expressed his desire that evening to befriend me, and gave orders that all Abyssinians whose acquaintance I had made at Massowah should be allowed to visit me and bring me any offering they liked. Owing to this permission, several merchants who had known me on the coast called upon me with a present of honey and sheep. All the courtiers came also to see me in the evening, introduced by Aito Samuel, and proffered their services and friendship as long as I remained in Abyssinia. I am bound to state, that every one of them served me most honestly and faithfully during my entire sojourn in the country.

Before proceeding further I must introduce Râs I'ngădă, the Prime Minister, and Aito Samuel, the King's Bâldărăbâ —personages whose names will frequently occur in the succeeding narrative—to the special notice of my readers. Râs I'ngădâ, the descendant of a wealthy and influential family in Agówmĕdĕr, was a man of most gentlemanly bearing, of strict integrity, and of an eminently humane disposition. If he had a fault, it was like that which Cardinal Wolsey deplored—he would have sacrificed anything to preserve the life of his royal master and to save his kingdom. So loyal and devoted was he to the man who seemed incapable of discriminating between friends and foes, that I verily believe he would have swallowed a draught of deadly poison at his bidding, out of deference to what he considered his bounden duty to his Sovereign. During the last four years of the King's reign, he never slept a night in his own house, but in a tent or a miserable hut, within call both by day and night, just large enough to give him shelter. He was fair in complexion, with handsome features, and so scrupulously neat and clean that he might have gone into any English drawing-room without betraying, by the odour of his garments, that he was an Abyssinian. He disliked the universal practice among his countrymen of drenching the head with butter, using it merely to keep his hair, which was always tidily dressed, free from impurities. He hated gossip; and its kindred vices, mischief-making and backbiting, he heartily detested. He eschewed all intoxicating drinks and a plurality of wives, and held those in disesteem who indulged in them, always excepting his royal master, alleging that it was beyond his competence as a subject to reflect upon the conduct of his " Anointed Sovereign." Although for four years he had held the highest position in the State, he never thought it below his dignity to associate freely with his old comrades, or with those above whom the King had raised him. To the Mission he was uniformly friendly, and he never lost an opportunity of speaking in my favour to his Majesty, and when I was in captivity of sending me his best wishes for my prosperity and happiness. He was, unfortunately, wanting in firmness; and a similar defect in other of the staunchest of the royal adherents proved the bane of Theodore; for had they been more resolute and united in their counsels, they might have arrested him in his downward career of misdoing. On our first arrival at the royal camp I sent to ask whether he would permit me to make him a present of silks, velvet and other articles befitting his rank. He begged to decline the proffered gift, on the ground that he detested gaudy vestments, and that it would be a disgrace if, after accepting them from me, he made them over to others. His wants, he said, were so few, that my liberality would be simply wasted on him, and he advised me to retain what I had at my disposal for more urgent occasions, which he forewarned me would not be lacking. He assured me, at the same time, of his unswerving friendship, remarking that it would be all the purer, and to him the more valuable, for not having been first contracted through a gift. This noble and disinterested man was eventually put in chains by his ungrateful master, whose only plea for the outrage was that, loving him as he did, he was afraid that he might be suborned to abandon him, and therefore took the most effectual means to prevent his escape! The poor man had to travel, wearing his chains, for months, during the time Theodore was making his way to Mágdala, at the beginning of 1868, and was not unshackled until my chains were also removed, in the middle of March of the same year, when the royal army approached that fortress. I had been informed that owing to the dearth which then prevailed in the army, Râs I'ngădă was on the point of starvation. In his grateful acknowledgment of the receipt of a few dollars which I sent him, he remarked, " He who helps a fellow-creature in distress is a friend indeed. Be under no apprehension, my friend; seek deliverance of the Lord only, and you will assuredly be saved." Notwithstanding all the ingratitude which this high-minded and trusty servant had received at the hands of his royal master, he stuck by him to the last, and fell at his side in the afternoon of that memorable day—the 13th of April, 1868—struck by a shot from the storming party. It has been alleged that he was one of the Chiefs who advised the King to have me and my fellow-captives killed, sooner than allow us to join the British camp. To credit this statement, I must disbelieve in the existence of a single good man in the world. The whole story is a fabrication. The real truth is, there was great rejoicing among the Chiefs generally when they heard of our having been sent away, for it inspired them with a confident hope .that nothing but peace was then in store for them. Alas! they were doomed to be disappointed.

Samuel, a native of Senâfé in Kállakozai, on the north-eastern border of Tigrê, is descended from good parentage belonging to the Shoho tribe — who are all Moham-medans—inhabiting that district. The local hereditary chiefdom rests in his family, and when Salt visited Abys-sinia, 'Ali, Samuel's father, was the ruling Chief, paying tribute sometimes to Dajjâj Oobê and sometimes to Dajjâj Sabagâdis. Samuel was reared as a boy with the two sons of the latter chieftain; the three lads mutually called each other "brother," took their meals and pursued their studies together. This, of course, led to Samuel being brought up as a Christian. On the death of Sabagâdis he became a great traveller, visited India, Egypt and Syria, and eventually entered the service of Theodore, after having successively served under different Chiefs whose jurisdiction fell under the sway of the King. He has a fair complexion, and is better informed than any of his countrymen, not excepting those who have been educated at Malta and Bombay. He has a keen intellect, surpassing in that respect every Abyssinian I have met with, and a most courteous deportment; in fact, few could outdo him in civility, when he is disposed to practise it. He has strong sympathies and antipathies: once induced to like a person, I believe he would risk life in his behalf; but woe-betide the man who insults him or treats him disdainfully. On our arrival in Abyssinia, Samuel was represented to me as a man not to be trusted, and, moreover, that he was the enemy of Europeans generally. He gave me this description of himself while we were riding together, behind Râs I'ngădă, on our way to the King's camp. "Mr. Rassam," he said, "you are a stranger, unacquainted with the manners and customs of the people of the country. Before you have been one week with his Majesty, you will hear all kinds of lies; every party, whether European or Abyssinian, will try to gain you over to its side. Take my friendly advice: keep aloof from any meddling with the questionable proceedings of others, or from giving ear to scandal or calumny. If you have not already been told so, you will soon be informed by the Europeans who are at Gáffat and Mágdala that Samuel is a bad man, a mischief-maker, a receiver of bribes, and the originator of the King's hatred to Europeans. Why all this should be said of me, I am at a loss to divine; unless, indeed, they conceive me to exercise an extraordinary influence over his Majesty, both for good and evil. But I shall leave it with yourself to judge, after a brief acquaintance with the King, whether you deem it probable that any one in the country can influence him towards either liking or disliking a visitor. Everything, with him, depends upon the impression which the new-comer makes upon him. He is a most wonderful man, as you will soon discover for yourself." My rejoinder to him was, that I had not come to Abyssinia to be a judge, or to find fault, or to interfere in any way between the King and his subjects; that it would not be right in me to believe anything to the disadvantage of another without adequate proof, and that even if he himself chose to carry false reports of me to Theodore, and his Majesty believed them, it was beyond my province to call him to account, inasmuch as he was the King's servant, not mine. I understood afterwards that the King was watching our advance with a telescope, and that, on perceiving Samuel at my side, he laughed and said to the bystanders, "Look! look! that artful dodger, Samuel, has already made friends with the new-comer. See how he rides close to Rassam!" From the time we had donned our uniforms, messenger after messenger had been dispatched to report progress; hence his Majesty could easily distinguish me from my companions, they having on their scarlet coats, I my blue political suit. It appears, moreover, that the King was much taken with the manner in which we received Râs I'ngădă, for being a vain man he was gratified that we showed so much respect to his deputy. Another trifling incident also, which occurred when we reached the red tent, pleased him so highly that he made Râs I'ngădă and Samuel repeat their report of it. On ushering us into the tent, the Râs begged us to be seated, and on my then requesting him to sit with us for a while, he declined, repeating his invitation to us. I replied that we could not possibly do so while he, the first Minister of State, remained standing. He then said that we were guests, and must be tired, and therefore he adjured us "by the death of the King" to sit down. Whereupon I assured him that we did not acquiesce because we were tired, but on account of the adjuration which he had used.

To return to Samuel. As the King had thought fit to appoint him interpreter between us, and had, moreover, made him my Bâldărăbâ, I was obliged to trust him in some measure. I made frequent inquiries, moreover, of different

Abyssinians why he was in such bad repute with the Europeans, but could never discover any adequate cause for their animosity towards him. A Copt, who certainly had no liking for Samuel, and an intelligent Abyssinian also, informed me that he was accused of having apprised the King of what the Rev. Mr. Stern and the other Missionaries had published to his disparagement in their books; but "Can you believe, Sir," they procee led to say, "that a man who is unable to read a word of English, or any other European language, could find out what the Missionaries wrote? It is the mutual hatred which exists among the Europeans themselves, and not Samuel, that has caused all the mischief. Every one envies Samuel because the King has a liking for him; but to suppose that he can sway his Majesty towards what is good, if he felt so disposed, is simply preposterous. It is notorious that the King persistently rejects all wise counsels; but if a bad man were to come forward and tell him that all the Missionaries hated him, that they write against him, and that he will undertake to prove it from their books, such an one he will readily listen to. It takes a long time to build a house, but it may be demolished within a very short space." I also heard, subsequently, that the Abûna had given Samuel a bad name; so when we were sent to Mágdala, and I was placed in a position which obliged me to confide in the man—as he was quartered close to my room, and without his co-operation I could not have communicated with the coast—I wrote to the Bishop, inquiring whether I might trust him implicitly; mentioning at the same time the charge which was alleged against him of having created mischief between the King and the Europeans. In reply, he stated that he certainly had heard, at the outset, when the Europeans were first imprisoned, that

Samuel had reported stories to the King both against the Consul and the Missionaries, but that it had been since proved to him beyond doubt that he was wholly innocent of the charge, and that the fault lay nearer home; I might therefore rely upon him without reserve. (I showed the Bishop's note to the Rev. Mr. Stern when it reached me; unfortunately, I had to burn it, with other papers, on the 29th of March, 1868, when Theodore came up to Mágdala). I had also heard that when the King sent Samuel with Consul Cameron, as Bâldă-răbâ, to the coast, on which occasion Cameron left him in Bogôs, while he himself went on to Cásala, that he had written in detraction of the Consul. I learnt, however, from those who had perused the letter referred to, that Samuel had simply written to complain that Cameron had left him in Bogôs, and had gone on to Cásala without telling him what to do, and he therefore applied for instructions from the King whether he should remain where he was or return to Góndar; whereupon his Majesty ordered him to return forthwith to the capital. I also questioned Samuel himself on the subject. He replied that he was the King's servant; that he had been sent specially to escort Consul Cameron to the coast; that instead of proceeding to Massowah, as the King expected, Cameron had gone alone to Cásala, without intending—so he was informed—to rejoin him; that, under these circumstances, it was his duty to report the matter to the King and await his orders, which were that he should return forthwith to Góndar. Just about that time, I'ngădă Wark —who, as has been already stated, was in Cameron's employ and had been sent on to Aden with the King's letter for transmission to England—returned to the capital, and I believe he was the man, in conjunction with unfriendly-disposed Europeans, who inflamed the King's temper against Consul Cameron.

Samuel's fidelity to me was so obvious, that those Europeans who had been previously prejudiced against him, and were determined not to be disabused of their prejudices, attributed his devotion solely to mercenary or self-interested motives. I am bound to say, in reply to this reflection on his character, that he never received a gratuity from me, either in the shape of money or otherwise, during my entire stay in Abyssinia. The only substantial reward accorded him was kindly presented to him by Sir Robert Napier, at my recommendation, after our release from captivity. It is true that, deprived as he was of all emolument from the King, who had transferred him to me, I provided for his establishment, but that was no more than I should have been obliged to do for any other individual, European or native, holding the appointment which he did; to say nothing of the important services which he was thereby enabled to render, not to the Mission only, but to the captives generally.

However, it does not concern me to attempt to exculpate Samuel from all the blame—mostly founded on hearsay—which has been cast upon him; what I can and do assert on his behalf, as regards the Mission, is that I could not have fallen in with a more faithful and trusty coadjutor, or one more devoted to our interests. He always gave his assistance cheerfully, and often placed himself in imminent danger to serve me. Even when I was disgraced, and in chains, he never assumed any airs of superiority over me, but uniformly presented himself before me in a respectful attitude. I must, moreover, do him the justice to testify, that from the time of my first interview with Theodore until, in conjunction with my companions, I was sent to prison at Mágdala, he never swerved in his duty or allegiance to his royal master; but after I was placed in chains, he came into my room weeping, and declared that as the King had dealt so treacher-ously with us, he swore that he would henceforth live or die with me, promising at the same time to do all in his power to effect our escape. He certainly did his best to accomplish that object, but failed through want of brave accomplices to carry it out. Through him I was enabled to keep up regular communications between Mágdala and the coast, and owing to his position as the King's agent—although his Majesty never employed him in that capacity after we left Debra Tábor, in July, 1866—I had it in my power to entertain Abyssinian Chiefs and others who proved of use to us.

I shall now resume the narrative of the Mission, and leave my readers to judge, from the conspicuous part which Samuel was destined to play in it, whether I have exagge-rated his meritorious services. I must here subjoin, however, two great failings of his, wherein his character contrasted most unfavourably with that of Rás I'ngădă. That sober and simple-minded Chief, as I have already stated, eschewed in-toxicating drinks and concubinage; Samuel indulged in both. Perhaps, as his father was a Mohammedan, whereas he him-self professed Christianity, he thought that something was due to paternal example as regards women, if he did not fail to act as a " Christian " in respect of strong mead and spirits.

Early the next morning the King sent for me to speak to me about the object of my Mission. I again took Dr. Blanc and Lieutenant Prideaux with me. We found his Majesty standing at the door of the tent, awaiting my arrival. After the usual exchange of salutations he asked us to go into the tent with him. As soon as we had sat down, he told all the bystanders to leave, and only allowed Rás I'ngădă, Aito Samuel and Alăkâ I'ngădă to remain. When we were left alone, he told me that he was much gratified with what I had said to him the day before, especially about the interpreters. He said he would like to speak to them, if I had no objection. On my consenting, they were called in, and the King inquired of each of what nationality he was. 'Omar 'Ali, the Mohammedan interpreter, said he was a native of Massowah; and the other, Wald-Gabriêl, whom I had only engaged a few days before at Matámma, informed the King that he was a native of Shoa, but had been brought up at Góndar. Whereupon his Majesty remarked to me that as Shoa was in rebellion against him, he could not trust Wald-Gabriêl, but he had no objection to the employment of 'Omar 'Ali as interpreter between us, he being a native of Massowah, which place was not inimical to him. I accordingly ordered the former to return to our tents, and told the latter to remain in attendance.

When this point was settled, the King told me that he could not sleep all night after what I had said to him the previous day, and he was glad to inform me that, for the sake of his friend, my Queen, and in return for the trouble I had taken in the matter of Mr. Cameron, he was pleased to pardon all the European captives. He informed me that he had ordered their immediate release, and that they should be made over to me, to be taken by me out of Abyssinia.

He then ordered the chief Amharic scribe, Alăkâ I'ngădă, to read the draft of an Amharic letter which he had written to the Queen, and Aito Samuel was directed to translate it word by word into Arabic. The following is a translation of the letter:—

"In the name of the Father, of the Son, and of the Holy Ghost—one God. Amen.

"From the servant of our Lord and his created being, the son of David, the son of Solomon, the King of kings, Theodorus.

"To Her whom God has exalted above all Sovereigns, and glorified above all Princes and peoples, and made the Defender of the Christian Faith, and the succour of the poor and oppressed, Victoria, the Queen of the United Kingdom of Great Britain and Ireland.

"Had the illustrious Hormuzd Rassam, whom your Majesty had mentioned to me in your letter, not been sent to me about the matter of Cameron and others, but the lowest of your servants, he would have been received graciously by me. I now send with Hormuzd Rassam, Cameron and all other Europeans about whom your Majesty has written. Your Majesty can learn from those who fear the Lord the ill-treatment and abuse which I have received at the hands of the above-mentioned Europeans, and the Copt who called himself Metropolitan, the Abûna Salâma.

"In my humble position I am not worthy to address your Majesty; but illustrious Princes and the deep ocean can bear everything. I, being an ignorant Ethiopian, hope that your Majesty will overlook my shortcomings and pardon my faults.

"The people, whom I have imprisoned for reviling and defaming me, did so because the Gallas had proved victorious over the royal Children of Israel and had humbled them; but God has empowered me, the son of one of the humble women of Israel, to regain that which had been lost by my forefathers.

"Doubtless, your Majesty has learnt how ignorant and blind the people of Ethiopia are; wherefore I beg of your Majesty not to take amiss the mistakes I may make in my correspondence with you. Counsel me, but do not blame me, O Queen, whose majesty God has glorified, and to whom He has given abundance of wisdom.

"Dated the 22nd day of January, 1858; corresponding to the 29th day of January, 1866."

As soon as the letter was read, I thanked his Majesty, on the part of our Queen and the British nation, for the friendship he had shown on that day. He replied, that he felt as happy as I did at the termination of the long-existing misunderstanding between himself and the English, and trusted that, in future, everything would go on well between the two countries. I had hoped that, after this explanation, I should hear no more of the past; but, to my great disappointment, I found that the King was not quite satisfied. He reverted to the ill-treatment he had received at the hands of Consul Cameron and the Missionaries. He said that on the arrival of the former at his Court, he had received him with great pomp for the sake of his friend, the Queen of England, and had treated him with great kindness and hospitality during his stay in Abyssinia; that he had been told that the Queen of England hated the Turks and liked Abyssinia and its Sovereign; he had also heard that the best way to cultivate the friendship of an European Power was by sending an Embassy to them, and as he had no ships in the Red Sea, and the Turks on the way were his enemies, he had written to ask the Queen for a vessel to convey his Agent, and to grant him safe-conduct through Egypt; that he had given the letter to Mr. Cameron, and had asked him to take it down to the coast and to bring up an answer himself; that he had provided him with the necessary funds for the road, and had ordered all the Chiefs of the different provinces between Góndar and Massowah to supply him and his followers with food, and to treat him with respect and honour; that instead of attending to his request, Mr. Cameron had gone to amuse himself with the Turks; that, after a long absence, Mr. Cameron, to his surprise, returned to Góndar without an answer; that he had said nothing at the time, but had allowed Mr. Cameron to remain peacefully in the country; that six months after, Mr. Cameron had sent him a letter, which he said he had received from his Government, and demanded his dismissal forthwith; that on hearing this he had sent to ask him why he had returned to Abyssinia if he wished to be at Massowah. " When I found," continued his Majesty, " I could not get a satisfactory answer to that question, I sent and told him that, by the power of God, you shall be detained in prison until I find out whether you are really the servant of the Queen or not."

The King also touched again upon the disturbed state of the country, and said that he was beset by enemies on every side. I thought it prudent to give no answer to these complaints.

Before I was dismissed I told the King that I had brought a few presents with me, which I hoped he would allow me to send to him. He said he was very sorry I had given myself so much trouble in conveying such heavy articles for him, and that he would communicate with me about them in the course of the day. He afterwards sent me the draft of his letter to the Queen to translate into English, and asked me to have it fairly copied, in order that he might sign and seal it. He did not wish to send an Amharic copy with it, as he said he wanted to show to the world how he trusted me, by signing a letter the contents of which he did not know, relying on me for its accuracy. Two days subsequently, however, I succeeded in obtaining from him an Amharic copy, urging that our Queen would prefer having the letter from him written in his own language.

Afterwards, the King sent Aito Samuel to ask whether the presents I had brought with me were from the Queen or from myself. I replied that, as I had to leave for Abyssinia in a hurry, there was no time to get anything from England, but that the articles which I had obtained partly at Aden and partly in Egypt were on the public account, and I had intended to present them as coming from her Majesty. He then sent to say that he would be happy to receive them in the afternoon. About 3 P.M. I was asked to go up with the presents to the King, who was ready to receive them. As usual, I took Dr. Blanc and Lieutenant Prideaux with me, and found his Majesty sitting in the open air outside his tent, waiting for me, with Râs I'ngădă and other attendants standing by. Every little present had to be exhibited separately and placed by itself in the field. When the whole was handed over to the officers in waiting, the King seemed very much pleased, and said, "I accept these presents not for their value, but for the sake of the giver, [the Queen], and in token of the renewal of friendship between me and the British nation."

That evening no less than four of the King's attendants came to make claims for money which they alleged to be owing to them by Consul Cameron, and partly on account of the late Consul Plowden. One of these men was I'ngădă Wark. I gave them to understand, once for all, that I had not come to Abyssinia to pay old debts, nor was I in a position to listen to such complaints; but I assured them, at the same time, that any just claim would be immediately satisfied by Consul Cameron, as soon as he was at large. As has been already stated, I'ngădă Wark played a conspicuous part in the misunderstanding between Theodore and ourselves, and I believe he was at the bottom of all the evil that brought on the late Abyssinian complications. On his return to Góndar, after carrying the King's letter to Aden, he reported that he had carried that letter to Aden and Egypt, but had not been treated well by the British authorities, and that at Aden, in particular, he was nearly starved. His companions subsequently received from Consul Cameron the amount of their respective claims, which were found to be correct; but his claim was disallowed, which irritated him so much that Aito Samuel threatened to report him to the King and have him flogged, if he did not behave himself properly.

Theodore having expressed distrust of Wald-Gabrîêl, I deemed it prudent to dispense with his services. Accordingly, on my return from the morning interview, I told the interpreter that, after what the King had said, I could not retain him in my employ. On hearing of this, his Majesty sent and begged me not to dismiss him, stating that he entertained no prejudice against the man, but merely objected to his acting as interpreter between us, suggesting at the same time that I might employ him in some other capacity. On this assurance, and not to disoblige the King, I retained Wald-Gabrîêl some time longer.

I had heard, both at Massowah and in Abyssinia, that Theodore understood Arabic well. As he had never spoken to me in that language, I was unable to gather how far the statement was correct; but when his letter to the Queen was being translated by Aito Samuel, his Majesty took him up on a nice point, which led me to infer that he was thoroughly acquainted with Arabic. When Samuel was translating that part of the letter where the writer styles himself "the son of one of the humble women of Israel," he rendered it "one of the sons of the humble women;" whereupon the King stopped him, and corrected him in Arabic. It is a remarkable fact, that during the entire period of my residence in the country the King never addressed me in that language, except when he wished to be particularly affectionate; on all other occasions he spoke to me through a native interpreter. He reads and writes Amharic fluently, but although he always peruses his letters he has never once subscribed even his name to any document since his accession to the throne.

When I presented his Majesty with the silks and other articles which I had obtained in Egypt and elsewhere, I mentioned that I had brought him a mirror for the use of the Queen. He sighed, and said in reply: "Unhappily, since the death of my good Queen I have been leading an un-Christian and disreputable life; but I have a person now whom I intend to make Queen, and I will present it to her. I thank you much for it."

The King sent me a message, after I had translated his letter to the Queen, to the effect that he had never hitherto allowed any European to interfere in the disputes which arose between Europeans and his own subjects; but that now, having perfect confidence in me, he fully empowered me to decide upon all such cases arising within the sphere of the Mission; that I was to award punishments, by imprisonment or otherwise, without reference to him; and that all Abyssinian officials were to aid me whenever I applied for their co-operation. It was eventually arranged with his Majesty that Samuel should be authorised to deal with all questions arising between the Abyssinians, while the Europeans and Indians should be left to my jurisdiction; and that, in the event of any dispute between an Indian and a native, if the case was not adjudged to the satisfaction of the former, he was to have the right of appeal to me. It is a noteworthy fact that the King never rescinded this arrangement; for even when I was myself a prisoner at Mágdala, he instructed the Chiefs of that fortress to support my authority, and to punish any of his own people in execution of an award by me.

A *Bâldárábá*, which means an Interpreter or Go-between, is quite indispensable in Abyssinia. Neither king nor peasant, bishop nor monk, Christian nor Mohammedan, can hold intercourse with each other, except through a third person—a domestic generally acting in that capacity. The usage, however, only applies to the upper classes, and, where the parties are strangers to one another, the functionary himself is appointed by the superior to be the medium of communication between him and the inferior. Nevertheless, it is not necessary that the Bâldărăbâ should be present on all occasions, or that, being present, the communications should pass through him, since the person who appointed him may dispense with his services, if so disposed. The chief advantage of having a Bâldărăbâ is this: he has free access at all times to the master of the house, or to the person who appointed him, whereas a stranger or guest has no such privilege. Although the King had appointed Samuel as Bâldărăbâ between him and myself, he never scrupled to employ other officers as mediums of communication. When I was sent to Mágdala, the Commandant of that fortress was officially directed to act in that capacity; yet, whenever I dispatched letters to his Majesty, my own messengers carried them, and they were ushered into the royal presence without an introducer. If one of them wished to say anything to the King, he had merely to stand up in front of his Majesty to obtain a hearing. On several occasions, Theodore employed my interpreters and messengers as Bâldărăbâ; for when he was in an angry mood, all his own people trembled at the idea of approaching him. On one occasion after we left Debra Tâbor, in the beginning of 1866, even Râs I'ngădă and Samuel feigned to be sick from this cause, whereupon the King sent for Dasta, my young interpreter, and directed him to act in that capacity, giving instructions that he should have free access to the royal presence whenever he came with a message from me. On the 13th of April, 1866, when my companions and I were arrested and disgraced, the King appointed his European artisans to be my Bâldărăbâ; but the poor fellows were in such terror at the time, that they hardly dared to look in the direction of our tent whenever they went to visit his Majesty. Had either of our party been taken ill under these circumstances, we should have been unable to communicate with the King.

30th.—The King sent me a message early this morning to say, that as he wished me to go to Korâta, where I was to wait until the captives from Mágdala joined me, he requested me and my party to be ready to start with him before noon, promising to escort us a day or two on our way to the Lake. The reason he assigned for sending us to Korâta was, that he knew we were fond of the sea-breeze, and that there we might also amuse ourselves in fishing. I found out afterwards that his real object was to plunder the few remaining villages in the once flourishing districts of Métcha and Dâmôt.

CHAPTER XI.

WITH THEODORE AND HIS ARMY.

Start from A'shfa — Encampment of the army — Soldiers' huts — Theodore's offer of funds — March of the army and plunder by the troops — Theodore's parentage — His Mother — Dajjâj Kánfu, his Father — His early training and warlike exploits — Receives a check at Kedârif — Marries the daughter of Râs 'Ali — Excites the jealousy of his father-in-law — Mr. Plowden's account of his subsequent career — He defeats Râs 'Ali and Dajazmâtsh Oobê — Is crowned King of kings of Ethiopia by the Abûna — Marches against the Gallas — Theodore's personal character — His reforms — Suppresses the Slave-Trade — Military discipline — Fosters commerce — His religious zeal — His jealousy of his sovereign rights — Remarks on Mr. Plowden's account of the Slave-Trade in Abyssinia — Causes of Theodore's declining power — His fits of melancholy — March again with the army — Encampment on the Abai or Blue Nile — Burning villages — Cross the Abai — Theodore's care for his troops — His questions on foreign politics — Why he delayed his invitation to the Mission — Orders an officer to proceed to Mágdala to release the captives — Theodore renews his complaints against Consul Cameron and the Missionaries — Party strife and treachery among the Europeans — The Mission to await the arrival of the Captives at Korâta — Theodore's views of our Treaty with Râs 'Ali — We take leave of the King — His letter and present to the Author — Explanation.

THE King left A'shfa at about 7 A.M., with the whole army, then estimated at 45,000 men; their attendant wives and children, male and female followers, amounted to double that number. No ladies of rank were present, the King having made it a rule that the wives of Chiefs should not accompany their husbands when on active service in the field; on the other hand, the Chiefs were allowed to take as many concubines with them as they pleased. Theodore set the example himself in this respect, having left all his establishment at Debra

Tâbor. When the troops were ordered to march, they set fire to the huts which they had erected, in accordance with his Majesty's command.   Blanc, Prideaux and I started from A'shfa at 10·45 A.M., after our luggage had been distributed amongst the soldiers who were told off to carry it. A Râs was appointed to take charge of it, and Samuel acted as Bâldărăbâ and escort.

At 12·30 P.M. we reached Sakôla, where we found the King already encamped. Before our arrival he had given directions that our camp should be pitched near him; also, that the red tent should be erected near the royal pavilion and our tents in a line with it, in order that our position might be the more conspicuous. These instructions had been scrupulously carried out, and our tents were ready for our reception the moment we arrived.

The whole army is formed into four divisions, which generally encamp at right angles to each other, in separate brigades and regiments—the ground permitting—thus making a hollow square, the Court occupying the centre of the same. The King's favourite division, consisting of his bravest followers, always takes up a position on his right. Most of the troops are without tents, but they never fail to provide themselves with shelter, even if halting for one night only. The rapidity with which thousands of huts are thus erected by the soldiers and their followers is truly astonishing. The privates of the different regiments put up their huts in a circle round those of their officers. On one occasion we saw not less than twenty thousand of these huts—"bowers" would be a more appropriate name—each capable of sheltering three or four persons, put up in regular order, within the space of two hours. Some soldiers carry the skeletons of these *tents d'abris* with them, but the majority cut the wood and grass on the line of march. On this occasion everything was conducted with such perfect order that it was a pleasure to travel with the royal army. Confusion seldom arose, except when the formidable mass reached a stream or narrow defile. As all strove to be first, none cared what obstruction was in the way, whether a laden mule or a laden woman, a horseman or a litter bearing a patient, or a mother with a child in her arms. The only wonder was that no one came to grief in the general crush.

On our arrival at Sakôla the King sent me a brace of partridges, also an antelope which his soldiers had caught alive on the road, and in the course of that day he sent his valet, Wald-Gâbir, with Aito Samuel, to ask me to allow him to supply me with money towards my daily disbursements. He said he did not know how much cash I had with me, but he thought it could not be ample, as he had kept me a long time waiting, and I must have spent all that I had brought with me from Massowah. He said, further, that he would be very much hurt if I borrowed from any of his subjects, as he should consider my doing so a most unfriendly act. "Does not all that I possess belong to your Queen?" the King ordered Wald-Gâbir to say; "and would it not be disgraceful in me to allow you, as the servant of my friend, to be in want? I know very well that I am a mere beggar compared with the English; but you are not in your own country, and it is very difficult for you to obtain funds from the coast. Let God be witness between me and you, that whatever you require you do not hesitate to send for, whether it be money, clothes or arms." I sent and thanked his Majesty for the kind message, but respectfully declined to accept any money; stating, in the first place, that I should otherwise infringe the standing regulations of my Government; and, secondly, that I was then amply supplied with funds; promising faithfully, however, to apply to him in case of want, and that I would always look upon his treasury as belonging to our Queen. To this the King sent an answer, expressing himself pleased with what I had said, and hoped that I should soon have recourse to him for supplies.

31st.—The King started at 8 this morning, and we followed about a quarter of an hour afterwards. We soon overtook the rear of the army, and found no small difficulty in forcing a passage through the moving masses, and a stream in the way brought us to a dead-lock for some time. Several rivulets on the route were actually arrested by the tread of the enormous multitude—a striking illustration of Sennacherib's boast, "With the soles of my feet I have dried up all the rivers of the besieged places," (Isaiah xxxvii. 25). At 12·40 P.M. we reached Bífâta, in the district of Métcha, and found that the Court had already taken up its quarters, our tent being pitched within fifty yards of the King's. The position selected was a high hill overlooking the two districts of Dâmôt and Métcha. It rained very heavily all the evening. For the last two days the soldiery had been engaged in laying waste every village and cultivated spot within reach; the former were generally set fire to, and the latter plundered of the standing crops. The reason alleged was that the inhabitants had rebelled against the King, and that unless he resorted to severe measures of repression they would aid the insurgents of Gójjam. Besides, he wished to make an example of these the two most flourishing districts in Abyssinia, for although they had already been devastated twice within the last two years, yet when we passed through them they still resembled a continuous park. His Majesty's last excuse for ravaging Dâmôt was, that on the occasion of

Tadla Gwâlu's advance into the district a few months before, the peasantry had supplied his troops with provisions. The unfortunate people had vainly appealed to the King, over and over again, against the Gójjam troops, whose inroads they were powerless to resist, begging either that succour might be afforded them, or that they might be allowed to purchase muskets to protect themselves; and now, because a host of those marauders had come into the district and helped themselves to everything they could lay hands on, the spoliation of the wretched peasants was to be consummated by their own Sovereign.

It is a great mistake to say that Theodore was ever a wise and beneficent ruler. Had he been endowed with the least talent for administration, the country over which he exercised undivided and absolute sway could never have been reduced to its present condition of utter disorganization and ruin. While yet a child, he was the favourite of a band of admiring and trusty adherents, who taught him the art of war, and led him on to victories of which he himself was unconscious. Born in Dámběa, of noble parentage, he was brought up in Kwâra, under the auspices of his father, Dajjâj Kánfu, the hereditary Chief of Kwâra, Chálga, and other districts bordering Abyssinia on the west, as far as Sennaar. As so much has been said about the mother of Theodore, and as the King is known to have been specially incensed against the Rev. Mr. Stern for having described her, in his 'Wanderings among the Falashas,' as a vendor of kósso, a native anthelmintic, I take this opportunity of recording what I learnt of the lady's descent from personal inquiry. Mr. Stern's statement is undoubtedly credited by different people in the country; nevertheless, I never met with a single individual who had been an eye-witness of the fact. On the other hand, adequate proof was afforded me that she was, by right of birth, a Princess, a daughter of the Râs of Amhâra-Seint, a district situated between Gójjam and the Wello-Gallas, whose family was in good circumstances when I was in Abyssinia. In all probability, the person mistaken for the mother of Theodore was the female to whose care he was committed in infancy, it being a prevailing custom in the country for children of the wealthy to be put out to nurse. In general, the children thus nurtured grow up more attached to their foster-mothers than to their maternal parents. Dajjâj 'Alamâyo, the legitimate son of King Theodore, now in England, is an instance in point. When, on the decease of their mistress, I had to dismiss her numerous attendants, the lad cried on parting with his nurse, though he did not shed a tear on the death of his mother.

Dajjâj Kánfu has been represented as merely the fraternal uncle of Theodore. How this extraordinary mistake originated it is difficult to say, but, like many other equally absurd stories concocted during the late Abyssinian complications, it has not lacked credence. The King always asserted that Dajjâj Kánfu was his father, from whom he inherited the sovereignty of the Amhâra country, which had been usurped for many years by Galla Chiefs. I made very particular inquiries on this subject of those who were brought up with the King, and of some of his relations also, and they unanimously declared that Theodore was the son of Dajjâj Kánfu; " if he is not his son," said some of them, laughingly, "whose son, then, is he?" Thus much may be said in extenuation of this and similar unfounded reports, that owing to the social condition of the people, and especially the constant change of wives which prevails among them, it is not always an easy matter even for an Abyssinian to know certainly who was his father, and therefore a stranger is excusable for confounding uncle with father, and *vice versâ*. However, accepting Theodore's version of his paternity, I shall proceed with the following brief sketch of his biography. Dajjâj Kánfu, it appears, having been infirm for many years, scarcely ever visiting his native district, Kwâra, the resident elders of the family took his son Kâsa in hand, and had him educated. An overweening pride, which brooked no dictation, characterised his disposition when only ten years old. Western Abyssinia had been so utterly neglected for a century prior to this period, that the Mohammedans of the lowlands were in the habit of making yearly raids into the adjoining country of Amhâra. Before Kâsa was out of the hands of his tutors, he entered heart and soul into the border warfare which ensued, frequently joining in repelling the inroads made upon his own district. When scarcely fifteen years old he headed an assault upon a large tribe which had been conspicuous for its depredations upon the inhabitants of Kwâra. The party barely consisted of three hundred men, but his extraordinary strategy ensured them a signal victory, and they returned home laden with booty, and without a single casualty—an event which had not occurred within the memory of his contemporaries, and which may be said to have laid the foundation of his future renown. Good descent is held in high esteem in Abyssinia, especially when accompanied with personal valour. Both these qualifications were eagerly recognized in the youthful Kâsa, who had already acquired the distinguished title of " Lij," and whose successful exploits drew fresh bands of warriors to join him on his marauding excursions. In the course of ten years, he subdued all the Mohammedan tribes to the west and north-west of Kwâra, the great object of his ambition being to reconquer Sennaar and the Soodân, both which districts, he alleged, belonged of right to the patrimony of his forefathers. But at Kedârif his career in that direction was checked in an encounter with a body of Irregulars. "Had the cowardly Turks not hid themselves behind a wall"—such was the King's bitter remark to me one day—"I would have utterly annihilated them. They invoked their Prophet, exclaiming, 'La ilah illa Allah, wa-Muhammed Rasûl-Allah!' [There is no god but the God, and Mohammed is the Apostle of God]. I retorted by invoking the Fountain-head of my faith and the faith of my forefathers, and bawled out to the infidels, 'In the name of the Father, Son, and Holy Ghost—one God for evermore,' to come forth and fight like men." On the death of his father, Lij Kâsa assumed the title of "Dajazmâtsh," by which time his fame had spread far and wide. Râs 'Ali, the then presiding ruler, who at this period was harassed on all sides, now made friendly overtures to him, judging that an alliance with the renowned Kâsa might enable him to cope with his numerous enemies, or that by securing him on his side he would at least be safe against molestation from Western Abyssinia. The alliance with Kâsa was further strengthened, on the advice of the Râs's mother, Wäízero Mínyen, by the gift to him, as a wife in the third degree, of their daughter "Tôbet," a name signifying "Blessed." Kwâra had been virtually independent for many years, and, as his power increased, the less disposed was Dajjâj Kâsa to tolerate any interference with the affairs of his native district by a "renegade Galla." He was too shrewd, however, openly to assume such a position until his plans were fully matured; he wanted to gain time, in order to enlist the friendship of the influential chiefs of Métcha, Bagámëdër, Dámbëa and

Wággără, before he threw off the mask. He accordingly subdued a number of disaffected tribes that had risen up in arms against Râs 'Ali in the neighbourhood of Góndar, and was so generally successful in these and similar enterprises that his name became a terror to the enemies of the State on all sides. His popularity eventually excited the jealousy of the Râs, who, judging it advisable to arrest the growing ambition of his son-in-law, sent a large army against him, under the command of a Chief renowned for gallantry and military strategy. But Kâsa proved more than a match for his distinguished antagonist. In the battle which ensued on that occasion, Râs 'Ali's general was slain, and two-thirds of his defeated army joined the ranks of the young aspirant.

Kâsa's subsequent military and political career, until he succeeded in reducing the whole country to his sway and caused himself to be crowned Emperor of Abyssinia, has been so ably narrated by the late Consul Plowden, in his official Report, dated June, 1855, that even at the risk of wearying my readers I cannot resist submitting the following quotation to their careful perusal, remarking, by the way, that I give the native names as spelt by the author :—

"From his earliest youth Dejajmatch Kasai regarded his present elevation as assuredly destined, but concealed his designs, with prudence equal to his daring, until ripe for execution. First, he denied the authority of the Queen, mother of Ras Ali, under whom he governed the provinces near Sennaar, defeated in succession all the troops she could send against him, and lastly herself, with tenfold his numbers. He protested, however, that he was still the faithful servant of Ras Ali, but refused to surrender, except on certain conditions of peace. The Ras then sent against him an immense force; the armies camped opposite to each other for some time, the Ras not wishing to drive matters to extremity, and in the interval Kasai fought several minor battles, detected and punished some traitors in his own camp, and introduced a little discipline into his army.

"The Ras having sworn to do him no injury, he surrendered and came to Debra Tabor, where he so completely lulled all suspicion that he received all his former honours and provinces from the Ras, the Queen being in a measure disgraced. He returned to Kwora, and attacked all the low countries towards Sennaar, Shankallas or Arabs, accustoming his soldiers to war and hardships.

"His projects not being yet matured, on several occasions when it was confidently reported that he had rebelled, he baffled his accusers by suddenly appearing in the Ras's camp, and following him to war in Godjam with about a third of his forces, thus quite winning his heart, though I ventured to point out to the Ras his dangerous character.

"At last, about two years and a half ago [1853], he threw off the mask, and the Ras having sent against him Dejajmatch Goscho, that prince was defeated and slain in battle.

"The Ras now became seriously alarmed, and ordered half his army under his best commanders to attack him; he also called upon Dejajmatch Oobeay, Chief of Tigré, for assistance, and that prince furnished a very large contingent. Though numbers were so overwhelming against him, Dejajmatch Kasai met these forces and gave them a signal defeat, killing most of the chiefs. Shortly after, he took the daring resolution of attacking the Ras, and arriving by forced marches near the camp of that prince in Godjam in the rainy season, sent him a defiance and met him, though so far superior in cavalry, in the open plains. The Ras fought with the utmost courage in person. The loss of life was considerable on both sides, but Kasai's determined valour again won the day, Ras Ali escaping.

"He then retired from Godjam, and afforded to Birro Goscho, who had been for five years besieged by the Ras in his mountain fort of Soma, an opportunity of leaving that stronghold.

"During some months Dejajmatch Kasai remained tranquil, amusing Dejajmatch Oobeay at first with friendly proposals, afterwards demanding of that chief the Aboona Salama, who had been banished by Ras Ali, with menaces in case of non-compliance. Oobeay becoming alarmed, sent first his son with proposals, and subsequently the Aboona; the latter was reinstated in his dignity at Gondar, and a peace was made between the chiefs. Dejajmatch Kasai then pursued Birro Goscho, even to the Galla provinces, where he had assembled a large force, defeated and took him prisoner.

" He was now strong in guns and troops, and on his return camped in the province of Waggera, from whence he declared war against Oobeay, reproaching him with his falsehood, which was proved, in having sent letters to encourage Birro Goscho. With some reluctance Oobeay at last put himself in motion to oppose Dejajmatch Kasai, who had advanced into Semen. The latter, by forced marches, fell suddenly upon his rival, and in two hours defeated him, taking prisoner all his sons and generals, with himself. Without delay he invested Oobeay's strongholds, which surrendered at once.

" The fruits of this last victory were large treasures accumulated for three generations; the submission or imprisonment of almost all the chiefs of Abyssinia; and the coronation of Dejajmatch Kasai by the Aboona Salama, under the title of Theodorus, King of Kings of Ethiopia.

" Discovering a plot against his life, the King only placed in durance those concerned, displaying in all things great clemency and generosity, and the ransom of Dejajmatch Oobeay was fixed at 120,000 dollars.

" With scarce a week's delay, and in spite of the murmurs of his soldiers, the King marched against the Mahomedan Gallas, who had during his absence burnt some churches, and assembled all the forces of Christian Abyssinia, Tigré included, in the province of Dillanta, on the borders of Worrahaimano, where I found him.

" He may have from 50,000 to 60,000 men of all arms.

" Such has been his adventurous and warlike career. I shall now say a few words on his personal character, the reforms he has effected, the designs he is contemplating, and the condition and prospects of the country.

" The King Theodorus is young in years, vigorous in all manly exercises, of a striking countenance, peculiarly polite and engaging when pleased, and mostly displaying great tact and delicacy. He is persuaded that he is destined to restore the glories of the Ethiopian Empire, and to achieve great conquests; of untiring energy, both mental and bodily, his personal and moral daring are boundless. The latter is well proved by his severity towards his soldiers, even when these, pressed by hunger, are mutinous, and he is in front of a powerful foe; more so even by his pressing reforms on a country so little used to any yoke, whilst engaged in unceasing hostilities, and his suppression of the power of the great feudal Chiefs, at a moment when any inferior man would have sought to conciliate them, as the stepping-stones to empire.

" When aroused, his wrath is terrible, and all tremble; but at all moments he possesses a perfect self-command. Indefatigable in business, he takes little repose night or day; his ideas and language are clear and precise; hesitation is not known to him, and he has neither counsellors nor go-betweens. He is fond of splendour, and receives in state, even on a campaign. He is unsparing in punishment—very necessary to restrain disorder, and to restore order in such a wilderness as Abyssinia. He salutes his meanest subject with courtesy; is sincerely, though often mistakenly, religious; and will acknowledge a fault committed toward his poorest follower in a moment of passion with sincerity and grace.

" He is generous to excess, and free from all cupidity, regarding nothing with pleasure or desire but munitions of war for his soldiers. He has hitherto exercised the utmost clemency towards the vanquished, treating them rather as his friends than his enemies. His faith is signal: ' without Christ,' he says, ' I am nothing; if He has destined me to purify and reform this distracted kingdom, with His aid who shall stay me?' nay, sometimes he is on the point of not caring for human assistance at all, and this is one reason why he will not seek, with much avidity, for assistance from or alliance with Europe.

" The worst points in his character are, his violent anger at times, his unyielding pride as regards his kingly and divine right, and his fanatical religious zeal.

" He has begun to reform even the dress of Abyssinia, all about his person wearing loose flowing trowsers, and upper and under vests, instead of the half-naked costume introduced by the Gallas. Married himself at the altar, and strictly continent, he has ordered or persuaded all who love him to follow his example, and exacts the greatest decency of manners and conversation: this system he hopes to extend to all classes.

" He has suppressed the slave-trade in all its phases, save that the slaves already bought may be sold to such Christians as shall buy them for charity : setting the example, he pays to the Mussulman dealers what price they please to ask for the slaves they bring to him, and then baptizes them.

" He has abolished the barbarous practice of delivering over murderers to the relatives of the deceased, handing over offenders, in public, to his own executioners, to be shot or decapitated.

" The arduous task of breaking the power of the great feudal Chiefs—a task achieved in Europe only during the reigns of many consecutive kings—he has commenced by chaining almost all who were dangerous, avowing his intention of liberating them when his power shall be consolidated. He has placed the soldiers of the different provinces under the command of his own trusty followers, to whom he has given high titles, but no power to judge or punish ; thus, in fact, creating Generals in place of feudal Chieftains more proud of their birth than of their monarch, and organising a new nobility, a legion of honour dependent on himself, and chosen specially for their daring and fidelity.

" To these he gives sums of money from time to time, accustoming them to his intention of establishing a regular pay ; his matchlock-men are numbered under officers commanding from 100 to 1000, and the King drills them in person. In the common soldiers he has effected a great reform, by paying them and ordering them to purchase their food, but in no way to harass and plunder the peasant as before ; the peasantry he is gradually accustoming to live quiet under the village judge, and to look no more to military rule. As regards commerce, he has put an end to a number of vexatious exactions, and has ordered that duty shall be levied only at three places in his dominions. All these matters cannot yet be perfected, but he intends also to disarm the people, and to establish a regular standing army, armed with muskets only, having declared that he will convert swords and lances into ploughshares and reaping-hooks, and cause a plough-ox to be sold dearer than the noblest war-horse.

" He has begun to substitute letters for verbal messages. After perusing the history of the Jesuits in Abyssinia, he has decided that no Roman Catholic priests shall teach in his dominions; and insisting on his right divine over those born his subjects, has ordered the Abyssinians who have adopted that creed to recant; to foreigners of all classes, however, he permits the free exercise of their religion, but prohibits all preaching contrary to the doctrine of the Coptic Church. To the Mahometans he has declared that he will first conquer the Gallas, who have seized on Christian lands, devastated churches, and by force converted the inhabitants to Islamism; and after that, the Mussulmans now residing in Abyssinia will have the option of being baptized or of leaving the country.

"He is peculiarly jealous, as may be expected, of his sovereign rights, and of anything that appears to trench on them; he wishes, in a short time, to send embassies to the great European Powers, to treat with them on equal terms. The most difficult trait in his character is this jealousy and the pride that, fed by ignorance, renders it impossible for him yet to believe that so great a monarch as himself exists in the world."

The character of Theodore, as portrayed in the foregoing masterly document, is true to the life, and I can bear personal testimony to the fact that, up to the last hours of his existence, that extraordinary man laboured under the delusion that he was destined to acquire a vast extension of power, to uproot Islamism from the world, and to prove by his future triumphs that he was the mighty Theodore who, according to a prediction contained in Abyssinian books, was to abolish heathenism.

There is one paragraph, however, in the extract above quoted, which calls for some remark. I refer to the passage where the King is said to have "suppressed the slave-trade in all its phases, save that the slaves already bought may be sold to such Christians as shall buy them for charity: setting the example, he pays to the Mussulman dealers what price they please to ask for the slaves they bring to him, and then baptizes them." Now it is a well-known fact, that the slave-trade, in the ordinary acceptation of the term, has ever been held to be unlawful by the Christians of Abyssinia: that is to say, no Christian can buy a slave and then dispose of him for money. Nevertheless, they are at perfect liberty to buy as many slaves as they please in order to Christianize them, and these, when once baptized, become absolutely free. Such is the law and such the prevailing practice in Abyssinia, and I regret to say that the objectionable example has found a number of imitators among the Europeans sojourning in those distant parts, who, regardless of the impulse which their misjudged support gives to the nefarious traffic, consider themselves justified in purchasing slaves for the sake of manumitting them and making them proselytes to Christianity. In a preceding part of his valuable Report, Consul Plowden writes:—"The slave-trade is carried on by Mahometans alone. Christians buy for domestic purposes, *but are not permitted to sell*, and the penalty of death by hanging is affixed to the act of selling a Christian child." This sufficiently bears out my account of Abyssinian law on the subject, although it is somewhat inconsistent with the writer's subsequent statement, which gives Theodore the credit of having "suppressed the slave-trade in all its phases."

Had Theodore kept faith with his adherents and devoted his energies to the civil administration of his kingdom, instead of locating himself at Debra Tâbor, where his whole time was occupied in carrying out the harshest measures—mostly from mere caprice—against the Chiefs who were still loyal to him, he might have retrieved his declining fortune, even as late as the year 1867. But for the last four years of his reign he had become increasingly suspicious, until at length the least success gained in the royal cause by any of his followers was requited with disgrace and chains; the same fate awaited them whenever they suffered a defeat. The Chiefs, consequently, began to think that their only safeguard was to keep out of his reach; and on the first favourable opportunity many of them deserted. Most of those, however, who had shared in his early victories remained with him to the last, submitting to starvation, chains, torture and other indignities, rather than forsake him. A more fortunate sovereign in that respect, and at the same time one more reckless in abusing the devoted attachment of his supporters, never existed. He uniformly rejected wise counsels, and generally followed those which precipitated his downfall; and the more he wronged a man, the more inveterate was his enmity towards him. He did everything by fits and starts, under the whim of the moment; insomuch that a Chief who had ably discharged some important duty was uncertain, on being summoned into his presence, whether his services would be approved and rerewarded, or visited with the infliction of the bastinado or the *jeráf*—a cow-hiding. On one occasion, something went wrong in the royal larder, and being unable at the time to fix upon a culprit on whom to vent his indignation, the King ordered his soldiery to plunder the kitchen establishment —an order which was promptly obeyed by the starving troops, who soon denuded it of everything in the shape of food. On coming to his senses, he asked for something to eat, and was told that the soldiers had left nothing behind them wherewith his Majesty could be served.

After this long digression, I return to the main narrative of my proceedings. During our stay at Bîfâta, in Métcha, two common rebels who had been found concealed in a thicket were seized and brought before the King. His Majesty reprimanded the captors for their officiousness, and bade them, if they had the pluck in them, go and catch Tadla Gwâlu, and not bother him with such insignificant matters. It was lucky for the captured, however, that the King happened to be in good humour at the time; and I have no doubt that they were agreeably surprised on finding themselves dismissed without the loss of their hands and feet.

Theodore was subject to attacks of hypochondriasis, and when the fit was on him he generally shut himself in his tent and remained alone. If a humane and sensible man happened to keep watch on such occasions, he advised all visitors on business to come again at a more propitious time—when the King was "awake." Reclining the head on the left shoulder, or, if near enough, whispering that his Majesty was "asleep," were the usual warnings given to those who had well-wishers at head-quarters. As almost every man about the Court was friendly-disposed towards me, my messengers were always kept from approaching the irascible Monarch when he was known to be in an angry mood.

1st February.—The King sent me word this morning that he intended to change his camping-ground, as the locality where they then were was too stony and too thickly covered with wood for the comfort of the troops. Knowing that we had been put to great inconvenience the day before in making our way through the crowd of soldiers which followed him, he invited us to ride in his company. His Majesty always rose early, and his message found me in bed. At half-past 7 he came to our camp and took us by surprise as we were standing by our tent, which was being packed up. After the usual interchange of salutations, he bade us mount and follow him. Luckily, our mules were ready, otherwise he might have been vexed at our delay; and, indeed, had we not started when we did, we could not have joined him, for ten minutes afterwards there was such a rush in his rear, that the wonder was how some of the pedestrians escaped being trodden down under the hoofs of the moving mass of horses and mules, especially as the ground was stony, and the rain of the previous night had made travelling more difficult. The King rode in front in a most graceful style, followed by two pages, one carrying his shield and the other a gun and a telescope. Next in order was Râs I'ngădă, and then my companions and myself, Samuel riding at my side ready to translate anything which the King might wish to address to me. Behind us came the interpreters, the royal stud, and a number of courtiers; and behind them again the advancing multitude, each party anxious to press forward, and yet retaining their relative position to one another, and never coming into collision. The King, of course, and his immediate cortège pursued the regular path, but the bulk of the army had to make the best way they could over hill and dale, always managing, however, to reach the rendezvous in good time. Unavoidable delay occasionally arose whenever a defile had to be passed; nevertheless, every straggler was brought into camp before the hour for retiring to rest. There can be no doubt that one of the main secrets of Theodore's successes was the skill and energy with which he directed a march, joined with the rapidity of his movements, whereby he frequently took his enemies by surprise. He has been known to march at the head of fifty thousand troops, over the most difficult country, for a week together, at the rate of thirty miles a-day, barely halting to give his men time to take their meals: always stopping himself to see his army safely through, whenever they came upon a narrow ravine where only a few could march abreast. The sight on the day we travelled with him was truly picturesque and grand. In the rear of the King, who rode onward at the rate of four miles an hour, came the mighty host, extending backwards as far as the eye could reach, all pressing forward in his wake, halting when he halted, and turning to the right or left as he changed his course in either direction, without noise or confusion, as if the living masses were moved by machinery. After travelling for about three miles we came to a halt, when the King himself indicated to Samuel the spot where our tents were to be pitched. The locality selected for the encampment—which, like the last, was also called Bîfâta—was an open plain on the banks of the Abai, the principal stream of the Blue Nile. A report coming in shortly after our arrival that a party of rebels had been seen in the neighbourhood, all the mounted troops, led by the King in person, moved towards the spot. The inhabitants of this district having abandoned their dwellings and fields on hearing of the approach of the royal army, his Majesty ordered all the villages to be burned, and all the standing crops to be appropriated by the soldiery—an order no sooner issued than it was eagerly carried into execution, volumes of smoke almost immediately rising up in all directions, darkening the atmosphere for miles around. A number of antelopes, unable to get clear of the dense masses of human beings in their way, were caught in the line of march this morning. After vainly attempting to bound through the serried ranks which hemmed them in on all sides, the poor creatures ran round and round until they fell, utterly exhausted. A number of guinea-fowl and spur-fowl, entangled in the same net, shared a similar fate; of some of these the King sent us a present during the day. There was more rain this afternoon.

2nd.—Left at 8 this morning, and in a few minutes reached the Abai. After his Majesty had forded the river on foot and ascended the opposite bank, he called out to me and my companions not to dismount. We accordingly crossed it on our mules, but finding that the bank on the opposite side was slippery we preferred walking up it. In climbing, my foot slipped, and I should certainly have fallen into the stream, had not the King ran and seized me by the arm, saying, in Arabic, "Cheer up; don't be afraid," helping me at the same time to reach the top of the bank. Having heard so much of the King's want of thought for his troops, treating them—so some alleged—as if they were his enemies, I was astonished to witness his care of them on this occasion, especially of their wives and children. Finding that the bank was too precipitous to be safe, he ordered it to be levelled, and forthwith went to work himself, Râs I'ngădă and the other Chiefs of rank following his example, some with spears, some with iron-pointed staves, and others with sticks. As the ground was soft, a good road was soon made, and the troops began to march up. We fancied every moment that some helpless child or unprotected female must inevitably be trodden down in the river by the onward rush of men, laden mules and litter-bearers; but not a soul was hurt. The King was on the bank, calling out ever and anon to Râs I'ngădă, "Mind that poor child: carry him up and help his poor mother." My companions and I stood by, and turning to us again and again he bade us come near him that we might receive no injury in the press. In fact, with all his haughtiness and inordinate vanity, Theodore, when he chose, could be most condescending and kind, and few could excel him in the art of pleasing. But for the vicious temper with which these qualities were unfortunately associated, what a pattern man he would have been! He honoured me to-day by wearing one of my own shirts with which I had presented him, and caused all the other gifts which I had given him as from the Queen to be carried on either side of him, in order to show his people how highly he appreciated them. I had also given him two dozen of Curaçoa: these he had taken out of their cases, and committed each separate bottle to a courtier, who was ordered to carry it in a conspicuous style, much to our suppressed amusement. At 9·10 A.M. we halted in a valley called Dánka in the district of Gôta. The King had altered the line of march to-day, diverging towards the east—for what reason none appeared to know; it was surmised, however, that he intended going to Gójjam, as we were then on the way thither from Métcha. As soon as the camp was pitched, his Majesty took all the fighting men and went in quest of rebel bands, but the magic name of "Theodore" had scared them miles away, while common freebooters were equally wary not to come within his reach. We had another heavy fall of rain this evening, with vivid lightning and tremendous claps of thunder.

3rd.—We started again at 9·45 A.M. in the King's company, and had not proceeded far when his Majesty moved in the direction of Agówmĕdĕr—the last district we had passed through on our way to join the royal Court. Our course, hitherto, since quitting Dâmôt, had been towards the north-east; this morning it was due east, and in following it we had to return to yesterday's camping-ground, and owing to the circuitousness of the route were obliged to cross the Abai twice, but by much better fords than on the first occasion. The King conversed with me to-day on the subject of European warfare, and touched also on the civil war in the United States, our hostilities against the Ashantees, and our war with Russia. He inquired whether the Czar Nicholas had died a natural death, or had been executed by us for having waged war against England? On my replying that, now-a-days, the usual practice in Europe was for the vanquished party to sue for peace and make the best terms they could with the conquerors, he asked, who paid the expenses? That, I told him, depended on the origin of the war, and against whom it was carried on; but that, generally speaking, both parties bore their own costs. He then referred to the government of Madagascar, and asked how the French managed to have one of their own people made Prime Minister there? I told him that the French Government had nothing whatever to do with the appointment; that the person had been elected to that office by the Sovereign of the country, who was entirely independent of foreign control. He next inquired whether there was a country called Dahomy, the ruler of which annually sacrificed several hundred human beings in some religious ceremony, and, if so, why the Christian Powers did not put a stop to such barbarity? I told him that, as a general rule, the civilized nations of Europe abstained from direct interference with other States, allowing them to act as they pleased towards their own subjects. He then reverted to my Mission, and gave the following as his reasons for having delayed to answer me for so long a time:—"Ever since the death of Plowden and Yuhannês" [Bell], he said, "all the English and Franks who have visited my country have proved themselves wanting in sincerity, ill-mannered and ill-tempered. I therefore said within myself, I will not see this English Agent until I find out that he is of a different disposition to those who have already created a breach between me and my friend, the Queen of England. Your patience in waiting so long for an answer convinced me of your worth; and now that you have happily established a renewal of the amicable relations between my country and England, I wish you to convey to your Queen and to her Council my anxious desire to cultivate the friendship of the English—an object which I have been intent upon ever since I ascended the throne of Abyssinia."

It has been proved to me beyond doubt, that the King had not the slightest intention to allow me to enter his territories, until Wald-Salassê Gobazê, the Abyssinian merchant who called upon me at Massowah and promised on his return home to speak with Theodore on the subject of my Mission, arrived at Mágdala, where his Majesty was staying when my third letter reached him. He gave the King a favourable account of me, and assured him that my sole object in seeking a personal audience was to cultivate his friendship. Both this man and Aito Samuel urged him either to send me permission to go up, or to bid me return to Aden with her Majesty's letter. Another merchant was seated by the side of my friend, in the presence of the King, on that occasion, who remarked to the former, "Wy! wy! Gobazê, we may take it for granted that you have been bribed by the Franks to speak so highly in their favour;" whereupon Wald-Salassê Gobazê gave the interlocutor a slap in the face, saying, "Who is your father? Prove what you say." This little affair greatly amused the King, who burst into a fit of laughter and said, "Well done, Gobazê!"   He then ordered that uncourteous letter to be written and dispatched at once to the coast which I received at Massowah in August, 1866. All my messengers, some of whom had been waiting at his Court for an answer nearly a year, were sent back at the same time.

On entering Agówmĕdĕr, the King dispatched officers through the district to protect the villagers from being molested by the soldiery. It was amusing to see the alacrity with which those whom his Majesty addressed by name obeyed the summons. They exclaimed at once "Abiát! Abiát!" tumbled off their horses or mules, which they let go, and ran on foot towards the Sovereign. They well knew, in fact, that any delay might have cost them their heads. At 11·15 we reached that part of Agówmĕdĕr which is called Fagâta, where the King and the Mission encamped on a hill, the army taking up a position in the plain below, in regular order, by divisions, brigades and regiments.

Although the King had communicated to me his decision to release Consul Cameron and his fellow-captives on the 29th of January, and a letter of apology which he had addressed to Queen Victoria had been delivered over to me, nevertheless no steps had been taken hitherto towards carrying out his Majesty's promise respecting the captives. I had repeatedly pressed the subject upon Samuel, but not till to-day did the King appoint an officer to go and unfetter them and bring them to me from Mágdala, and I had barely dismounted when he sent me a message directing me to write to the Consul to acquaint him with his release and that of the other captives, requesting me at the same time to send one of my followers with the officer, in order that he might see that they were well taken care of on the road. Agafâri Gôlam, a chamberlain—the person selected by his Majesty for this duty—was ordered to proceed to Mágdala forthwith, and to conduct the captives to me, either at Korâta or Debra Tâbor. On his coming to me for further instructions, I simply requested him to make all speed to the fortress, to unfetter the captives at once, and to return with them as quickly as possible. After I had written the letter to Cameron, however, and both Agafâri Gôlam and my man were ready to start, the King countermanded the order for their immediate departure, on the plea that he had not yet fixed on the place where we were to meet. This intelligence was a great disappointment to me, as I felt most anxious that the poor fellows should be free from their chains with the least possible delay; but there was no help for it. If I importuned the King on the subject, he was just the man to act in an adverse direction.

4*th*.—The King sent to me this morning to say, that he wished to have a conversation with me before I left him for the Lake. I went to him at once, with Dr. Blanc and Lieutenant Prideaux. We found him standing in the open air, awaiting our arrival. Two carpets were then brought: one he occupied, and the other he ordered to be spread a few yards from him. My companions and I sat on one, in accordance with his directions. He began again about the ill-behaviour of the Mágdala captives, and related to me all his doings from childhood, when he attacked the Turks in the Soodân, declaring that he had defeated them, and would have utterly annihilated them had they not, as cowards, taken refuge behind a wall. He said that he had placed implicit confidence in me, and considered us three (Dr. Blanc, Lieutenant Prideaux and myself) like his own brothers. He asked me again to express to her Majesty the Queen and her Parliament the friendly sentiments he entertained towards them, and his love to the English in general. He hoped that in future he would prove himself worthy of their friendship and goodwill. He said, further, that he had done his best to cultivate the friendship of the Queen, and had gone so far as to order a number of curious articles to be made to send to her Majesty, which, although worthless in England, would serve to show the skill and customs of his people. " But, ah! " he said, "Mr. Cameron has spoiled the whole. However," he continued, "let the past be forgotten; and now I wish to make you a present of some Abyssinian curiosities, such as an Abyssinian saddle, shields and other articles, which I hope you will accept as a token of our friendship, though they will be a mean present from me to you."

The King then renewed his complaints against the Missionaries, and began by recounting the history of the Rev. Mr. Stern's disgrace. He said, that when the reverend gentleman visited Abyssinia the second time, he had treated him with the same consideration as formerly, and that after he (Mr. Stern) had stayed some time in the country, he applied for leave to depart, and a passport was supplied him in accordance with the rules of the country. Some time after that, he (the King) had to go on a war expedition; and while he was encamping in the neighbourhood of Góndar, it was reported to him that an European wished to see him. He was then inside a tent, and came out at once to see what the European required. On finding that Mr. Stern was the visitor, the King asked him what he wanted, and why he had intruded on his privacy without a Bâldărăbâ (Introducer), especially after he had given him permission to leave Abyssinia. On Mr. Stern giving him an unsatisfactory answer, the King turned towards two Abyssinian attendants whom Mr. Stern had taken with him, and asked them why they allowed their master to appear there without a Bâldărăbâ, contrary to the custom of the country.

The servants, the King alleged, gave him an impertinent answer, whereupon he ordered them to be beaten until they died; that when Mr. Stern saw what had taken place, he bit his finger, which seemed to the King a gesture of defiance, whereupon he ordered him also to be beaten; that while Mr. Stern was under the stick, a little book fell from his pocket, in which it was found that he (the King) was called a murderer; that Mr. Stern was then sent a prisoner to Góndar, and that as the King suspected him of having written more against him, he had all his papers seized and examined; that it was then further discovered that Mr. Stern had abused the King's mother, by alleging that she had sold *kósso*; that in the possession of Mr. Stern two letters were found, one addressed by Mrs. Flad to him, and the other from Mr. Rosenthal to a friend in England; that in Mrs. Flad's letter he found that she had ridiculed him by saying that he had been heard to boast that he was bent on fighting the English and French in their country. "On hearing this," the King continued, "I said to myself why do these people tell such falsehoods? Who am I, a weak and ignorant Ethiopian, to think of such an aggression, when the English and French might only send against me a few ships, and utterly destroy me? Had she not been a woman, I would have punished her."

With regard to Mr. Rosenthal, the King said that he had not been two months in the country before he professed to know all that took place in the royal "Ilfing" (this word, like the *Harím* in Turkey and the East, means the female establishment), and had given his opinion about different customs of the country, which even the Abyssinians themselves were quite ignorant of. He said that Mr. Rosenthal had written to his friends, ridiculing the habit the King had of using the name of the Holy Trinity in the beginning of every letter he wrote; that he (Mr. Rosenthal) had asserted, on good authority, that the British Government had laughed at him (the King) because Mr. Barroni, the late Consular Agent at Massowah, had written to them to say that his Majesty had invited him to come up and get drunk with him; and last, but not least, that Mr. Rosenthal had called his Majesty, in his letter, "King of the Wild Beasts."

It was quite ludicrous to witness the King's description of Mr. Rosenthal. Asking me first if I knew that gentleman, and receiving my reply in the negative, he raised his left hand about four feet from the ground, and said, "Why, the man who has designated me as King of the Wild Beasts does not stand higher than that!" Then, looking towards Samuel, who was translating at the time, he asked him if he had not correctly measured Mr. Rosenthal's height. "No, your Majesty," remarked the confidant; "you must raise your hand somewhat higher." The royal arm was then uplifted about half a foot; but Samuel said, "A little higher, your Majesty." Theodore accordingly condescended to allow the person indicated an additional six inches; but Samuel giving his opinion that Mr. Rosenthal was "a little taller" still, the King was rather annoyed, and said pettishly, "No, Samuel; I cannot raise my hand any higher." Then turning to me, he said, "I assure you, Mr. Rassam, that he is not taller than *that*." Mr. Rosenthal, however, had not given Theodore the obnoxious title; but, in writing to friends in England, conscious at the time that such a fact as the seizure of private letters by the King and his causing them to be read to him, had never yet been known to occur, alluded to him as "his Savage Majesty"—a designation which a malevolent translator had rendered into the more offensive epithet "King of the Wild Beasts." In his correspondence,'Mr. Rosenthal had also mentioned having heard that Mr. Barroni had written officially to the Foreign Office, stating that the King had invited him to go up to Abyssinia from Massowah, in order that they might get drunk together, and that such an expression, coming from a King, had made the clerks laugh. When this passage came to be translated into Amharic by the same malicious interpreter, he substituted the word "Government" for "clerks," thereby giving Theodore to understand that he had been made a subject of ridicule by the English Ministry. It was found afterwards that the whole story was a fabrication, as no such letter had been received at the Foreign Office.

The King got so excited while repeating these different grievances against Messrs. Stern and Rosenthal, that I began to fear something disastrous was coming. His face grew ashy pale and his hands shook, especially when I tried to soothe him. Before Aito Samuel began to translate my remarks, the King thought that I was defending the Missionaries, because I had used the Arabic word *Masákin*, the literal meaning of which is "poor," but it is also commonly used to express sympathy. (I had pleaded, on behalf of the Missionaries, who are all styled "Priests" in Abyssinia, "Why should his Majesty, who is a great Sovereign, be vexed at what poor priests may say?") On hearing my reply, however, Theodore smiled, and said, "I do not care about the past, but must only think of the friendship of you three."

It may be asked, how the King became aware of the existence of the letters and books above referred to, and how they were translated to him? I can answer these questions in a few words. Although, since the late Expedition under

Sir Robert Napier to Mágdala, all Europeans who were located there, whether in chains, or persons in the King's employ, are called "captives," there were individuals among them who had gone to Abyssinia as mere adventurers—men who did not care a straw what evil befel the rest, provided that they were safe, and could bask for a time in the sunshine of the royal favour. So intense was party hatred among some of them, that all probity and all fear of God were set aside, whenever either had a chance of doing the other an ill turn—no matter if it involved the risk of the antagonist's life. When the documents in question were found, two Abyssinians who knew English refused to read them, on the plea that they could not decipher the handwriting; but an European was forthcoming to undertake the treacherous task. I believe, however, that the King's mind had been previously poisoned against the Rev. Mr. Stern; for his 'Wanderings among the Falashas' had never been seen by any Abyssinian before it was read by M. Bardel. It is, moreover, singular, and, to say the least, suspicious, that of all the books which were seized on the occasion, the King should have lighted upon that particular volume, and that out of all its contents the obnoxious passage relating to his maternal origin should have fallen under his special notice. It was a common practice, when two contending European parties wished to make matters up, to cast the blame of their antecedent differences upon some Abyssinian in authority, mutually agreeing, it would seem, to ignore the source from whence the native must have derived the information which he communicated to the King.

When the King had somewhat cooled down, he said he wished me to get ready to leave the camp early next morning, and left it with me to choose my resting-place, until

Consul Cameron and his party joined me, observing that I might stay either at Koráta or Debra Tâbor; but I begged his Majesty to choose the locality himself. It was then agreed that Koráta should be our head-quarters, from whence we might visit Debra Tâbor and other places.

We had sat nearly two hours in the sun, and the King was so excited all the time that he forgot to send for umbrellas for us, as he generally did. Before we were dismissed, the King told me that Mr. Plowden had spoken to him about a treaty which he had made with Râs 'Ali; and, moreover, that he had wished to hoist the English flag at Góndar, and that to these proposals his Majesty had replied: "What! do you consider me like that menial servant, Râs 'Ali, that you speak to me in this way? Can a renegade Galla slave enter into agreements with foreign nations on behalf of Emperors?" Plowden, he remarked, had not reverted to the matter again; but, if I wished, he would make a regular treaty with me. My answer to this was, that I was not sent by the British Government to make a treaty with his Majesty; that such a mission required authority and particular instructions; nevertheless, I felt convinced that when I returned to England, and represented to her Majesty's Government how well-disposed he was towards it, due consideration would be given to all his Majesty's propositions. On leaving he said to me, "I wish you to tell your Queen that I consider her too great a personage for me to communicate with; but as I learn she has a great number of Governors in India, who are her servants, I hope she will appoint one of them to correspond with me, because I consider myself only on equality with those rulers, and it will also be more convenient for us both, India being nearer my country than England."

When I took leave, I asked the King to appoint a trustworthy agent to be always with me, to assist in my requirements, and also to facilitate my communication with him, as we were now to be some distance from each other. He inquired whether I would like to have Aito Samuel. I replied, that whoever his Majesty liked and trusted, him I would prefer. He smiled and said, "*I'sh-shi;* take Aito Samuel, because I both love and trust him."

A short time after I had left the King, he sent me the following polite letter, with a present of muskets and pistols, and the sum of 5,000 dollars was ordered to be supplied to me on my way to Korâta:—

"In the name of the Father, and of the Son, and of the Holy Ghost—one God.   Amen.

"The servant of God, and His created being, the son of David, the son of Solomon, the King of kings, Theodorus.

"To the servant of Her whom God has exalted above all sovereigns, and glorified above all princes and peoples, and made the Defender of the Christian faith, and the succour of the poor and oppressed, Hormuzd Rassam, who is, by the power of God, endowed with wisdom and a benevolent heart.

"Be it known to you that by your favour [*i. e.*, by the favour of the English] I have abundance of fire-arms. I send you one single-barrelled and four double-barrelled muskets, and five single-barrelled pistols; and if besides these you require more to give to persons who ask you for them, by the power of God I will supply you with them. I am the Sovereign of my country, and you are the servant of the Queen, my friend, and I should feel hurt if any one asked you for anything that you refused him. I do not do this because you cannot afford to make such presents; but, having been sent in haste, you had no time to bring such things. When you arrive at your destination, whatever arms or other articles you require, Aito Samuel, the agent appointed between you and myself, will supply them.

"Between this and Korâta, Aito Samuel will also supply you with 5,000 dollars, to be spent in any way you like, except in a manner unpleasing to God.

"When the men [prisoners] shall be delivered to you, if God permit, I will come and wish you farewell; but if I am not able to come to you in person, I will give orders to have you sent to the frontier in safety and honour."

This letter put me in an awkward position, having been given to understand that I must not refuse the King's munificent gift, especially after he had accepted the presents which I had made him on the part of her Majesty and from myself; that such a course might upset the good understanding I had established with the King, and lead to disastrous consequences. On that score, I felt compelled to accept the presents, and I sent to notify the same to his Majesty.

The passage about my spending the money in any way I liked, " except in a manner unpleasing to God," was explained to me by different Abyssinians to mean, that I ought not to give any of it to the donor's European enemies who were coming from Mágdala, or allow any of the rebels to benefit by it. For my own part, I believe the King meant that I should not pay any of his courtiers to betray his secrets. The same expression, as will be seen farther on, occurs in another of the King's letters to me, dated the 28th of February, and confirms that idea.

In accordance with the rules of the service, I at once credited Government with the sum mentioned, and in June of the same year it was publicly known in England that I had accepted the present on the public account. Even that notification, however, did not restrain adverse criticisms on my conduct in the matter from certain irresponsible individuals at home, who, it may be, measured my corn in their own bushel.

CHAPTER XII.

OVER LAKE TÂNA TO KORÂTA.

Theodore is "asleep"—Departure from the Royal Camp—Visit from Abyssinian Chiefs—Entertainment by the Governor of Wandígé—Bulrush Canoes—The Abyssinians relish our cookery—Abyssinian Fasts—Communicants—The Author shoots a Hippopotamus—The Waitos—We embark on the Lake—The Island of Dák—How reduced by Theodore—A canoe race—Reception of the Mission at Korâta—A native Joan of Arc—Sanctity of Korâta—Church of Waldt-Máryam—Toleration of the Abyssinians—The Mission quarters at Korâta.

It was reported to me this afternoon, 6th of February, that the King was in an awful mood—in fact, that he was "asleep." No one had approached him during the previous night, and although it had been decided that my companions and I should start for the Lake early the following morning, owing to his Majesty having "overslept himself" we did not get away before one in the afternoon. Aito Samuel and Agafâri Gôlam accompanied us by order of the King, as did also our old Chálga escort and other Chiefs of Agówmĕdĕr. Râs I'ngădă had also been directed to escort us a short distance from the camp, but as the order did not reach him till long after we had set out, he was obliged to follow with fifty mounted troopers a distance of five miles, that he might be able to tell the King that he had seen us off. We reached Zûgda at 2·30 P.M., where we halted for the night.

7th.—Samuel and Agafâri Gôlam having some business to transact at Zûgda for the King, we spent the day there.

An Abyssinian merchant called upon me, who informed me that he was going to Góndar. I availed myself of his proffered services to send a note through him to the Resident at Aden, reporting the progress of the Mission.

8th.—Received a polite message which the King sent me by the old Governor of Góndar. A number of Chiefs from Agówmĕdĕr and Bagámĕdĕr called on me this morning—introduced, of course, by Samuel, the King's Bâldărăbâ. This was the first visit I had received from district or local Chiefs. His Majesty having given orders that no Abyssinian was to approach me unless he was perfectly clean and well-dressed, all the Chiefs came habited in grand style, with fine silk shirts and new *shámmas*—the latter the common robe of the country—girt round the loins, in token of their inferiority to the Sovereign's guest.

Left Zûgda at 10·45 A.M., crossed the Kilté river at noon, and after a rest in the shade of a tree reached Nafâsa at 2·15 P.M. Started again the following day at 10·45 A.M., but as the escort were afraid that the carriers would not be able to travel far, they ordered a halt at Yasmâla at 12·45 P.M., on the southern side of which we encamped. There is an extensive marsh about half a mile from the village which swarmed with snipe. I managed to bag a few, and Lij Tasámma shot two ducks, which he presented to us.

10th.—Left Yasmâla at 9·30 A.M. and passed Dankôra at 11. As it was the King's wish that we should proceed from Wandígê to Korâta by water, we diverged from Lake Dámbĕa two miles below Kanôha and reached Adîna, situated on the north-western extremity of the Lake, at 2 P.M. Owing to the length of the day's march, our carriers did not arrive till after dusk. Balambarâs Gabra-Mádhanê-'Âlam, the Governor of Wandígê, and cousin to Lij Tasámma, came out to meet us about a mile from Farôhê. After we had seated ourselves in the shade of a thicket, which was festooned on all sides with the lovely flowers of a luxuriant creeper, the Balambarâs set some boiled beef, stewed fish, and excellent *téf* bread before us, and being hungry we enjoyed the repast exceedingly. In the evening he brought us a supply of green chick-peas, beans and fish. The father of this Balambarâs was a great favourite with the King, whose affection for him was so strong that he used to call him "father." He was one of those influential Chiefs who had superintended the education of Theodore, and had fought by his side in many a battle. On one occasion, when his Majesty was in pursuit of a formidable enemy, and was about to relinquish the chase, deeming his antagonist too strong for him, the father of this young Chief drew his sword and threatened to hamstring the King's horse, unless he persisted in the adventure and emboldened his adherents by his example. When the old man died, Theodore is said to have mourned for him two whole days. His son, whom the King styles a "good-for-nothing vagabond," because he was given to falling in love with every pretty girl he met, was raised to his present post for his father's sake. He rebelled against his Sovereign at the beginning of 1868.

11th.—As the requisite number of canoes had not been brought from Korâta and the island of Dák, we were obliged to spend the day at Adîna. The Balambarâs took me out in the afternoon to try one of the canoes in which we were to cross the Lake. It was by no means comfortable. These vessels are made of bulrushes, in the centre of which is a heap of the same material piled up so high that the passenger, who is forced to sit upon it in a crouching position, must be careful to maintain his equilibrium, otherwise he is sure of a ducking. The rower sits at the prow—if I may use the expression—holding a long reed in his hand, which he plunges deep into the water, alternately on the right side and on the left. (Perhaps the ships made of bulrushes, mentioned by Isaiah as having carried ambassadors to Egypt, were constructed in a similar style.) These canoes are very safe, it being next to impossible for them to sink when properly laden, and they never upset so long as the cargo, whatever it may chance to be, is kept steady. Some carry three passengers and as many rowers; but, for dispatch, the best trim is two rowers in front, with only one passenger seated in the hull. One drawback to this mode of conveyance is, that the passengers get thoroughly drenched by the splash from the sculls, unless they take the precaution of being well covered during the passage. A cow-hide is the usual native substitute for a Mackintosh.

Wäizero Denké, Lij Tasámma's mother, called this evening, bringing me an Abyssinian dinner, of which, to gratify the old lady, I was constrained to taste. As Samuel and the rest of the royal escort had expressed a wish to try some of our cookery, and to-morrow being the beginning of the Abyssinian Lent, after which they are forbidden to eat meat for fifty days, I ordered a mixed European and Turkish dinner to be prepared for them, including a large dish of *pilau*. To prove how much they had enjoyed it, they consumed every atom. I heard afterwards that our guests on this occasion acquired thenceforward a disrelish for *Brundo* and Abyssinian dishes generally; Samuel especially always preferred ours, whenever he could get them. On a subsequent occasion, at Mágdala, several native ladies expressed a similar desire to taste our *cuisine*, and with the exception of any dish containing custard — which they abominated — they ate

heartily of all that my butler sent them.   Open tarts,
particularly when made of apricot jam, were most liked by
the ladies and children; the men preferred tipsy-pudding,
provided the flavour of eggs was not perceptible.   The only
Abyssinian dish which one accustomed to an European diet
can eat with relish is a curried fowl, to which hard-boiled
eggs are added.   Curried beef or mutton—a common native
dish—is also passable, when eaten with thin *téf* bread.
Greens are simply stewed in butter—the only dish which is
not made pungent with their red-pepper paste; but as these
are generally eaten in conjunction with the hot dishes above-
mentioned, the absence of the caustic condiment is not missed.
The compliment which I used to pay the Abyssinian ladies
at Mágdala in sending them samples of our dinners, was
always reciprocated on their part, and in course of time we
began to like the stews, with the accompaniment of fine
white *téf* bread, which they sent us, preferring them to the
lean beef and mutton, which, when simply roasted in our
style, were most insipid.

12th.—Lij Tasámma and the rest of our old escort left us
to return to their respective posts, but as the King had given
orders that they should see our mules and horses safely conveyed round the Lake to Koráta, they undertook the charge
of them as far as Dámbĕa.

This being the first day of a very long fast, the Abyssinians
looked rather downcast.   Unlike all other communities both
in the East and West, who reckon Lent from Ash-Wed-
nesday, the Abyssinian Church begins that season to-day,
Monday.   With the exception, however, of this prolonged
fast, and the Wednesdays and Fridays throughout the year,
the Abyssinians generally are by no means rigid in their
observance of the other days whereon the eating of meat is

prohibited, which happen to be as numerous as those on which no such restriction is placed. Fish is permissible on fast-days, but a strict communicant never allows himself that indulgence. No man having more than one wife, and no woman being other than the sole wife of her husband, whose marriage was duly solemnized in the church, can partake of the Holy Communion. All priests and monks, however, who are expected to lead exemplary lives, and all children, are admitted as communicants. Abyssinians, on the whole, are not bigoted, and are generally ready to concede anything which is proved to them out of the Sacred Scriptures, even when it is opposed to the teaching of their priests, whom they are in the habit of styling " ignorant." Of late years the King has given up fasting in Lent, and intimated to his soldiers that they were at perfect liberty to follow the dictates of their own consciences in such matters. The rule is, that on fast-days nothing whatever must be eaten before one o'clock in the afternoon; but I did not meet with many who adhered to the restriction.

Incidents occurring on our journey have led me to the foregoing digression on two or three religious usages prevailing in the country.

The Governor informed me this morning that several hippopotami were sunning themselves near the beach, not far from our camp. Prideaux, Samuel and I accordingly accompanied him to the spot indicated. We had not proceeded a mile when we saw three huge beasts, standing up to the neck in water, evidently dozing, since we approached to within two hundred yards without their seeming to notice us. I was carrying an Enfield rifle, which I discharged, aiming at the head of one of the trio. A tremendous commotion in the water immediately succeeded. Being quite a novice in such sport, I concluded that the game had dived beneath the surface on hearing the report of the gun ; 'but a *Waito*, whose occupation it is to hunt these animals on the Lake, began capering about, and affirmed that one of them was hit, as it was lying on its back and "swallowing water." I found afterwards that the man's inference was correct, for, when wounded, these monsters, instead of making for the shore, dive in a state of stupefaction, and are suffocated. As soon as the Waitos heard—there were many of them at hand—that there was the chance of a feast in store for them, they volunteered to fetch the carcass on shore. At this stage of the proceedings, I certainly thought that the men were joking, but one of them soon convinced me to the contrary, for, jumping out of his canoe, and standing upon what appeared to be a firm substance, he exclaimed "Here is the Gumârê!" Ten of their number managed to roll the huge mass into a deep basin formed by two rocks projecting into the Lake, and with the assistance of a score more hands it was hauled into shallow water, where we had a good view of its proportions. The Waitos were delighted on my telling them that they might have the body, provided they gave me the tusks and a part of the hide. The carcass measured 12 feet 9 inches round the body, 11 feet 1 inch from the tail to the nostrils, and 6 feet $1\frac{1}{2}$ inch round the jaws. The bullet had barely fractured the skull, without penetrating through the bone. Four arrows were found in different parts of the body, two of which were recognized by a couple of the fishermen as severally belonging to them. There was more than an inch of fat between the skin and the flesh, and the skin itself was nearly of the same thickness, some parts of it so hard as to be almost impervious to a bullet. The teeth were twelve in number, the largest measuring eight inches outside the jaw.

The whips, called "kûrbâshes" in the East, are made out
of the hide, and a clever Waito manufactured upwards of
fifty, of different shapes and sizes, from that of the strange
beast which I had most unexpectedly shot. The softer parts
of the hide are as ductile as wax, and may be readily moulded
into any form, but, on being exposed to dry, they become
exceedingly tough and indurated. The Waitos attack the
hippopotamus with poisoned arrows, which they discharge
from their canoes. Sometimes the poison does not take effect
for a week, when the wounded animal repairs to shallow
water to die. It is a recognized point of honour with the
Waitos inhabiting the southern and western shores of the Lake,
that the carcass should be made over to those who claim the
arrows, each tribe having its own particular arrows. When
two fresh arrows are found in the body, the booty is divided
equally between the owners of the same. The Waitos are
Mussulmans of the Mâliky sect, and although Mohamme-
danism recognizes no castes among its adherents, nevertheless
these people, who subsist upon the flesh of the hippopotamus,
are looked down upon by their co-religionists, who consider
it a degradation to associate with them. A few among them
cultivate a little grain, but the flesh of the hippopotamus
forms their staple food. I was assured by those to whom I
gave it, that the carcass of the one I had shot would support
fifty families for a week. I was unable to obtain any satisfactory account of the origin of this peculiar people. It is
just possible, however, that there may be some relationship
between them and the *Wâtos*, a tribe of Gallas inhabiting the
banks of the Hawâsh, south of Shoa, who are also said to live
on the flesh of the hippopotamus.

We had been told that 120 canoes would be ready for transporting ourselves and our baggage across the Lake ; but this

morning only half that number was forthcoming. However, as our escort were against any further delay, we started at eight o'clock, after no end of bustle and worry, taking an easterly direction towards the island of Dák. As the wherry in which Agafâri Gôlam and I had embarked was well paddled by some of our Waito friends of yesterday, we reached Dák at 1·15 P.M., and after coasting along the island for about an hour entered the creek called Sarmoutsh, situated at its southern extremity. The island, which is about ten miles in circumference, contains four villages, with a church attached to each. There are two other islets to the south, and another towards the east, which rises much higher above the Lake. In the latter there is an old church, the monks attached to which never leave their isolated abode, and live exclusively on the fruits of their own husbandry. The Dákites are renowned for bravery both by sea and land, and are said to have resisted every attempt to coerce them until Theodore reduced them in the following characteristic manner. He was in pursuit, it appears, of a refractory Chief under Râs 'Ali, who had taken refuge on the island. In less than twenty-four hours he had two hundred canoes constructed, in which he suddenly appeared off the place with five hundred chosen warriors. The inhabitants, deeming their position secure from an attack by water, were taken by surprise. In directing the mode of assault, Theodore, then Dajjâj Kâsa, telling his men that death would be preferable to the disgrace of failure, ordered them to secure their spears by a rope tied round the waist, whereby they would be able to wield their weapons freely, and be in no danger of losing them; for that if they lost them, being surrounded by the Lake on all sides, they would inevitably be slaughtered, there being no succour at hand. He chose the south-western corner of the island for the assault, where there was no cover for the enemy. The landing was bravely contested, but no sooner had the dreaded Kâsa touched the shore than a general panic seized the defenders, and before the day was over the victor had executed those whom he considered worthy of death, amnestied the remainder, and returned to the mainland in greater triumph than ever. His star was then in the ascendant, and every fresh feat of valour exalted him in the estimation of his devoted adherents.

My companions and Samuel did not arrive till 4·10 P.M., when we took up our quarters for the night in the open air.

As the islanders had been ordered to contribute 1,000 dollars towards the 5,000 which the King had ordered Aito Samuel to give me, they came in the evening to say that they had no money, but offered to hand me over the chalice and some gold crosses belonging to the church, in lieu of cash payment. I told them that I had never asked the King for the money, nor was I in want of it; and I declined all interference in the matter. I then remonstrated with Aito Samuel on the impropriety of the proceeding, and told him once for all that I was not in need of money, and that I should be disgraced in our country if I received such a gift. My protest had the desired effect, for Aito Samuel listened to me at once, and told the inhabitants of Dák that they might retain their sacred vessels.

14*th*.—Embarked at 6·15 A.M. Our course was south-easterly to Korâta, which we reached a little before noon. Canoes are generally propelled at the rate of three miles an hour; but our paddlers must have made at least four to-day, in the hope of winning a prize of ten dollars which I had promised to the foremost in the race. Having two stalwart Waitos in my canoe, we might have easily distanced the rest by a mile, had we not been obliged to wait for the escort to join us when we approached the land. In accordance with orders from the King, the two principal merchants of the place, Aito Kâsa and Aito Wandé—the latter, as mentioned at page 230, the person on whom Theodore had bestowed Lij Tasámma's sister, one of his favourite concubines—came out in a wherry to meet us about a mile from the shore, clad in gorgeous habiliments. After an interchange of civilities, we followed them to a small plateau which rises above the Lake about two miles to the south of the town, where upwards of a hundred ecclesiastics from the neighbourhood were assembled to welcome us, his Majesty having directed the clergy to receive me with royal honours, and to take care that their persons and garments were scrupulously clean. They were in full canonicals, and greeted us with prayers and psalmody, conducting us with the same accompaniments to a tent which had been erected for the occasion, a few yards from our landing-place. The glitter of the pageant was heightened by a grand display of crosses, croziers, mitres, church umbrellas, David's-harps and censers, which were borne aloft in the procession. After spending a short time witnessing their religious dances, and listening to their discordant chants, the benediction was pronounced, and the Lord's Prayer wound up the service, when we accompanied the merchants to their dwellings on mules provided for our use. Korâta rejoices in a patron saint of great celebrity—a native Joan of Arc, in fact—called Waldt-Máryam. She was a resident nun when a formidable Galla Chief, who had overrun a great part of the country, appeared before Korâta. She encouraged her townsmen to defend the place, and their valour combined with her powerful intercessions availed to withstand the repeated assaults of the infidel hosts, who were eventually obliged to retreat with great loss. Since that time the town has been placed under her special patronage, and to show their veneration for the locality Abyssinians generally dismount on approaching it, and walk on foot through the streets. Although Samuel had ridiculed the tradition to me, and intimated that not being a worshipper of saints I was at perfect liberty to ride through the town, I declined to do so just then, for two reasons: first, because I did not wish to excite the prejudices of the people against the Mission; and secondly, having been led to understand that the King himself was in the habit of respecting the local superstition, I did not deem it prudent to assume any appearance of superiority to his Majesty. Soon afterwards, however, when my visits to the town became frequent, I was obliged to forego the practice; but the residents were polite enough to assure me that, being a stranger, and, moreover, not a communicant in the Abyssinian Church, Waldt-Máryam would not be offended by my riding over the hallowed ground. How little regard Theodore really entertained for such legends was proved by his conduct eighteen months later, when he not only rode into the town, but sacked it, and desecrated the temple dedicated to the patron saint. The church of Waldt-Máryam has been a fine structure—the best of the kind I have seen in Abyssinia. Noticing, on my frequent visits to witness the services, that the veil before the sanctuary was made of a very common material, which was awkwardly lifted up by a reed whenever the officiating priests administered the Eucharist to the communicants, I had a better one made for them, and fixed it in such a way that it could be readily opened or closed by barely pulling a rope. This most simple mechanical contrivance was the wonder of the neighbourhood for some time. Even the King had heard of it, and when the arch-priest, who was also the local Governor, visited the Court, his Majesty told him that such an act on my part merited their special prayers—an attention which the clergy never omitted whenever I was present. As I have mentioned before, the Abyssinians in general are not bigoted, provided nothing is said against the worship of saints and angels. The priests at Korâta carried their toleration so far that they allowed Mr. Waldmeier to preach in the church from the *Más-haf-Kedús*, the Sacred Scriptures.

On our first arrival at Korâta we were taken to Aito Wandé's house, which was considered the best in the place; but finding that it was too small for our whole party, I resigned it to my companions, and took up my quarters in the adjoining house, belonging to Aito Kâsa; Aito Samuel and Agafâri Gôlam locating themselves in a third, a short distance from us. Aito Wandé had prepared an Abyssinian luncheon for us, consisting of *téf* bread and stewed fish. A plentiful supply of strong mead was also provided, which our servants and followers were allowed to partake of without any restriction as to quantity, and although the drinking-bout lasted for two hours I did not notice a single case of intoxication. The dwellings of our hospitable entertainers are square, built of stone and mud covered with cement; the windows and doors, though clumsily made, are well fitted to the walls. The conical roofs, however, like all other Abyssinian houses, are covered with grass thatch, beautifully finished, and surmounted with an apex of neatly-designed pottery. The floors of the rooms were well carpeted, and we were accommodated with large bedsteads, covered with damask. These, however, we soon discovered, to our great discomfort, were infested with vermin.

15th.—The remainder of our baggage did not arrive from

Wandígê until this afternoon. Finding that our stay in this neighbourhood might be prolonged for some time, I spoke to Aito Samuel about relinquishing the rations which the poor peasants were expected to supply us with, suggesting that we should pay for everything we wanted, more especially as the King had presented me with five thousand dollars, a sum quite ample to meet all our requirements. I was glad to find that neither Samuel nor the local Chiefs demurred to this proposition; and thenceforward every article obtained was paid for in ready money.

What we most ardently longed for now, was to hear of the release of the Mágdala captives, and to welcome them at Korâta.

END OF VOL. I.

LONDON: PRINTED BY WILLIAM CLOWES AND SONS, DUKE STREET, STAMFORD STREET,
AND CHARING CROSS.

MR. MURRAY'S

GENERAL LIST OF WORKS.

ALBERT'S (PRINCE) SPEECHES AND ADDRESSES ON PUBLIC OCCASIONS; with an Introduction giving some Outlines of his Character. Portrait. 8vo. 10s. 6d.; or *Popular Edition.* Portrait. Fcap. 8vo. 1s.

ABBOTT'S (REV. J.) Philip Musgrave; or, Memoirs of a Church of England Missionary in the North American Colonies. Post 8vo. 2s.

ABERCROMBIE'S (JOHN) Enquiries concerning the Intellectual Powers and the Investigation of Truth. 14th *Edition.* Fcap. 8vo. 6s. 6d.

———————————— Philosophy of the Moral Feelings. 13th *Edition.* Fcap. 8vo. 4s.

ACLAND'S (REV. CHARLES) Popular Account of the Manners and Customs of India. Post 8vo. 2s.

ÆSOP'S FABLES. A New Translation. With Historical Preface. By Rev. THOMAS JAMES. With 100 Woodcuts, by TENNIEL and WOLF. 60th *Thousand.* Post 8vo. 2s. 6d.

AGRICULTURAL (THE ROYAL) SOCIETY'S JOURNAL. 8vo. *Published half-yearly.*

AIDS TO FAITH: a Series of Theological Essays. By various Writers. Edited by WILLIAM THOMSON, D.D., Archbishop of York. 8vo. 9s.

AMBER-WITCH (THE). A most interesting Trial for Witch- craft. Translated from the German by LADY DUFF GORDON. Post 8vo. 2s.

ARCHITECTURE OF AHMEDABAD, with Historical Sketch and Architectural Notes by T. C. HOPE, and JAMES FERGUSSON. With Maps, Photographs, and Woodcuts. 4to. 5l. 5s.

———————————— BEJAPOOR, with Historical Sketch and Architectural Essay by Col. MEADOWS TAYLOR and JAS. FERGUSSON. With Maps, Photographs, and Woodcuts. Folio. 10l. 10s.

———————————— DHARWAR and MYSORE. With Historical Sketch and Architectural Essay by Col. MEADOWS TAYLOR and JAS. FERGUSSON. With Maps, Photographs, and Woodcuts. Folio. 12l. 12s.

ARMY LIST (THE). *Published Monthly by Authority.* 18mo. 1s. 6d.

ARTHUR'S (LITTLE) History of England. By LADY CALLCOTT. *New Edition, continued to* 1862. Woodcuts. Fcap. 8vo. 2s. 6d.

ATKINSON'S (MRS.) Recollections of Tartar Steppes and their Inhabitants. Illustrations. Post 8vo. 12s.

AUNT IDA'S Walks and Talks; a Story Book for Children. By a LADY. Woodcuts. 16mo. 5s.

B

AUSTIN'S (JOHN) LECTURES ON JURISPRUDENCE; or, the Philosophy of Positive Law. 3 Vols. 8vo. 39s.

———— (SARAH) Fragments from German Prose Writers. With Biographical Notes. Post 8vo. 10s.

ADMIRALTY PUBLICATIONS; Issued by direction of the Lords Commissioners of the Admiralty:—

A MANUAL OF SCIENTIFIC ENQUIRY, for the Use of Travellers. Edited by Sir JOHN F. HERSCHEL, and Rev. ROBERT MAIN, M.A. *Third Edition*. Woodcuts. Post 8vo. 9s.

AIRY'S ASTRONOMICAL OBSERVATIONS MADE AT GREENWICH. 1836 to 1847. Royal 4to. 50s. each.

———— ASTRONOMICAL RESULTS. 1848 to 1858. 4to. 8s. each.

———— APPENDICES TO THE ASTRONOMICAL OBSERVATIONS.

1836.—I. Bessel's Refraction Tables.
   II. Tables for converting Errors of R.A. and N.P.D. } 8s.
     into Errors of Longitude and Ecliptic P.D.
1837.—I. Logarithms of Sines and Cosines to every Ten } 8s.
     Seconds of Time.
   II. Table for converting Sidereal into Mean Solar Time. }
1842.—Catalogue of 1439 Stars. 8s.
1845.—Longitude of Valentia. 8s.
1847.—Twelve Years' Catalogue of Stars. 14s.
1851.—Maskelyne's Ledger of Stars. 6s.
1852.—I. Description of the Transit Circle. 5s.
   II. Regulations of the Royal Observatory. 2s.
1853.—Bessel's Refraction Tables. 8s.
1854.—I. Description of the Zenith Tube. 3s.
   II. Six Years' Catalogue of Stars. 10s.
1856.—Description of the Galvanic Apparatus at Greenwich Observatory. 8s.
1862.—I. Seven Years' Catalogue of Stars. 10s.
   II. Plan of the Building and Ground of the Royal Ob- } 3s.
     servatory, Greenwich.
   III. Longitude of Valentia.

———— MAGNETICAL AND METEOROLOGICAL OBSERVATIONS. 1840 to 1847. Royal 4to. 50s. each.

———— ASTRONOMICAL, MAGNETICAL, AND METEOROLOGICAL OBSERVATIONS, 1848 to 1864. Royal 4to. 50s. each.

———— ASTRONOMICAL RESULTS. 1848 to 1864. 4to.

———— MAGNETICAL AND METEOROLOGICAL RESULTS. 1848 to 1864. 4to. 8s. each.

———— REDUCTION OF THE OBSERVATIONS OF PLANETS. 1750 to 1830. Royal 4to. 50s.

———————————————— LUNAR OBSERVATIONS. 1750 to 1830. 2 Vols. Royal 4to. 50s. each.

———————————————— 1831 to 1851. 4to. 20s.

BERNOULLI'S SEXCENTENARY TABLE. *London*, 1779. 4to.

BESSEL'S AUXILIARY TABLES FOR HIS METHOD OF CLEARING LUNAR DISTANCES. 8vo.

————FUNDAMENTA ASTRONOMIÆ: *Regiomontii*, 1818. Folio. 60s.

BIRD'S METHOD OF CONSTRUCTING MURAL QUADRANTS. *London*, 1768. 4to. 2s. 6d.

———— METHOD OF DIVIDING ASTRONOMICAL INSTRUMENTS. *London*, 1767. 4to. 2s. 6d.

COOK, KING, AND BAYLY'S ASTRONOMICAL OBSERVATIONS *London*, 1782. 4to. 21s.

ADMIRALTY PUBLICATIONS—*continued.*

ENCKE'S BERLINER JAHRBUCH, for 1830. *Berlin*, 1828. 8vo. 9s.

GROOMBRIDGE'S CATALOGUE OF CIRCUMPOLAR STARS. 4to. 10s.

HANSEN'S TABLES DE LA LUNE. 4to. 20s.

HARRISON'S PRINCIPLES OF HIS TIME-KEEPER. PLATES. 1797. 4to. 5s.

HUTTON'S TABLES OF THE PRODUCTS AND POWERS OF NUMBERS. 1781. Folio. 7s. 6d.

LAX'S TABLES FOR FINDING THE LATITUDE AND LONGI-TUDE. 1821. 8vo. 10s.

LUNAR OBSERVATIONS at GREENWICH. 1783 to 1819. Compared with the Tables, 1821. 4to. 7s. 6d.

MASKELYNE'S ACCOUNT OF THE GOING OF HARRISON'S WATCH. 1767. 4to. 2s. 6d.

MAYER'S DISTANCES of the MOON'S CENTRE from the PLANETS. 1822, 3s.; 1823, 4s. 6d. 1824 to 1835, 8vo. 4s. each.

———— THEORIA LUNÆ JUXTA SYSTEMA NEWTONIANUM. 4to. 2s. 6d.

———— TABULÆ MOTUUM SOLIS ET LUNÆ. 1770. 4to. 5s.

———— ASTRONOMICAL OBSERVATIONS MADE AT GOT-TINGEN, from 1756 to 1761. 1826. Folio. 7s. 6d.

NAUTICAL ALMANACS, from 1767 to 1870. 8vo. 2s. 6d. each.

———— SELECTIONS FROM THE ADDITIONS up to 1812. 8vo. 5s. 1834-54. 8vo. 5s.

———— SUPPLEMENTS, 1828 to 1833, 1837 and 1838. 8vo. 2s. each.

———— TABLE requisite to be used with the N.A. 1781. 8vo. 5s.

POND'S ASTRONOMICAL OBSERVATIONS. 1811 to 1835. 4to. 21s. each.

RAMSDEN'S ENGINE for DIVIDING MATHEMATICAL INSTRUMENTS. 4to. 5s.

———— ENGINE for DIVIDING STRAIGHT LINES. 4to. 5s.

SABINE'S PENDULUM EXPERIMENTS to DETERMINE THE FIGURE OF THE EARTH. 1825. 4to. 40s.

SHEPHERD'S TABLES for CORRECTING LUNAR DISTANCES. 1772. Royal 4to. 21s.

———— TABLES, GENERAL, of the MOON'S DISTANCE from the SUN, and 10 STARS. 1787. Folio. 5s. 6d.

TAYLOR'S SEXAGESIMAL TABLE. 1780. 4to. 15s.

———— TABLES OF LOGARITHMS. 4to. 3l.

TIARK'S ASTRONOMICAL OBSERVATIONS for the LONGITUDE of MADEIRA. 1822. 4to. 5s.

———— CHRONOMETRICAL OBSERVATIONS for DIFFERENCE of LONGITUDE between DOVER, PORTSMOUTH, and FALMOUTH. 1823. 4to. 5s.

VENUS and JUPITER: OBSERVATIONS of, compared with the TABLES. *London*, 1822. 4to. 2s.

WALES' AND BAYLY'S ASTRONOMICAL OBSERVATIONS. 1777. 4to. 21s.

WALES' REDUCTION OF ASTRONOMICAL OBSERVATIONS MADE IN THE SOUTHERN HEMISPHERE. 1764—1771. 1788. 4to. 10s. 6d.

BARBAULD'S (MRS.) Hymns in Prose for Children. With 112
Original Designs. Small 4to. 5s. ; or *Fine Paper*, 7s. 6d.

BARROW'S (SIR JOHN) Autobiographical Memoir. From Early
Life to Advanced Age. Portrait. 8vo. 16s.

———— (JOHN) Life, Exploits, and Voyages of Sir Francis
Drake. With numerous Original Letters. Post 8vo. 2s.

BARRY'S (SIR CHARLES) Life. By Alfred Barry, D.D. With
Portrait, Plans, and Illustrations. 8vo. 24s.

BATES' (H. W.) Records of a Naturalist on the River Amazons
during eleven years of Adventure and Travel. *Second Edition.* Illustrations. Post 8vo. 12s.

BEES AND FLOWERS. Two Essays. By Rev. Thomas James.
Reprinted from the "Quarterly Review." Fcap. 8vo. 1s. each.

BERTHA'S Journal during a Visit to her Uncle in England.
Containing a Variety of Interesting and Instructive Information. *Seventh Edition.* Woodcuts. 12mo. 7s. 6d.

BERTRAM'S (JAS. G.) Harvest of the Sea: a Contribution to the
Natural and Economic History of British Food Fishes. With 50 Illustrations.

BIRCH'S (SAMUEL) History of Ancient Pottery and Porcelain :
Egyptian, Assyrian, Greek, Roman, and Etruscan. With 200 Illustrations. 2 Vols. Medium 8vo. 42s.

BISSET'S (ANDREW) History of the Commonwealth of England,
from the Death of Charles I. to the Expulsion of the Long Parliament
by Cromwell. Chiefly from the MSS. in the State Paper Office. 2 vols.
8vo. 30s.

BLAKISTON'S (CAPT.) Narrative of the Expedition sent to ex-
plore the Upper Waters of the Yang-Tsze. Illustrations. 8vo. 18s.

BLOMFIELD'S (BISHOP) Memoir, with Selections from his Correspondence. By his Son. *2nd Edition.* Portrait, post 8vo. 12s.

BLUNT'S (REV. J. J.) Undesigned Coincidences in the Writings of
the Old and New Testament, an Argument of their Veracity : containing
the Books of Moses, Historical and Prophetical Scriptures, and the
Gospels and Acts. *9th Edition.* Post 8vo. 6s.

———— History of the Church in the First Three Centuries.
Third Edition. Post 8vo. 7s. 6d.

———— Parish Priest ; His Duties, Acquirements and Obligations. *Fourth Edition.* Post 8vo. 7s. 6d.

———— Lectures on the Right Use of the Early Fathers.
Second Edition. 8vo. 15s.

———— Plain Sermons Preached to a Country Congregation.
Second Edition. Post 8vo. 7s. 6d. each.

———— Essays on various subjects. 8vo. 12s.

BOOK OF COMMON PRAYER. Illustrated with Coloured
Borders, Initial Letters, and Woodcuts. A new edition. 8vo. 18s.
cloth ; 31s. 6d. calf ; 36s. morocco.

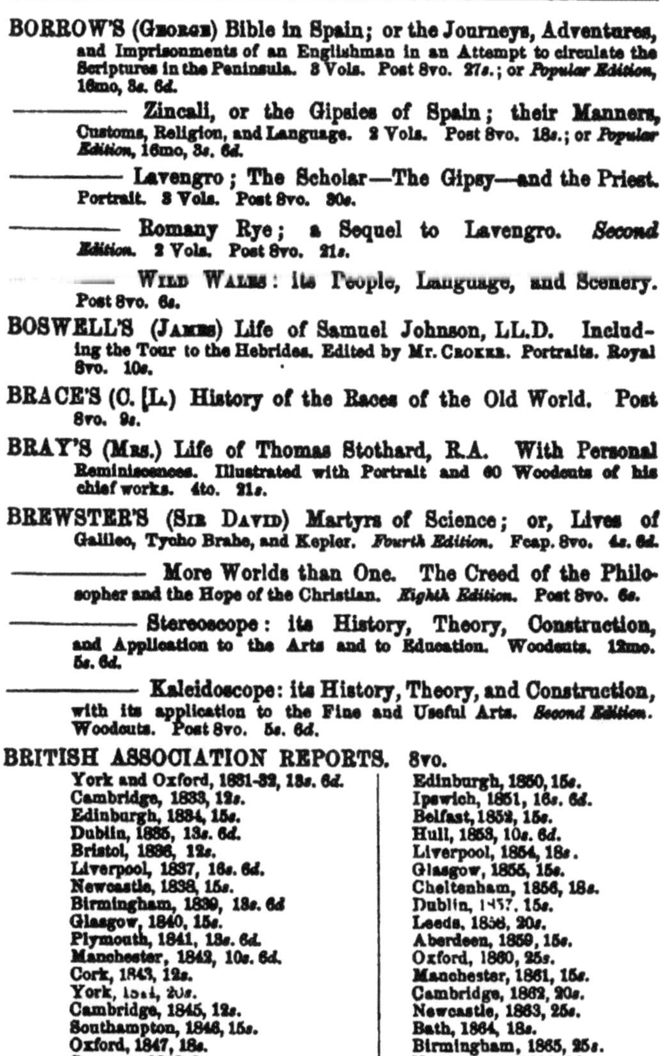

BORROW'S (GEORGE) Bible in Spain; or the Journeys, Adventures, and Imprisonments of an Englishman in an Attempt to circulate the Scriptures in the Peninsula. 3 Vols. Post 8vo. 27s.; or *Popular Edition*, 16mo, 3s. 6d.

———— Zincali, or the Gipsies of Spain; their Manners, Customs, Religion, and Language. 2 Vols. Post 8vo. 18s.; or *Popular Edition*, 16mo, 3s. 6d.

———— Lavengro; The Scholar—The Gipsy—and the Priest. Portrait. 3 Vols. Post 8vo. 30s.

———— Romany Rye; a Sequel to Lavengro. *Second Edition*. 2 Vols. Post 8vo. 21s.

———— WILD WALES: its People, Language, and Scenery. Post 8vo. 6s.

BOSWELL'S (JAMES) Life of Samuel Johnson, LL.D. Including the Tour to the Hebrides. Edited by Mr. CROKER. Portraits. Royal 8vo. 10s.

BRACE'S (C. L.) History of the Races of the Old World. Post 8vo. 9s.

BRAY'S (MRS.) Life of Thomas Stothard, R.A. With Personal Reminiscences. Illustrated with Portrait and 60 Woodcuts of his chief works. 4to. 21s.

BREWSTER'S (SIR DAVID) Martyrs of Science; or, Lives of Galileo, Tycho Brahe, and Kepler. *Fourth Edition*. Fcap. 8vo. 4s. 6d.

———— More Worlds than One. The Creed of the Philosopher and the Hope of the Christian. *Eighth Edition*. Post 8vo. 6s.

———— Stereoscope: its History, Theory, Construction, and Application to the Arts and to Education. Woodcuts. 12mo. 5s. 6d.

———— Kaleidoscope: its History, Theory, and Construction, with its application to the Fine and Useful Arts. *Second Edition*. Woodcuts. Post 8vo. 5s. 6d.

BRITISH ASSOCIATION REPORTS. 8vo.

York and Oxford, 1831-32, 13s. 6d.	Edinburgh, 1850, 15s.
Cambridge, 1833, 12s.	Ipswich, 1851, 16s. 6d.
Edinburgh, 1834, 15s.	Belfast, 1852, 15s.
Dublin, 1835, 13s. 6d.	Hull, 1853, 10s. 6d.
Bristol, 1836, 12s.	Liverpool, 1854, 18s.
Liverpool, 1837, 16s. 6d.	Glasgow, 1855, 15s.
Newcastle, 1838, 15s.	Cheltenham, 1856, 18s.
Birmingham, 1839, 13s. 6d	Dublin, 1857. 15s.
Glasgow, 1840, 15s.	Leeds, 1858, 20s.
Plymouth, 1841, 13s. 6d.	Aberdeen, 1859, 15s.
Manchester, 1842, 10s. 6d.	Oxford, 1860, 25s.
Cork, 1843, 12s.	Manchester, 1861, 15s.
York, 1844, 20s.	Cambridge, 1862, 20s.
Cambridge, 1845, 12s.	Newcastle, 1863, 25s.
Southampton, 1846, 15s.	Bath, 1864, 18s.
Oxford, 1847, 18s.	Birmingham, 1865, 25s.
Swansea, 1848, 9s.	Nottingham, 1866, 24s.
Birmingham, 1849, 10s.	Dundee, 1867.

BROUGHTON'S (LORD) Journey through Albania and other Provinces of Turkey in Europe and Asia, to Constantinople, 1809—10. *Third Edition*. Illustrations. 2 Vols. 8vo. 30s.

———— Visits to Italy. *3rd Edition*. 2 Vols. Post 8vo. 18s.

BRITISH CLASSICS. A Series of Standard English Authors, printed from the most correct text, and edited with notes. 8vo.

Already Published.

I. GOLDSMITH'S WORKS. Edited by Peter Cunningham, F.S.A. Vignettes. 4 Vols. 30s.

II. GIBBON'S DECLINE AND FALL OF THE ROMAN EMPIRE. Edited by William Smith, LL.D. Portrait and Maps. 8 Vols. 60s.

III. JOHNSON'S LIVES OF THE ENGLISH POETS. Edited by Peter Cunningham, F.S.A. 8 Vols. 22s. 6d.

IV. BYRON'S POETICAL WORKS. Edited, with Notes. 6 vols. 45s.

In Preparation.

LIFE AND WORKS OF POPE. Edited by Rev. Whitwell Elwin.

HUME'S HISTORY OF ENGLAND. Edited, with Notes.

LIFE AND WORKS OF SWIFT. Edited by John Forster.

LIFE AND WORKS OF DRYDEN. Edited, with Notes.

BROWNLOW'S (Lady) Reminiscences of a Septuagenarian. From 1802 to 1815. *Third Edition.* Post 8vo. 7s. 6d.

BUBBLES FROM THE BRUNNEN OF NASSAU. By Sir Francis B. Head, Bart. *7th Edition,* with Illustrations. Post 8vo. 7s. 6d.

BUNYAN (John) and Oliver Cromwell. Select Biographies. By Robert Southey. Post 8vo. 2s.

BURGON'S (Rev. J. W.) Memoir of a Christian Gentleman (Patrick Fraser Tytler). *Second Edition.* Post 8vo. 9s.

———— Letters from Rome. Illustrations. Post 8vo. 12s.

BURN'S (Col.) Dictionary of Naval and Military Technical Terms, English and French, and French and English. *Fourth Edition.* Crown 8vo. 15s.

BURR'S (G. D.) Instructions in Practical Surveying, Topographical Plan Drawing, and on sketching ground without Instruments. *Fourth Edition.* Woodcuts. Post 8vo. 6s.

BUTTMAN'S LEXILOGUS; a Critical Examination of the Meaning of numerous Greek Words, chiefly in Homer and Hesiod. Translated by Rev. J. R. Fishlake. *Fifth Edition.* 8vo. 12s.

———— CATALOGUE OF IRREGULAR GREEK VERBS. With all the Tenses extant—their Formation, Meaning, and Usage, accompanied by an Index. Translated, with Notes, by Rev. J. R. Fishlake. *Fifth Edition.* Revised by Rev. E. Venables. Post 8vo. 6s.

BUXTON'S (Sir Fowell) Memoirs. With Selections from his Correspondence. By his Son. Portrait. 8vo. 16s. *Abridged Edition.* Portrait. Fcap. 8vo. 2s. 6d.

———— (Charles) Ideas of the Day on Policy. *Third Edition.* 8vo. 6s.

BYRON'S (LORD) Life, Letters, and Journals. By THOMAS MOORE. Plates. 6 Vols. Fcap. 8vo. 18s.

———— Life, Letters, and Journals. By THOMAS MOORE. Portraits. Royal 8vo. 9s.

———— Poetical Works. Portrait. 6 Vols. 8vo. 45s.

———— Poetical Works. Plates. 10 Vols. Fcap. 8vo. 30s.

———— Poetical Works. 8 Vols. 24mo. 20s.

———— Poetical Works. Plates. Royal 8vo. 9s.

———— Poetical Works. (PEARL EDITION.) Crown 8vo. 2s. 6d.

———— Childe Harold. With 80 Engravings. Small 4to. 21s.

———— Childe Harold. 16mo. 2s. 6d.

———— Childe Harold. Vignettes. 16mo. 1s.

———— Childe Harold. Portrait. 16mo. 6d.

———— Tales and Poems. 24mo. 2s. 6d.

———— Miscellaneous. 2 Vols. 24mo. 5s.

———— Dramas and Plays. 2 Vols. 24mo. 5s.

———— Don Juan and Beppo. 2 Vols. 24mo. 5s.

———— Beauties. Poetry and Prose. Portrait. Fcap. 8vo. 3s. 6d.

CALLCOTT'S (LADY) Little Arthur's History of England. *New Edition, brought down to* 1862. With Woodcuts. Fcap. 8vo. 2s. 6d.

CAMPBELL'S (LORD) Lives of the Lord Chancellors and Keepers of the Great Seal of England. From the Earliest Times to the Death of Lord Eldon in 1838. *Fourth Edition.* 10 Vols. Crown 8vo. 6s. each.

———— Lives of the Chief Justices of England. From the Norman Conquest to the Death of Lord Tenterden. *Second Edition.* 3 Vols. 8vo. 42s.

———— Shakspeare's Legal Acquirements Considered. 8vo. 5s. 6d.

———— Life of Lord Chancellor Bacon. Fcap. 8vo. 2s. 6d.

———— (GEORGE) Modern India. A Sketch of the System of Civil Government. With some Account of the Natives and Native Institutions. *Second Edition.* 8vo. 16s.

———— India as it may be. An Outline of a proposed Government and Policy. 8vo. 12s.

———— (THOS.) Short Lives of the British Poets. With an Essay on English Poetry. Post 8vo. 3s. 6d.

CARNARVON'S (LORD) Portugal, Gallicia, and the Basque Provinces. From Notes made during a Journey to those Countries. *Third Edition.* Post 8vo. 3s. 6d.

———— Recollections of the Druses of Lebanon. With Notes on their Religion. *Third Edition.* Post 8vo. 5s. 6d.

CASTLEREAGH (THE) DESPATCHES, from the commencement of the official career of the late Viscount Castlereagh to the close of his life. Edited by the MARQUIS OF LONDONDERRY. 12 Vols. 8vo. 14s. each.

CATHCART'S (SIR GEORGE) Commentaries on the War in Russia and Germany, 1812-13. Plans. 8vo. 14s.

CAVALCASELLE AND CROWE'S History of Painting in Italy, from the Second to the Sixteenth Century, from recent researches, as well as from personal inspection of the Works of Art in that Country. With 100 Illustrations. Vols. I. to III. 8vo. 63s.

———— ———— History of Painting in North Italy, including Venice, Lombardy, Padua, Vicenza, Verona, Parma, Friuli, Ferrara, and Bologna. With Illustrations. 2 Vols. 8vo. (*In preparation.*)

———— ———— Notices of the Lives and Works of the Early Flemish Painters. Woodcuts. Post 8vo. 12s.

CHILD (G. CHAPLIN, M.D.) Benedicite; or, Song of the Three Children; being Illustrations of the Power, Wisdom, and Goodness of the Creator. 2 Vols. Fcap. 8vo. 12s.

CHORLEY'S (H. F.) STUDIES OF THE MUSIC OF MANY NATIONS; including the Substance of a Course of Lectures delivered at the Royal Institution. 8vo. (*In the Press.*)

CHURTON'S (ARCHDEACON) Gongora. An Historical Essay on the Age of Philip III. and IV. of Spain. With Translations. Portrait. 2 Vols. Small 8vo. 15s.

CICERO'S LIFE AND TIMES. With his Character viewed as a Statesman, Orator, and Friend, and a Selection from his Correspondence and Orations. By WILLIAM FORSYTH, Q.C. *New Edition.* With Illustrations. 8vo. 16s.

CLIVE'S (LORD) Life. By REV. G. R. GLEIG, M.A. Post 8vo. 3s. 6d.

COLCHESTER (THE) PAPERS. The Diary and Correspondence of Charles Abbott, Lord Colchester, Speaker of the House of Commons, 1802-1817. Portrait. 3 Vols. 8vo. 42s.

COLERIDGE'S (SAMUEL TAYLOR) Table-Talk. *New Edition.* Portrait. Fcap. 8vo. 6s.

COLLINGWOOD'S (CUTHBERT) Rambles of a Naturalist on the Shores and Waters of the China Seas, during a Voyage to China, Formosa, Borneo, Singapore, &c. With Illustrations. 8vo.

COLONIAL LIBRARY. [See Home and Colonial Library.]

COOK'S (Canon) Sermons Preached at Lincoln's Inn Chapel, and on Special Occasions. 8vo. 9s.

COOKERY (MODERN DOMESTIC). Founded on Principles of Economy and Practical Knowledge, and adapted for Private Families. By a Lady. *New Edition.* Woodcuts. Fcap. 8vo. 5s.

CORNWALLIS (THE) Papers and Correspondence during the American War,—Administrations in India,—Union with Ireland, and Peace of Amiens. *Second Edition.* 3 Vols. 8vo. 63s.

COWPER'S (MARY, COUNTESS) Diary while Lady of the Bedchamber to Caroline Princess of Wales, 1714—20. Edited by Hon. SPENCER COWPER. *Second Edition.* Portrait. 8vo. 10s. 6d.

CRABBE'S (REV. GEORGE) Life. By his Son. Portrait. Fcap. 8vo. 3s.

———— Life and Poetical Works. Plates. 8 Vols. Fcap. 8vo. 24s. Or complete in One Volume. Plates. Royal 8vo. 7s.

CREE'S (Rev. E. D.) Portrait of the Primitive Church. Fcap. 8vo. 1s.

CROKER'S (J. W.) Progressive Geography for Children. *Fifth Edition.* 18mo. 1s. 6d.

———— Stories for Children, Selected from the History of England. *Fifteenth Edition.* Woodcuts. 16mo. 2s. 6d.

— — — Boswell's Life of Johnson. Including the Tour to the Hebrides. Portraits. Royal 8vo. 10s.

———— Essays on the Early Period of the French Revolution. 8vo. 15s.

———— Historical Essay on the Guillotine. Fcap. 8vo. 1s.

CROMWELL (OLIVER) and John Bunyan. By ROBERT SOUTHEY. Post 8vo. 2s.

CROWE'S AND CAVALCASELLE'S Notices of the Early Flemish Painters; their Lives and Works. Woodcuts. Post 8vo. 12s.

- - ———— History of Painting in Italy, from 2nd to 16th Century. Derived from Historical Researches as well as Inspection of the Works of Art in that Country. With 100 Illustrations. Vols. I. II. and III. 8vo. 21s. each.

———— History of Painting in North Italy, including Venice, Lombardy, Padua, Vicenza, Verona, Parma, Friuli, Ferrara, and Bologna. With Illustrations. Vols. 8vo. (*In Preparation*).

CUMMING'S (R. GORDON) Five Years of a Hunter's Life in the Far Interior of South Africa; with Anecdotes of the Chace, and Notices of the Native Tribes. *New Edition.* Woodcuts. Post 8vo. 5s.

CUNNINGHAM'S (ALLAN) Poems and Songs. Now first collected and arranged, with Biographical Notice. 24mo. 2s. 6d.

CURTIUS' (PROFESSOR) Student's Greek Grammar, for Colleges and the Upper Forms. Edited by DR. WM. SMITH. *2nd Edition.* Post 8vo. 6s.

———— Smaller Greek Grammar for the Middle and Lower Forms, abridged from the above. 12mo. 3s. 6d.

CURZON'S (HON. ROBERT) ARMENIA AND ERZEROUM. A Year on the Frontiers of Russia, Turkey, and Persia. *Third Edition.* Woodcuts. Post 8vo. 7s. 6d.

———— Visits to the Monasteries of the Levant. *Fifth Edition.* Illustrations. Post 8vo. 7s. 6d.

CUST'S (GENERAL) Warriors of the 17th Century—The Thirty Years' War—and the Civil Wars of France and England. 4 Vols. Post 8vo. 8s. each.

———— Annals of the Wars of the 18th & 19th Centuries. 9 Vols. Fcap. 8vo. 5s. each.

DARWIN'S (CHARLES) Journal of Researches into the Natural History of the Countries visited during a Voyage round the World. Post 8vo. 9s.

- — - - —— Origin of Species by Means of Natural Selection; or, the Preservation of Favoured Races in the Struggle for Life. *Fourth Edition, revised.* Post 8vo. 15s.

———— Fertilization of Orchids through Insect Agency, and as to the good of Intercrossing. Woodcuts. Post 8vo. 9s.

———— Variation of Animals and Plants under Domestication; With Illustrations. 2 Vols. 8vo. 28s.

DAVIS'S (NATHAN) Visit to the Ruined Cities of Numidia and Carthaginia. Illustrations. 8vo. 16s.

———— (SIR J. F.) Chinese Miscellanies: a Collection of Essays and Notes. Post 8vo. 6s.

DAVY'S (SIR HUMPHRY) Consolations in Travel; or, Last Days of a Philosopher. *Fifth Edition*. Woodcuts. Fcap. 8vo. 6s.

———— Salmonia; or, Days of Fly Fishing. *Fourth Edition*. Woodcuts. Fcap. 8vo. 6s.

DELEPIERRE'S (OCTAVE) History of Flemish Literature. From the Twelfth Century. 8vo. 9s.

———— Historical Difficulties and Contested Events: Being Notes on some Doubtful Points of History. Post 8vo. 6s.

DERBY'S (EDWARD, EARL OF) Translation of the Iliad of Homer into English Blank Verse. *Sixth Edition*. 2 Vols. Fcap. 8vo. 10s. Or Library Edition, 2 Vols. 8vo. 24s.

DE ROS'S (LORD) Memorials of the Tower of London. *Second Edition*, with Additions. With Illustrations. Crown 8vo. 12s.

DIXON'S (W. HEPWORTH) Story of the Life of Lord Bacon. *Second Edition*. Portrait. Fcap. 8vo. 7s. 6d.

DOG-BREAKING; the Most Expeditious, Certain, and Easy Method, whether great excellence or only mediocrity be required. With a Few Hints for those who Love the Dog and the Gun. By LIEUT.-GEN. HUTCHINSON. *Fourth Edition*. With 40 Woodcuts. Crown 8vo. 15s.

DOMESTIC MODERN COOKERY. Founded on Principles of Economy and Practical Knowledge, and adapted for Private Families. *New Edition*. Woodcuts. Fcap. 8vo. 5s.

DOUGLAS'S (GENERAL SIR HOWARD) Life and Adventures; From Notes, Conversations, and Correspondence. By S. W. FULLOM. Portrait. 8vo. 15s.

———— Theory and Practice of Gunnery. *5th Edition*. Plates. 8vo. 21s.

———— Military Bridges, and the Passage of Rivers in Military Operations. *Third Edition*. Plates. 8vo. 21s.

———— Naval Warfare with Steam. *Second Edition*. 8vo. 8s. 6d.

———— Modern Systems of Fortification. Plans. 8vo. 12s.

DRAKE'S (SIR FRANCIS) Life, Voyages, and Exploits, by Sea and Land. By JOHN BARROW. *Third Edition*. Post 8vo. 2s.

DRINKWATER'S (JOHN) History of the Siege of Gibraltar, 1779-1783. With a Description and Account of that Garrison from the Earliest Periods. Post 8vo. 2s.

DU CHAILLU'S (PAUL B.) EQUATORIAL AFRICA, with Accounts of the Gorilla, the Nest-building Ape, Chimpanzee, Crocodile, &c. Illustrations. 8vo. 21s.

———— Journey to Ashango Land; and Further Penetration into Equatorial Africa. Illustrations. 8vo. 21s.

DUFFERIN'S (Lord) Letters from High Latitudes; an Account of a Yacht Voyage to Iceland, Jan Mayen, and Spitzbergen. *Fifth Edition.* Woodcuts. Post 8vo. 7s. 6d.

DYER'S (Dr. Thos. H.) History of Modern Europe, from the taking of Constantinople by the Turks to the close of the War in the Crimea. 4 Vols. 8vo.

EASTLAKE'S (Sir Charles) Italian Schools of Painting. From the German of Kugler. Edited, with Notes. *Third Edition.* Illustrated from the Old Masters. 2 Vols. Post 8vo. 30s.

EASTWICK'S (E. B.) Handbook for Bombay and Madras, with Directions for Travellers, Officers, &c. Map. 2 Vols. Post 8vo. 24s.

EDWARDS' (W. H.) Voyage up the River Amazon, including a Visit to Para. Post 8vo. 2s.

ELDON'S (Lord) Public and Private Life, with Selections from his Correspondence and Diaries. By Horace Twiss. *Third Edition.* Portrait. 2 Vols. Post 8vo. 21s.

ELLESMERE'S (Lord) Two Sieges of Vienna by the Turks. Translated from the German. Post 8vo. 2s.

ELLIS (Rev. W.) Visits to Madagascar, including a Journey to the Capital, with notices of Natural History, and Present Civilisation of the People. *Fifth Thousand.* Map and Woodcuts. 8vo. 16s.

—— — Madagascar Revisited. Setting forth the Persecutions and Heroic Sufferings of the Native Christians, and the eventual Toleration of Christianity. Illustrations. 8vo. 16s.

—— (Mrs.) Education of Character, with Hints on Moral Training. Post 8vo. 7s. 6d.

ELPHINSTONE'S (Hon. Mountstuart) History of India—the Hindoo and Mahomedan Periods. *Fifth Edition.* Map. 8vo. 18s.

ENGEL'S (Carl) Music of the Most Ancient Nations; particularly of the Assyrians, Egyptians, and Hebrews; with Special Reference to the Discoveries in Western Asia and in Egypt. With 100 Illustrations. 8vo. 16s.

ENGLAND (History of) from the Peace of Utrecht to the Peace of Versailles, 1713—83. By Lord Mahon (now Earl Stanhope). *Library Edition,* 7 Vols. 8vo. 93s.; or *Popular Edition,* 7 Vols. Post 8vo. 35s.

———— From the First Invasion by the Romans. By Mrs. Markham. *New and Cheaper Edition, continued to 1863.* Woodcuts. 12mo. 4s.

———— From the Invasion of Julius Cæsar to the Revolution of 1688. By David Hume. Corrected and continued to 1858. Edited by Wm. Smith, LL.D. Woodcuts. Post 8vo. 7s. 6d.

———— (A Smaller History of). By Wm. Smith, LL.D. *New Edition, continued to 1865.* Woodcuts. 18mo. 3s. 6d.

———— Little Arthur's. By Lady Callcott. *New Edition, continued to 1862.* Woodcuts. 18mo. 2s. 6d.

ENGLISHWOMAN IN AMERICA. Post 8vo. 10s. 6d.

ESKIMAUX and English Vocabulary, for Travellers in the Arctic Regions. 16mo. 3s. 6d.

ESSAYS FROM "THE TIMES." Being a Selection from the LITERARY PAPERS which have appeared in that Journal. 2 vols. Fcap. 8vo. 8s.

ETHNOLOGICAL (THE) SOCIETY'S TRANSACTIONS. New Series. Vols. I. to VI. 8vo. 10s. 6d. each.

EXETER'S (BISHOP OF) Letters to Charles Butler, on his Book of the Roman Catholic Church. *New Edition.* Post 8vo. 6s.

FAMILY RECEIPT-BOOK. A Collection of a Thousand Valuable and Useful Receipts. Fcap. 8vo. 5s. 6d.

FARRAR'S (REV. A. S.) Critical History of Free Thought in reference to the Christian Religion. Being the Bampton Lectures, 1862. 8vo. 16s.

———— (F. W.) Origin of Language, based on Modern Researches. Fcap. 8vo. 5s.

FEATHERSTONHAUGH'S (G. W.) Tour through the Slave States of North America, from the River Potomac to Texas and the Frontiers of Mexico. Plates. 2 Vols. 8vo. 26s.

FERGUSSON'S (JAMES) Palaces of Nineveh and Persepolis Restored. Woodcuts. 8vo. 16s.

———— History of Architecture in all Countries: from the Earliest Times to the Present Day. With 1200 Illustrations and an Index. Vols. I. and II. 8vo. 42s. each.

———— History of Architecture. Vol. III.—The Modern Styles. With 312 Illustrations, and an Index. 8vo. 31s. 6d.

———— Holy Sepulchre and the Temple at Jerusalem; being the Substance of Two Lectures delivered at the Royal Institution, 1862 and '65. Woodcuts. 8vo. 7s. 6d.

FISHER'S (REV. GEORGE) Elements of Geometry, for the Use of Schools. *Fifth Edition.* 18mo. 1s. 6d.

———— First Principles of Algebra, for the Use of Schools. *Fifth Edition.* 18mo. 1s. 6d.

FLEMING (WM., D.D.) Student's Manual of Moral Philosophy. Post 8vo. 7s. 6d.

FLOWER GARDEN (THE). By REV. THOS. JAMES. Fcap. 8vo. 1s.

FONNEREAU'S (T. G.) Diary of a Dutiful Son. Fcap. 8vo. 4s. 6d.

FORBES' (C. S.) Iceland; its Volcanoes, Geysers, and Glaciers. Illustrations. Post 8vo. 14s.

FORSTER'S (JOHN) Arrest of the Five Members by Charles the First. A Chapter of English History re-written. Post 8vo. 12s.

———— Grand Remonstrance, 1641. With an Essay on English freedom under the Plantagenet and Tudor Sovereigns. *Second Edition.* Post 8vo. 12s.

———— Sir John Eliot: a Biography, 1590—1632. With Portraits. 2 Vols. Crown 8vo. 30s.

———— Biographies of Oliver Cromwell, Daniel De Foe, Sir Richard Steele, Charles Churchill, Samuel Foote. *Third Edition.* Post 8vo. 12s.

FORD'S (RICHARD) Handbook for Spain, Andalusia, Ronda, Valencia, Catalonia, Granada, Gallicia, Arragon, Navarre, &c. *Third Edition.* 2 Vols. Post 8vo. 30s.

———— Gatherings from Spain. Post 8vo. 3s. 6d.

FORSYTH'S (WILLIAM) Life and Times of Cicero. With Selections from his Correspondence and Orations. *New Edition.* Illustrations. 8vo. 16s.

FORTUNE'S (ROBERT) Narrative of Two Visits to the Tea Countries of China, 1843-52. *Third Edition.* Woodcuts. 2 Vols. Post 8vo. 18s.

———— ———— Third Visit to China. 1853-6. Woodcuts. 8vo. 16s.

———— ———— Yedo and Peking. With Notices of the Agriculture and Trade of China, during a Fourth Visit to that Country. Illustrations. 8vo. 16s.

FOSS' (Edward) Judges of England. With Sketches of their Lives, and Notices of the Courts at Westminster, from the Conquest to the Present Time. 9 Vols. 8vo. 126s.

———— Tabulæ Curiales; or, Tables of the Superior Courts of Westminster Hall. Showing the Judges who sat in them from 1066 to 1864; with the Attorney and Solicitor Generals of each reign. To which is prefixed an Alphabetical List of all the Judges during the same period. 8vo. 10s. 6d.

FRANCE (HISTORY OF). From the Conquest by the Gauls. By Mrs. MARKHAM. *New and Cheaper Edition, continued to* 1856. Woodcuts. 12mo. 4s.

———— From the Earliest Times to the Establishment of the Second Empire, 1852. By W. H. PEARSON. Edited by WM. SMITH, LL.D. Woodcuts. Post 8vo. 7s. 6d.

FRENCH (THE) in Algiers; The Soldier of the Foreign Legion— and the Prisoners of Abd-el-Kadir. Translated by Lady DUFF GORDON. Post 8vo. 2s.

FRERE (SIR BARTLE). Old Deccan Days; or Hindoo Fairy Legends. Collected by M. FRERE, and Illustrated by C. F. FRERE. With Introduction and Notes, by SIR BARTLE FRERE. Crown 8vo. 12s.

GALTON'S (FRANCIS) Art of Travel; or, Hints on the Shifts and Contrivances available in Wild Countries. *Fourth Edition.* Woodcuts. Post 8vo. 7s. 6d.

GEOGRAPHY (ANCIENT). By Rev. W. L. BEVAN. Woodcuts. Post 8vo. 7s. 6d.

———— ———— (MODERN). By Rev. W. L. BEVAN. Woodcuts. Post 8vo. *In the Press.*

———— ———— Journal of the Royal Geographical Society of London. 8vo.

GERMANY (HISTORY OF). From the Invasion by Marius, to Recent times. By Mrs. MARKHAM. *New and Cheaper Edition.* Woodcuts. 12mo. 4s.

GIBBON'S (EDWARD) History of the Decline and Fall of the Roman Empire. *A New Edition.* Preceded by his Autobiography. And Edited, with Notes, by Dr. WM. SMITH. Maps. 8 Vols. 8vo. 60s.

———— (The Student's Gibbon); Being an Epitome of the above work, incorporating the Researches of Recent Commentators. By Dr. WM. SMITH. Woodcuts. Post 8vo. 7s. 6d.

GIFFARD'S (EDWARD) Deeds of Naval Daring; or, Anecdotes of the British Navy. Fcap. 8vo. 3s. 6d.

GLADSTONE'S (W. E.) Financial Statements of 1853, 60, 63, and 64; with Speeches on Tax-Bills and Charities. *Second Edition.* 8vo. 12s.

———————— Speeches on Parliamentary Reform. *Third Edition.* Post 8vo. 6s.

GLEIG'S (Rev. G. R.) Campaigns of the British Army at Washington and New Orleans. Post 8vo. 2s.

———— Story of the Battle of Waterloo. Post 8vo. 3s. 6d.

———— Narrative of Sale's Brigade in Affghanistan. Post 8vo. 2s.

———— Life of Robert Lord Clive. Post 8vo. 3s. 6d.

———— Sir Thomas Munro. Post 8vo. 3s. 6d.

GOLDSMITH'S (Oliver) Works. A New Edition. Edited by Peter Cunningham, F.S.A. Vignettes. 4 Vols. 8vo. 30s.

GONGORA; An Historical Essay on the Times of Philip III. and IV. of Spain. With Illustrations. By Archdeacon Churton. Portrait. 2 vols. Post 8vo. 15s.

GORDON'S (Sir Alex. Duff) Sketches of German Life, and Scenes from the War of Liberation. From the German. Post 8vo. 3s. 6d.

———————— (Lady Duff) Amber-Witch: A Trial for Witchcraft. From the German. Post 8vo. 2s.

———————— French in Algiers. 1. The Soldier of the Foreign Legion. 2. The Prisoners of Abd-el-Kadir. From the French. Post 8vo. 2s.

GOUGER'S (Henry) Personal Narrative of Two Years' Imprisonment in Burmah. *Second Edition.* Woodcuts. Post 8vo. 12s.

GRAMMARS (Latin and Greek). See Curtius; Smith; King Edward VIth., &c. &c.

GREECE (History of). From the Earliest Times to the Roman Conquest. By Wm. Smith, LL.D. Woodcuts. Post 8vo. 7s. 6d.

———————— (A Smaller History of). By Wm. Smith, LL.D. Woodcuts. 16mo. 3s. 6d.

GRENVILLE (The) PAPERS. Being the Public and Private Correspondence of George Grenville, including his Private Diary. Edited by W. J. Smith. 4 Vols. 8vo. 16s. each.

GREY'S (Earl) Correspondence with King William IVth. and Sir Herbert Taylor, from November, 1830, to the Passing of the Reform Act in 1832. 2 Vols. 8vo. 30s.

———————— Parliamentary Government and Reform; with Suggestions for the Improvement of our Representative System. *Second Edition.* 8vo. 9s.

———————— (Sir George) Polynesian Mythology, and Ancient Traditional History of the New Zealand Race. Woodcuts. Post 8vo. 10s. 6d.

GRUNER'S (Lewis) Terra-Cotta Architecture of North Italy, From careful Drawings and Restorations. Engraved and printed in Colours. With Coloured Illustrations. Small folio

GROTE'S (George) History of Greece. From the Earliest Times to the close of the generation contemporary with the death of Alexander the Great. *Fourth Edition.* Maps. 8 Vols. 8vo. 112*s.*

———————— Plato, and the other Companions of Socrates. *Second Edition.* 3 Vols. 8vo. 45*s.*

— ——— (Mrs.) Memoir of Ary Scheffer. Post 8vo. 8*s.* 6*d.*

GUIZOT'S (M.) Meditations on Christianity, and on the Religious Questions of the Day. Part I. The Essence. Part II. The Present State. 2 Vols. Post 8vo. 21*s.*

HALLAM'S (Henry) Constitutional History of England, from the Accession of Henry the Seventh to the Death of George the Second. *Seventh Edition.* 3 Vols. 8vo. 30*s.*

——————— History of Europe during the Middle Ages. *Tenth Edition.* 3 Vols. 8vo. 30*s.*

——————— Literary History of Europe, during the 15th, 16th and 17th Centuries. *Fourth Edition.* 3 Vols. 8vo. 36*s.*

——————— Historical Works. Containing History of England, —Middle Ages of Europe,—Literary History of Europe. 10 Vols. Post 8vo. 6*s.* each.

——————— (Arthur) Remains; in Verse and Prose. With Preface, Memoir, and Portrait. Fcap. 8vo. 7*s.* 6*d.*

HAMILTON'S (James) Wanderings in North Africa. With Illustrations. Post 8vo. 12*s.*

HANNAH'S (Rev. Dr.) Bampton Lectures for 1863; the Divine and Human Elements in Holy Scripture. 8vo. 10*s.* 6*d.*

HART'S ARMY LIST. (*Quarterly and Annually.*) 8vo.

HAY'S (J. H. Drummond) Western Barbary, its Wild Tribes and Savage Animals. Post 8vo. 2*s.*

HEAD'S (Sir Francis) Horse and his Rider. Woodcuts. Post 8vo. 5*s.*

——— Rapid Journeys across the Pampas. Post 8vo. 2*s.*

——— Bubbles from the Brunnen of Nassau. Illustrations. Post 8vo. 7*s.* 6*d.*

——— Emigrant. Fcap. 8vo. 2*s.* 6*d.*

——— Stokers and Pokers; or, the London and North Western Railway. Post 8vo. 2*s.*

——— (Sir Edmund) Shall and Will; or, Future Auxiliary Verbs. Fcap. 8vo. 4*s.*

HEBER'S (Bishop) Journey through the Upper Provinces of India, from Calcutta to Bombay, with an Account of a Journey to Madras and the Southern Provinces. *Twelfth Edition.* 2 Vols. Post 8vo. 7*s.*

——————— Poetical Works, including Palestine, Europe, The Red Sea, Hymns, &c. *Sixth Edition.* Portrait. Fcap. 8vo. 6*s.*

——————— Hymns adapted to the Weekly Church Service of the Year. 16mo. 1*s.* 6*d.*

HERODOTUS. A New English Version. Edited, with Notes and Essays, historical, ethnographical, and geographical, by Rev. G. Rawlinson, assisted by Sir Henry Rawlinson and Sir J. G. Wilkinson. *Second Edition.* Maps and Woodcuts. 4 Vols. 8vo. 48*s.*

HAND-BOOK—TRAVEL-TALK. English, French, German, and Italian. 18mo. 3s. 6d.

———— - —- NORTH GERMANY,—HOLLAND, BELGIUM, and the Rhine to Switzerland. Map. Post 8vo. 10s.

———————— SOUTH GERMANY, Bavaria, Austria, Styria, Salzberg, the Austrian and Bavarian Alps, the Tyrol, Hungary, and the Danube, from Ulm to the Black Sea. Map. Post 8vo. 10s.

—————————— KNAPSACK GUIDE TO THE TYROL. Post 8vo. 6s.

—————————— PAINTING. German, Flemish, and Dutch Schools. Edited by Dr. WAAGEN. Woodcuts. 2 Vols. Post 8vo. 24s.

- - ————— LIVES OF THE EARLY FLEMISH PAINTERS. By CROWE and CAVALCASELLE. Illustrations. Post 8vo. 12s.

—————————— SWITZERLAND, Alps of Savoy, and Piedmont. Maps. Post 8vo. 10s.

—————————— KNAPSACK GUIDE TO SWITZERLAND. Post 8vo. 5s.

—————————— FRANCE, Normandy, Brittany, the French Alps, the Rivers Loire, Seine, Rhone, and Garonne, Dauphiné, Provence, and the Pyrenees. Maps. Post 8vo. 12s.

—————————— PARIS, and its Environs. Map and Plans. Post 8vo. 3s. 6d.

₊ MURRAY'S PLAN OF PARIS, mounted on canvas in a case. 3s. 6d.

—————————— SPAIN, Andalusia, Ronda, Granada, Valencia, Catalonia, Gallicia, Arragon, and Navarre. Maps. 2 Vols. Post 8vo. 30s.

—————————— PORTUGAL, LISBON, &c. Map. Post 8vo. 9s.

—————— NORTH ITALY, Piedmont, Liguria, Venetia, Lombardy, Parma, Modena, and Romagna. Map. Post 8vo. 12s.

—————————— CENTRAL ITALY, Lucca, Tuscany, Florence, The Marches, Umbria, and the Patrimony of St. Peter's. Map. Post 8vo. 10s.

——————— ROME AND ITS ENVIRONS. Map. Post 8vo. 9s.

—————————— SOUTH ITALY, Two Sicilies, Naples, Pompeii, Herculaneum, and Vesuvius. Map. Post 8vo. 10s.

———————— KNAPSACK GUIDE TO ITALY. Post 8vo. 6s.

—————————— SICILY, Palermo, Messina, Catania, Syracuse, Etna, and the Ruins of the Greek Temples. Map. Post 8vo. 12s.

——————— - PAINTING. The Italian Schools. Edited by Sir CHARLES EASTLAKE, R.A. Woodcuts. 2 Vols. Post 8vo. 30s.

—————————— LIVES OF ITALIAN PAINTERS, FROM CIMABUE to BASSANO. By Mrs. JAMESON. With 60 Portraits. Post 8vo. 12s.

—————————— NORWAY. Map. Post 8vo. 5s.

- - ————— DENMARK, SWEDEN, and NORWAY. Maps. Post 8vo. 15s.

—————————— GREECE, the Ionian Islands, Albania, Thessaly, and Macedonia. Maps. Post 8vo. 15s.

—————— -- TURKEY, Malta, Asia Minor, Constantinople, Armenia, Mesopotamia, &c. Maps. Post 8vo.

HAND-BOOK—EGYPT, Thebes, the Nile, Alexandria, Cairo, the Pyramids, Mount Sinai, &c. Map. Post 8vo. 15s.

——————— HOLY LAND—Syria and Palestine, Peninsula of Sinai, Edom, and Syrian Desert. Maps. 2 Vols. Post 8vo. 24s.

——————— INDIA. — Bombay and Madras. Map. 2·Vols. Post. 8vo. 24s.

——————— RUSSIA, Poland, and Finland. Maps. Post 8vo. 12s.

——————— MODERN LONDON. Map. 16mo. 3s. 6d.

——————— WESTMINSTER ABBEY. Woodcuts. 16mo. 1s.

——————— KENT AND SUSSEX, Canterbury, Dover, Ramsgate, Sheerness, Rochester, Chatham, Woolwich, Brighton, Chichester, Worthing, Hastings, Lewes, Arundel, &c. Map. Post 8vo. 10s.

——————— SURREY AND HANTS, Kingston, Croydon, Reigate, Guildford, Winchester, Southampton, Portsmouth, and Isle of Wight. Maps. Post 8vo. 10s.

——————— WILTS, DORSET, AND SOMERSET, Salisbury, Chippenham, Weymouth, Sherborne, Wells, Bath, Bristol, Taunton, &c. Map. Post 8vo.

——————— DEVON AND CORNWALL, Exeter, Ilfracombe, Linton, Sidmouth, Dawlish, Teignmouth, Plymouth, Devonport, Torquay, Launceston, Truro, Penzance, Falmouth, &c. Maps. Post 8vo. 10s.

——————— BERKS, BUCKS, AND OXON, Windsor, Eton, Reading, Aylesbury, Uxbridge, Wycombe, Henley, the City and University of Oxford, and the Descent of the Thames. Map. Post 8vo. 7s. 6d.

——————— GLOUCESTER, HEREFORD, and WORCESTER, Cirencester, Cheltenham, Stroud, Tewkesbury, Ledbury, Bromyard, Leominster, Ross, Malvern, Stourbridge, Kidderminster, Dudley, Droitwich, Bromsgrove, Evesham, &c. Map. Post 8vo. 6s. 6d.

——————— CATHEDRALS OF GLOUCESTER, HEREFORD AND WORCESTER. Illustrations. Post 8vo. 6s. 6d.

——————— NORTH AND SOUTH WALES, Bangor, Carnarvon, Beaumaris, Snowdon, Conway, Menai Straits, Carmarthen, Pembroke, Tenby, Swansea, The Wye, &c. Maps. 2 Vols. Post 8vo. 12s.

——————— STAFFORD, DERBY, NOTTS, AND LEICESTER, Chesterfield, Matlock, Chatsworth, Buxton, Ashborne, Southwell, Mansfield, Retford, Burton, Belvoir, Melton Mowbray, Wolverhampton, Lichfield, Walsall, Tamworth. Map. Post 8vo. (*Just Ready.*)

——————— EASTERN COUNTIES, Essex, Suffolk, Norfolk, and Cambridge. Map. Post 8vo. (*In the Press.*)

——————— YORKSHIRE, York, Doncaster, Hull, Selby, Beverley, Scarborough, Whitby, Malton, Harrogate, Ripon, Barnard Castle, Leeds, Wakefield, Bradford, Halifax, Huddersfield, Sheffield. Map. Post 8vo. 12s.

——————— DURHAM AND NORTHUMBERLAND, Newcastle, Darlington, Gateshead, Bishop Auckland, Stockton, Hartlepool, Sunderland, Shields, Berwick-on-Tweed, Morpeth, Tynemouth, Coldstream, Alnwick, &c. Map. Post 8vo. 9s.

——————— WESTMORELAND, CUMBERLAND, and THE LAKES, Lancaster, Furness Abbey, Ambleside, Kendal, Windermere, Coniston, Keswick, Grasmere, Carlisle, Cockermouth, Penrith, Kirby-Lonsdale, Appleby. Map. Post 8vo. 6s.

*** Murray's Large Map of the Lake District, for Pedestrians and Travellers, in a case. 3s. 6d.

HANDBOOK—SCOTLAND, Edinburgh, Melrose, Kelso, Glasgow, Dumfries, Ayr, Stirling, Arran, The Clyde, Oban. Inverary, Loch Lomond, Loch Katrine and Trossachs, Caledonian Canal, Inverness, Perth, Dundee, Aberdeen, Braemar, Skye, Caithness, Ross, Sutherland, &c. Maps and Plans. Post 8vo.

———————— IRELAND, Dublin, Belfast, Donegal, Galway, Wexford, Cork, Limerick, Waterford, the Lakes of Killarney, Coast of Munster, &c. Maps. Post 8vo. 12s.

———————— CATHEDRALS of Oxford, Peterborough, Norwich, Ely, and Lincoln. With 90 Illustrations. Crown 8vo. 18s.

———————— of Winchester, Salisbury, Exeter, Wells, Chichester. Rochester, Canterbury. With 110 Illustrations. 2 Vols. Crown 8vo. 24s.

———————— of Bristol, Gloucester, Hereford, Worcester and Lichfield. With 50 Illustrations. Crown 8vo. 16s.

———————— of York, Ripon, Durham, Carlisle, Chester, and Manchester. With Illustrations. Crown 8vo. (*In Preparation.*)

———————— FAMILIAR QUOTATIONS. From English Authors. *Third Edition.* Fcap. 8vo. 5s.

HESSEY (REV. DR.). Sunday—Its Origin, History, and Present Obligations. Being the Bampton Lectures for 1860. *Second Edition.* 8vo. 16s. Or *Popular Edition.* Post 8vo. 9s.

HICKMAN'S (WM.) Treatise on the Law and Practice of Naval Courts-Martial. 8vo. 10s. 6d.

HILLARD'S (G. S.) Six Months in Italy. 2 Vols. Post 8vo. 16s.

HOLLWAY'S (J. G.) Month in Norway. Fcap. 8vo. 2s.

HONEY BEE (THE). An Essay. By REV. THOMAS JAMES. Reprinted from the "Quarterly Review." Fcap. 8vo. 1s.

HOOK'S (DEAN) Church Dictionary. *Ninth Edition.* 8vo. 16s.

———————— (THEODORE) Life. By J. G. LOCKHART. Fcap. 8vo. 1s.

HOPE'S (A. J. BERESFORD) English Cathedral of the Nineteenth Century. With Illustrations. 8vo. 12s.

HORACE Edited by DEAN MILMAN. With Woodcuts. Post 8vo. 7s. 6d.

———————— (Life of). By DEAN MILMAN. Woodcuts, and coloured Borders. 8vo. 9s.

HOUGHTON'S (LORD) Poetical Works. Fcap. 8vo. 6s.

HUME'S (THE STUDENT'S) History of England, from the Invasion of Julius Cæsar to the Revolution of 1688. Corrected and continued to 1858. Edited by DR. WM. SMITH. Woodcuts. Post 8vo. 7s. 6d.

HUTCHINSON (GEN.) on the most expeditious, certain, and easy Method of Dog-Breaking. *Fourth Edition.* Enlarged and revised, with 40 Illustrations. Crown 8vo. 15s.

HUTTON'S (H. E.) Principia Græca; an Introduction to the Study of Greek. Comprehending Grammar, Delectus, and Exercise-book, with Vocabularies. *Third Edition.* 12mo. 3s. 6d.

IRBY AND MANGLES' Travels in Egypt, Nubia, Syria, and the Holy Land. Post 8vo. 2s.

JAMES' (REV. THOMAS) Fables of Æsop. A New Translation, with Historical Preface. With 100 Woodcuts by TENNIEL and WOLF. *Fiftieth Thousand.* Post 8vo. 2s. 6d.

JAMESON'S (MRS.) Lives of the Early Italian Painters— and the Progress of Painting in Italy—Cimabue to Bassano. With 60 Portraits. Post 8vo. 12s.

JENNINGS' (LOUIS) Eighty Years of Republican Government in the United States. Post 8vo. 10s. 6d.

HOME AND COLONIAL LIBRARY. A Series of Works adapted for all circles and classes of Readers, having been selected for their acknowledged interest and ability of the Authors. Post 8vo. Published at 2*s.* and 3*s.* 6*d.* each, and arranged under two distinctive heads as follows :—

CLASS A.

HISTORY, BIOGRAPHY, AND HISTORIC TALES.

1. SIEGE OF GIBRALTAR. By JOHN DRINKWATER. 2*s.*
2. THE AMBER-WITCH. By LADY DUFF GORDON. 2*s.*
3. CROMWELL AND BUNYAN. By ROBERT SOUTHEY. 2*s.*
4. LIFE OF SIR FRANCIS DRAKE. By JOHN BARROW. 2*s.*
5. CAMPAIGNS AT WASHINGTON. By REV. G. R. GLEIG. 2*s.*
6. THE FRENCH IN ALGIERS. By LADY DUFF GORDON. 2*s.*
7. THE FALL OF THE JESUITS. 2*s.*
8. LIVONIAN TALES. 2*s.*
9. LIFE OF CONDE. By LORD MAHON. 3*s.* 6*d.*
10. SALE'S BRIGADE. By REV. G. R. GLEIG. 2*s.*
11. THE SIEGES OF VIENNA. By LORD ELLESMERE. 2*s.*
12. THE WAYSIDE CROSS. By CAPT. MILMAN. 2*s.*
13. SKETCHES OF GERMAN LIFE. By SIR A. GORDON. 3*s.* 6*d.*
14. THE BATTLE OF WATERLOO. By REV. G. R. GLEIG. 3*s.* 6*d.*
15. AUTOBIOGRAPHY OF STEFFENS. 2*s.*
16. THE BRITISH POETS. By THOMAS CAMPBELL. 3*s.* 6*d.*
17. HISTORICAL ESSAYS. By LORD MAHON. 3*s.* 6*d.*
18. LIFE OF LORD CLIVE. By REV. G. R. GLEIG. 3*s.* 6*d.*
19. NORTH - WESTERN RAILWAY. By SIR F. B. HEAD. 2*s.*
20. LIFE OF MUNRO. By REV. G. R. GLEIG. 3*s.* 6*d.*

CLASS B.

VOYAGES, TRAVELS, AND ADVENTURES.

1. BIBLE IN SPAIN. By GEORGE BORROW. 3*s.* 6*d.*
2. GIPSIES OF SPAIN. By GEORGE BORROW. 3*s.* 6*d.*
3 & 4. JOURNALS IN INDIA. By BISHOP HEBER. 2 Vols. 7*s.*
5. TRAVELS IN THE HOLY LAND. By IRBY and MANGLES. 2*s.*
6. MOROCCO AND THE MOORS. By J. DRUMMOND HAY. 2*s.*
7. LETTERS FROM THE BALTIC. By a LADY. 2*s.*
8. NEW SOUTH WALES. By MRS. MEREDITH. 2*s.*
9. THE WEST INDIES. By M. G. LEWIS. 2*s.*
10. SKETCHES OF PERSIA. By SIR JOHN MALCOLM. 3*s.* 6*d.*
11. MEMOIRS OF FATHER RIPA. 2*s.*
12. 13. TYPEE AND OMOO. By HERMANN MELVILLE. 2 Vols. 7*s.*
14. MISSIONARY LIFE IN CANADA. By REV. J. ABBOTT. 2*s.*
15. LETTERS FROM MADRAS. By a LADY. 2*s.*
16. HIGHLAND SPORTS. By CHARLES ST. JOHN. 3*s.* 6*d.*
17. PAMPAS JOURNEYS. By SIR F. B. HEAD. 2*s.*
18. GATHERINGS FROM SPAIN. By RICHARD FORD. 3*s.* 6*d.*
19. THE RIVER AMAZON. By W. H. EDWARDS. 2*s.*
20. MANNERS & CUSTOMS OF INDIA. By REV. C. ACLAND. 2*s.*
21. ADVENTURES IN MEXICO. By G. F. RUXTON. 3*s.* 6*d.*
22. PORTUGAL AND GALLICIA. By LORD CARNARVON. 3*s.* 6*d.*
23. BUSH LIFE IN AUSTRALIA. By REV. H. W. HAYGARTH. 2*s.*
24. THE LIBYAN DESERT. By BAYLE ST. JOHN. 2*s.*
25. SIERRA LEONE. By a LADY. 3*s.* 6*d.*

*** Each work may be had separately.

JESSE'S (EDWARD) Gleanings in Natural History. *Eighth Edition.* Fcp. 8vo. 6s.

JOHNS' (REV. B. G.) Blind People; their Works and Ways. With Sketches of the Lives of some famous Blind Men. With Illustrations. Post 8vo. 7s. 6d.

JOHNSON'S (DR. SAMUEL) Life. By James Boswell. Including the Tour to the Hebrides. Edited by MR. CROKER. Portraits. Royal 8vo. 10s.

———— Lives of the English Poets. Edited by PETER CUNNINGHAM. 3 vols. 8vo. 22s. 6d.

KEN'S (BISHOP) Life. By a LAYMAN. *Second Edition.* Portrait. 2 Vols. 8vo. 18s.

———— Exposition of the Apostles' Creed. Extracted from his "Practice of Divine Love." Fcap. 1s. 6d.

———— Approach to the Holy Altar. Extracted from his "Manual of Prayer" and "Practice of Divine Love." Fcap. 8vo. 1s. 6d.

KENNEDY'S (GENERAL SHAW) Notes on the Battle of Waterloo. With a Memoir of his Life. Plans. 8vo. 7s. 6d.

KERR'S (ROBERT) GENTLEMAN'S HOUSE; OR, HOW TO PLAN ENGLISH RESIDENCES, FROM THE PARSONAGE TO THE PALACE. With Tables and Cost. Views and Plans. *Second Edition.* 8vo. 24s.

———— Ancient Lights; a Book for Architects, Surveyors, Lawyers, and Landlords. 8vo. 5s. 6d.

———— (R. MALCOLM) Student's Blackstone. A Systematic Abridgment of the entire Commentaries, adapted to the present state of the law. Post 8vo. 7s. 6d.

KING'S (REV. C. W.) Antique Gems; their Origin, Use, and Value, as Interpreters of Ancient History, and as illustrative of Ancient Art. *Second Edition.* Illustrations. 8vo. 24s.

KING EDWARD VITH's Latin Grammar; or, an Introduction to the Latin Tongue. *Seventeenth Edition.* 12mo. 3s. 6d.

———— First Latin Book; or, the Accidence, Syntax, and Prosody, with an English Translation. *Fifth Edition.* 12mo. 2s. 6d.

KING GEORGE THE THIRD'S CORRESPONDENCE WITH LORD NORTH, 1769-82. Edited, with Notes and Introduction, by W. BODHAM DONNE. 2 vols. 8vo. 32s.

KIRK'S (J. FOSTER) History of Charles the Bold, Duke of Burgundy. Portrait. Vols. I. and II. 8vo. 30s. Vol. III. 15s.

KUGLER'S Italian Schools of Painting. Edited, with Notes, by SIR CHARLES EASTLAKE. *Third Edition.* Woodcuts. 2 Vols. Post 8vo. 30s.

———— German, Dutch, and Flemish Schools of Painting. Edited, with Notes, by DR. WAAGEN. *Second Edition.* Woodcuts. 2 Vols. Post 8vo. 24s.

LAYARD'S (A. H.) Nineveh and its Remains. Being a Narrative of Researches and Discoveries amidst the Ruins of Assyria. With an Account of the Chaldean Christians of Kurdistan; the Yezedis, or Devil-worshippers; and an Enquiry into the Manners and Arts of the Ancient Assyrians. *Sixth Edition.* Plates and Woodcuts. 2 Vols. 8vo. 36s.

⁎ A POPULAR EDITION of the above Work. With Illustrations. Post 8vo. 7s. 6d.

———— Nineveh and Babylon; being the Narrative of a Second Expedition to Assyria. Plates. 8vo. 21s.

⁎ A POPULAR EDITION of the above Work. With Illustrations. Post 8vo. 7s. 6d.

LEATHES' (Rev. Stanley) Short Practical Hebrew Grammar. Post 8vo.

LENNEP'S (Rev. H. J. Van) Missionary Travels in Asia Minor. With Illustrations. 2 Vols. Post 8vo. (*In preparation.*)

LESLIE'S (C. R.) Handbook for Young Painters. With Illustrations. Post 8vo. 10s. 6d.

———— Autobiographical Recollections, with Selections from his Correspondence. Edited by Tom Taylor. Portrait. 2 Vols. Post 8vo. 18s.

———— Life and Works of Sir Joshua Reynolds. Portraits and Illustrations. 2 Vols. 8vo. 42s.

LETTERS FROM THE BALTIC. By a Lady. Post 8vo. 2s.

———— Madras. By a Lady. Post 8vo. 2s.

———— Sierra Leone. By a Lady. Post 8vo. 3s. 6d.

LEVI'S (Leone) Wages and Earnings of the Working Classes. With some Facts Illustrative of their Economic Condition. 8vo. 6s.

LEWIS (Sir G. C.) On the Government of Dependencies. 8vo. 12s.

———— Glossary of Provincial Words used in Herefordshire, &c. 12mo. 4s. 6d.

———— (M. G.) Journal of a Residence among the Negroes in the West Indies. Post 8vo. 2s.

LIDDELL'S (Dean) History of Rome. From the Earliest Times to the Establishment of the Empire. With the History of Literature and Art. 2 Vols. 8vo. 28s.

———— Student's History of Rome, abridged from the above Work. With Woodcuts. Post 8vo. 7s. 6d.

LINDSAY'S (Lord) Lives of the Lindsays; or, a Memoir of the Houses of Crawfurd and Balcarres. With Extracts from Official Papers and Personal Narratives. *Second Edition.* 3 Vols. 8vo. 24s.

LISPINGS from LOW LATITUDES; or, the Journal of the Hon. Impulsia Gushington. Edited by Lord Dufferin. With 24 Plates. 4to. 21s.

LITTLE ARTHUR'S HISTORY OF ENGLAND. By Lady Callcott. *New Edition, continued to* 1862. With 20 Woodcuts. Fcap. 8vo. 2s. 6d.

LIVINGSTONE'S (Dr.) Popular Account of his Missionary Travels in South Africa. Illustrations. Post 8vo. 6s.

———— Narrative of an Expedition to the Zambezi and its Tributaries; and of the Discovery of Lakes Shirwa and Nyassa. 1858-64. Map and Illustrations. 8vo. 21s.

LIVONIAN TALES. By the Author of "Letters from the Baltic." Post 8vo. 2s.

LOCKHART'S (J. G.) Ancient Spanish Ballads. Historical and Romantic. Translated, with Notes. *New Edition.* Post 8vo. 2s. 6d.

———— Life of Theodore Hook. Fcap. 8vo. 1s.

LONDON (OLD). A series of Essays on its Archæology and Antiquities, by Dean Stanley; A. J. Beresford Hope, M.P.; G. G. Scott, R.A.; R. Westmacott. R.A.; E. Foss, F.S.A.; G. T. Clark: Joseph Burtt; Rev. J. R Green; and G. Scharf, F.S.A. 8vo. 12s.

LONDON'S (BISHOP OF) Dangers and Safeguards of Modern Theology. Containing Suggestions to the Theological Student under present difficulties. *Second Edition.* 8vo. 9s.

LONSDALE'S (BISHOP) Life. With Selections from his Writings. Edited by E. B. DENISON, Q. C. With Portrait. Crown 8vo.

LOUDON'S (MRS.) Instructions in Gardening. With Directions and Calendar of Operations for Every Month. *Eighth Edition.* Woodcuts. Fcap. 8vo. 5s.

LUCAS' (SAMUEL) Secularia; or, Surveys on the Main Stream of History. 8vo. 12s.

LUCKNOW: a Lady's Diary of the Siege. Fcap. 8vo. 4s. 6d.

LYELL'S (SIR CHARLES) Elements of Geology; or, the Ancient Changes of the Earth and its Inhabitants considered as illustrative of Geology. *Sixth Edition.* Woodcuts. 8vo. 18s.

———————— Principles of Geology; or, the Ancient Changes of the Earth and its Inhabitants considered as illustrative of Geology. *Tenth Edition.* With Illustrations. 2 Vols. 8vo. 16s. each.

———————— Geological Evidences of the Antiquity of Man. *Third Edition.* Illustrations. 8vo. 14s.

LYTTELTON'S (LORD) Ephemera. Post 8vo. 10s. 6d.

LYTTON'S (LORD) Poems. *New Edition.* Post 8vo. 10s. 6d.

———————— Lost Tales of Miletus. *Second Edition.* Post 8vo. 7s. 6d.

MACPHERSON'S (MAJOR S. C.) Memorials of Service in India, while Political Agent at Gwalior during the Mutiny. With Portrait and Illustrations. 8vo. 12s.

MAHON'S (LORD) History of England, from the Peace of Utrecht to the Peace of Versailles, 1713—83. *Library Edition,* 7 Vols. 8vo. 93s. *Popular Edition,* 7 Vols. Post 8vo. 35s.

———————— Life of William Pitt, with Extracts from his MS. Papers. Portraits. 4 Vols. Post 8vo. 24s.

———————— Condé, surnamed the Great. Post 8vo. 3s. 6d.

——————————— Belisarius. Post 8vo. 10s. 6d.

———————— Miscellanies. Post 8vo. 5s. 6d.

———————— "Forty-Five;" a Narrative of the Rebellion in Scotland. Post 8vo. 3s.

———————— History of British India from its Origin till the Peace of 1783. Post 8vo. 3s. 6d.

———————— Spain under Charles the Second; 1690 to 1700. Post 8vo. 6s. 6d.

———————— Historical and Critical Essays. Post 8vo. 3s. 6d.

———————— Story of Joan of Arc. Fcap. 8vo. 1s.

McCLINTOCK'S (CAPT. SIR F. L.) Narrative of the Discovery of the Fate of Sir John Franklin and his Companions in the Arctic Seas. Illustrations. 8vo. 16s.

McCULLOCH'S (J. R.) Collected Edition of RICARDO'S Political Works. With Notes and Memoir. 8vo. 16s.

MacDOUGALL'S (COL.) Modern Warfare as Influenced by Modern Artillery. With Plans. Post 8vo. 12s.

MAINE (H. SUMNER) On Ancient Law: its Connection with the Early History of Society, and its Relation to Modern Ideas. 8vo. 12s.

MALCOLM'S (SIR JOHN) Sketches of Persia. Post 8vo. 3s. 6d.

MANSEL (CANON) Limits of Religious Thought Examined. Being the Bampton Lectures for 1858. Post 8vo. 8s. 6d.

MANSFIELD (SIR WILLIAM) On a Gold Currency for India. 8vo. 3s. 6d.

MANTELL'S (GIDEON A.) Thoughts on Animalcules; or, the Invisible World, as revealed by the Microscope. Plates. 16mo. 6s.

MANUAL OF SCIENTIFIC ENQUIRY. For the Use of Travellers. Edited by Sir J. F. HERSCHEL and Rev. R. MAIN. Maps. Post 8vo. 9s. (Published by order of the Lords of the Admiralty.)

MARKHAM'S (MRS.) History of England. From the First Invasion by the Romans, down to Recent Times. New Edition, continued to 1863. Woodcuts. 12mo. 4s.

———————— History of France. From the Conquest by the Gauls, to Recent Times. New Edition, continued to 1856. Woodcuts. 12mo. 4s.

———————— History of Germany. From the Invasion by Marius, to Recent Times. New Edition. Woodcuts. 12mo. 4s.

———————— (CLEMENTS R.) Travels in Peru and India. Maps and Illustrations. 8vo. 16s.

MARRYAT'S (JOSEPH) History of Modern and Mediæval Pottery and Porcelain. Third Edition. Plates and Woodcuts. 8vo.

———————— (HORACE) Jutland, the Danish Isles, and Copenhagen. Illustrations. 2 Vols. Post 8vo. 24s.

———————— Sweden and Isle of Gothland. Illustrations. 2 Vols. Post 8vo. 28s.

MARSH'S (G. P.) Student's Manual of the English Language. Post 8vo. 7s. 6d.

MAUREL'S (JULES) Essay on the Character, Actions, and Writings of the Duke of Wellington. Second Edition. Fcap. 8vo. 1s. 6d.

MAYNE'S (CAPT.) Four Years in British Columbia and Vancouver Island. Its Forests, Rivers, Coasts, and Gold Fields, and Resources for Colonisation. Illustrations. 8vo. 16s.

MELVILLE'S (HERMANN) Typee and Omoo; or, Adventures amongst the Marquesas and South Sea Islands. 2 Vols. Post 8vo. 7s.

MILLS' (REV. JOHN) Three Months' Residence at Nablus, with an Account of the Modern Samaritans. Illustrations. Post 8vo. 10s. 6d.

MILMAN'S (DEAN) Historical Works. Containing: 1. History of the Jews, 3 Vols. 2. History of Early Christianity, 3 Vols. 3. History of Latin Christianity, 9 Vols. Post 8vo. 6s. each.

———————— Character and Conduct of the Apostles considered as an Evidence of Christianity. 8vo. 10s. 6d.

———————— Translations from the Agamemnon of Æschylu and Bacchanals of Euripides. With Illustrations, crown 8vo. 12s.

———————— Horace. With 100 woodcuts. Post 8vo. 7s. 6d.

———————— Life of Horace. Woodcuts. 8vo. 9s.

———————— Poetical Works. Plates. 3 Vols. Fcap. 8vo. 18s.

———————— Fall of Jerusalem. Fcap. 8vo. 1s.

———————— (CAPT. E. A.) Wayside Cross. A Tale of the Carlist War. Post 8vo. 2s.

MEREDITH'S (Mrs. Charles) Notes and Sketches of New South Wales. Post 8vo. 2s.

MESSIAH (THE): A Narrative of the Life, Travels, Death, Resurrection, and Ascension of our Blessed Lord. By the Author of "Life of Bishop Ken." Map. 8vo. 18s.

MICHIE'S (Alexander) Siberian Overland Route from Peking to Petersburg, through the Deserts and Steppes of Mongolia, Tartary, &c. Maps and Illustrations. 8vo. 16s.

MODERN DOMESTIC COOKERY. Founded on Principles of Economy and Practical Knowledge and adapted for Private Families. *New Edition.* Woodcuts. Fcap. 8vo. 5s.

MOORE'S (Thomas) Life and Letters of Lord Byron. Plates. 6 Vols. Fcap. 8vo. 18s.; or 1 Vol. Portraits. Royal 8vo. 9s.

MOTLEY'S (J. L.) History of the United Netherlands: from the Death of William the Silent to the Twelve Years' Truce, 1609. Embracing the English-Dutch struggle against Spain; and a detailed Account of the Spanish Armada. Portraits. 4 Vols. 8vo. 60s.

MOUHOT'S (Henri) Siam, Cambojia, and Lao; a Narrative of Travels and Discoveries. Illustrations. 2 vols. 8vo. 32s.

MOZLEY'S (Rev. J. B.) Treatise on Predestination. 8vo. 14s.

———— Primitive Doctrine of Baptismal Regeneration. 8vo. 7s.6d.

MUNDY'S (General) Pen and Pencil Sketches in India. *Third Edition.* Plates. Post 8vo. 7s. 6d.

MUNRO'S (General Sir Thomas) Life and Letters. By the Rev. G. R. Gleig. Post 8vo. 3s. 6d.

MURCHISON'S (Sir Roderick) Russia in Europe and the Ural Mountains. With Coloured Maps, Plates, Sections, &c. 2 Vols. Royal 4to. 5l. 5s.

———————— Siluria; or, a History of the Oldest Rocks containing Organic Remains. *Fourth Edition.* Map and Plates. 8vo. 30s.

MURRAY'S RAILWAY READING. Containing:—

Wellington. By Lord Ellesmere. 6d.	Hallam's Literary Essays. 2s.
Nimrod on the Chase, 1s.	Mahon's Joan of Arc. 1s.
Essays from "The Times." 2 Vols. 8s.	Head's Emigrant. 2s. 6d.
Music and Dress. 1s.	Nimrod on the Road. 1s.
Layard's Account of Nineveh. 5s.	Croker on the Guillotine. 1s.
Milman's Fall of Jerusalem. 1s.	Hollway's Norway. 2s.
Mahon's "Forty-Five." 3s.	Maurel's Wellington. 1s. 6d.
Life of Theodore Hook. 1s.	Campbell's Life of Bacon. 2s. 6d.
Deeds of Naval Daring. 2s. 6d.	The Flower Garden. 1s.
The Honey Bee. 1s.	Lockhart's Spanish Ballads. 2s. 6d.
James' Æsop's Fables. 2s. 6d.	Taylor's Notes from Life. 2s.
Nimrod on the Turf. 1s. 6d.	Rejected Addresses. 1s.
Art of Dining. 1s. 6d.	Penn's Hints on Angling. 1s.

MUSIC AND DRESS. By a Lady. Reprinted from the "Quarterly Review." Fcap. 8vo. 1s.

NAPIER'S (Sir Chas.) Life; chiefly derived from his Journals and Letters. By Sir W. Napier. *Second Edition.* Portraits. 4 Vols. Post 8vo. 48s.

———— (Sir Wm.) Life and Letters. Edited by H. A. Bruce, M.P. Portraits. 2 Vols. Crown 8vo. 28s.

———————— English Battles and Sieges of the Peninsular War. *Fourth Edition.* Portrait. Post 8vo. 9s.

NAUTICAL (The) ALMANACK. Royal 8vo. 2s. 6d. (By
Authority.)

NAVY LIST (The). (Published Quarterly, by Authority.) 16mo.
2s. 6d.

NEW (The Illustrated) TESTAMENT. With a Plain Explanatory
Commentary. Edited by Archdeacon Churton, M.A., and Basil
Jones, M.A. With 110 authentic Views of Sacred Places, from Sketches
and Photographs taken on the spot. 2 Vols. Crown 8vo. 30s. cloth;
52s. 6d. calf; 63s. morocco.

NICHOLLS' (Sir George) History of the English, Irish and
Scotch Poor Laws. 4 Vols. 8vo.

——————— (Rev. H. G.) Historical Account of the Forest of
Dean. Woodcuts, &c. Post 8vo. 10s. 6d.

NICOLAS' (Sir Harris) Historic Peerage of England. Exhi-
biting the Origin, Descent, and Present State of every Title of Peerage which has existed in this Country since the Conquest. By
William Courthope. 8vo. 30s.

NIMROD On the Chace—The Turf—and The Road. Woodcuts.
Fcap. 8vo. 3s. 6d.

OXENHAM'S (Rev. W.) English Notes for Latin Elegiacs; designed
for early Proficients in the Art of Latin Versification, with Prefatory
Rules of Composition in Elegiac Metre. Fourth Edition. 12mo. 3s. 6d.

OXFORD'S (Bishop of) Life of William Wilberforce. Condensed
from the larger Biography. With Portrait. Post 8vo.

PARIS' (Dr.) Philosophy in Sport made Science in Earnest;
or, the First Principles of Natural Philosophy inculcated by aid of the
Toys and Sports of Youth. Ninth Edition. Woodcuts. Post 8vo. 7s. 6d.

PARKYNS' (Mansfield) Life in Abyssinia: During a Three Years'
Residence and Travels in that Country. With Illustrations. Post
8vo. 7s. 6d.

PEEL'S (Sir Robert) Memoirs. Edited by Earl Stanhope
and Mr. Cardwell. 2 Vols. Post 8vo. 7s. 6d. each.

PENN'S (Richard) Maxims and Hints for an Angler and Chess-
player. New Edition. Woodcuts. Fcap. 8vo. 1s.

PENROSE'S (F. C.) Principles of Athenian Architecture, and the
Optical Refinements exhibited in the Construction of the Ancient
Buildings at Athens, from a Survey. With 40 Plates. Folio. 5l. 5s.

PERCY'S (John, M.D.) Metallurgy of Fuel, Coal, Fire-Clays,
Copper, Zinc, Brass, &c. Illustrations. 8vo.

——————— Iron and Steel. Illustrations. 8vo. 42s.

——————— Lead, Silver, Gold, Platinum, Tin, Nickel, Cobalt, Anti-
mony, Bismuth, Arsenic, &c. Illustrations. 8vo. (In the Press.)

PHILLIPP (C. S. M.) On Jurisprudence. 8vo. 12s.

PHILLIPS' (John) Memoirs of William Smith, (the Father of Geology). Portrait. 8vo. 7s. 6d.

——————— Geology of Yorkshire, The Coast, and Limestone
District. Plates. 4to. Part I., 20s.—Part II., 30s.

——————— Rivers, Mountains, and Sea Coast of Yorkshire.
With Essays on the Climate, Scenery, and Ancient Inhabitants.
Second Edition. Plates. 8vo. 15s.

PHILPOTTS' (Bishop) Letters to the late Charles Butler, on his
" Book of the Roman Catholic Church." New Edition. Post 8vo. 6s.

POPE'S (ALEXANDER) Life and Works. *A New Edition.* Containing nearly 500 unpublished Letters. Edited, with a NEW LIFE, Introductions and Notes, by REV. WHITWELL ELWIN. Portraits 8vo. (*In the Press.*)

PORTER'S (REV. J. L.) Five Years in Damascus. With Travels to Palmyra, Lebanon and other Scripture Sites. Map and Woodcuts. 2 Vols. Post 8vo. 21s.

———— Handbook for Syria and Palestine : including an Account of the Geography, History, Antiquities, and Inhabitants of these Countries, the Peninsula of Sinai, Edom, and the Syrian Desert. Maps. 2 Vols. Post 8vo. 24s.

PRAYER-BOOK (THE ILLUSTRATED), with Borders, Initials, Vignettes, &c. Edited, with Notes, by REV. THOS. JAMES. Medium 8vo. 18s. cloth ; 31s. 6d. calf ; 36s. morocco.

PUSS IN BOOTS. With 12 Illustrations. By OTTO SPECKTER. 16mo. 1s. 6d. or Coloured, 2s. 6d.

QUARTERLY REVIEW (THE). 8vo. 6s.

RAMBLES among the Turkomans and Bedaweens of the Syrian Deserts. Post 8vo. 10s. 6d.

RANKE'S (LEOPOLD) History of the Popes of Rome during the 16th and 17th Centuries. Translated from the German by SARAH AUSTIN. 3 Vols. 8vo. 30s.

RAWLINSON'S (REV. GEORGE) Herodotus. A New English Version. Edited with Notes and Essays. Assisted by SIR HENRY RAWLINSON and SIR J. G. WILKINSON. *Second Edition.* Maps and Woodcut. 4 Vols. 8vo. 48s.

———— Five Great Monarchies of the Ancient World, Chaldæa, Assyria, Media, Babylonia, and Persia. With Maps and 650 Illustrations. 4 Vols. 8vo. 16s. each.

———— Historical Evidences of the truth of the Scripture Records stated anew. *Second Edition.* 8vo. 14s.

REJECTED ADDRESSES (THE). By JAMES AND HORACE SMITH. Fcap. 8vo. 1s.

RENNIE'S (D. F.) British Arms in Peking, 1860 ; Kagosima, 1862. Post 8vo. 12s.

———— Peking and the Pekingese : Being a Narrative of the First Year of the British Embassy in China. Illustrations. 2 Vols. Post 8vo. 24s.

———— Story of Bhotan and the Dooar War ; including Sketches of a Residence in the Himalayas and Visit to Bhotan in 1865. Map and Woodcut. Post 8vo. 12s.

REYNOLDS' (SIR JOSHUA) Life and Times. Commenced by C. R. LESLIE, R.A., continued and concluded by TOM TAYLOR. Portraits and Illustrations. 2 Vols. 8vo. 42s.

———— Descriptive Catalogue of his Works. With Notices of their present owners and localities. By TOM TAYLOR and CHARLES W. FRANKS. With Illustrations. Fcap. 4to. (*In the Press.*)

RICARDO'S (DAVID) Political Works. With a Notice of his Life and Writings. By J. R. M'CULLOCH. *New Edition.* 8vo. 16s.

RIPA'S (FATHER) Memoirs during Thirteen Years' Residence at the Court of Peking. From the Italian. Post 8vo. 2s.

ROBERTSON'S (Canon) History of the Christian Church, from the Apostolic Age to the Death of Boniface VIII., A.D. 1122—1304. 3 Vols. 8vo. 54s.

ROBINSON'S (Rev. Dr.) Biblical Researches in the Holy Land. Maps. 3 Vols. 8vo. 42s.

———— Physical Geography of the Holy Land. Post 8vo. 10s. 6d.

ROME (The Student's History of). From the Earliest Times to the Establishment of the Empire. By Dean Liddell. Woodcuts. Post 8vo. 7s. 6d.

———— (A Smaller History of). By Wm. Smith, LL.D. Woodcuts. 16mo. 3s. 6d.

ROWLAND'S (David) Manual of the English Constitution; Its Rise, Growth, and Present State. Post 8vo. 10s. 6d.

———— Laws of Nature the Foundation of Morals. Post 8vo. 6s.

RUNDELL'S (Mrs.) Domestic Cookery, adapted for Private Families. New Edition. Woodcuts. Fcap. 8vo. 5s.

RUSSELL'S (Rutherfurd) History of the Heroes of Medicine. Portraits. 8vo. 14s.

RUXTON'S (George F.) Travels in Mexico; with Adventures among the Wild Tribes and Animals of the Prairies and Rocky Mountains. Post 8vo. 3s. 6d.

SALE'S (Sir Robert) Brigade in Affghanistan. With an Account of the Defence of Jellalabad. By Rev. G. R. Gleig. Post 8vo. 2s.

SALLESBURY'S (Edward) "Children of the Lake." A Poem. Fcap. 8vo. 4s. 6d.

SANDWITH'S (Humphry) Siege of Kars. Post 8vo. 3s. 6d.

SCOTT'S (G. Gilbert) Secular and Domestic Architecture, Present and Future. 8vo. 9s.

———— (Master of Baliol) University Sermons, preached at Oxford. Post 8vo. 8s. 6d.

SCROPE'S (G. P.) Geology and Extinct Volcanoes of Central France. Illustrations. Medium 8vo. 30s.

SEDDON'S (J. P.) Rhine and the Moselle: Being Rambles in the Rhine Provinces. With Chromo-lithographs, Photographs, and Woodcuts. 4to. 42s.

SHAW'S (T. B.) Manual of English Literature. Edited, with Notes and Illustrations, by Dr. Wm. Smith. Post 8vo. 7s. 6d.

———— Specimens of English Literature. Selected from the Chief Writers. Edited by Wm. Smith, LL.D. Post 8vo. 7s. 6d.

SHIRLEY (Evelyn P.) on Deer and Deer Parks, or some Account of English Parks, with Notes on the Management of Deer. Illustrations. 4to. 21s.

SIERRA LEONE; Described in Letters to Friends at Home. By A Lady. Post 8vo. 3s. 6d.

SIMMONS (Capt. T. F.) on the Constitution and Practice of Courts-Martial; with a Summary of the Law of Evidence. Sixth and Revised Edition. 8vo. (In the Press.)

SOUTH'S (John F.) Household Surgery; or, Hints on Emergencies. Seventeenth Thousand. Woodcuts. Fcp. 8vo. 4s. 6d.

SMILES' (Samuel) Lives of British Engineers; from the Earliest Period to the Death of Robert Stephenson; with an account of their Principal Works; including Lives of Boulton and Watt, and a History of the Invention of the Steam Engine. With 9 Portraits and 300 Illustrations. 4 Vols. 8vo. 21s. each.

———— Huguenots in England and Ireland: their Churches, Settlements, and Industries. 8vo. 16s.

———— Lives of George and Robert Stephenson. With Portraits and Illustrations. 8vo. 21s. Or *Popular Edition*, with Woodcuts. Post 8vo. 6s.

———— Brindley and the Early Engineers. With Portrait and 50 Woodcuts. Post 8vo. 6s.

———— Thomas Telford. Portrait and Woodcuts. Post 8vo. **6s.**

———— Self-Help. With Illustrations of Character and Conduct. Post 8vo. 6s. Or translated into French as a School Reading-Book. 5s.

——— Industrial Biography: Iron-Workers and Tool Makers. A sequel to "Self-Help." Post 8vo. 6s.

———— Workmen's Earnings—Savings—and Strikes. Fcap. 8vo. 1s. 6d.

SOMERVILLE'S (Mary) Physical Geography. *Fifth Edition.* Portrait. Post 8vo. 9s.

———————— Connexion of the Physical Sciences. *Ninth Edition.* Woodcuts. Post 8vo. 9s.

———————— Molecular and Microscopic Science. Illustrations. 2 Vols. Post 8vo. (*In the Press.*)

SOUTHEY'S (Robert) Book of the Church. *Seventh Edition.* Post 8vo. 7s. 6d.

SPECKTER'S (Otto) Puss in Boots. With 12 Woodcuts. Square 12mo. 1s. 6d. plain, or 2s. 6d. coloured.

STANLEY'S (Dean) Sinai and Palestine, in Connexion with their History. Map. 8vo. 14s.

———— Bible in the Holy Land; being Extracts from the above Work. Woodcuts, Fcap. 8vo, 2s. 6d.

———— St. Paul's Epistles to the Corinthians. With Dissertations and Notes. 8vo. 18s.

———— History of the Eastern Church. Plans. 8vo. 12s.

———————— Jewish Church. First and Second Series. 8vo. 16s. each.

———— Historical Memorials of Canterbury. Woodcuts. Post 8vo. 7s. 6d.

———— Memorials of Westminster Abbey. Woodcuts. 8vo. 16s.

———— Sermons in the East, with Notices of the Places Visited. 8vo. 9s.

———————— on Evangelical and Apostolical Teaching. Post 8vo. 7s. 6d.

———— Addresses and Charges of Bishop Stanley. With Memoir. 8vo. 10s. 6d.

———— Lives of Bunyan and Cromwell. Post 8vo. 2s.

SMITH'S (Dr. Wm.) Dictionary of the Bible; its Antiquities, Biography, Geography, and Natural History. Illustrations. 3 Vols. 8vo. 105s.

———— Concise Bible Dictionary, for Families and Students. Illustrations. Medium 8vo. 21s.

———— Smaller Bible Dictionary, for Schools and Young Persons. Illustrations. Post 8vo. 7s. 6d.

———— Dictionary of Christian Antiquities: from the Times of the Apostles to the Age of Charlemagne. Illustrations. Medium. 8vo. (*In preparation.*)

———— Biblical Atlas. Folio. (*In preparation.*)

———— Classical Atlas. Folio. (*In preparation.*)

———— Dictionary of Greek and Roman Antiquities. Woodcuts. 8vo. 42s.

———— Smaller Dictionary of Greek and Roman Antiquities, compiled from the above Work. Woodcuts. Crown 8vo. 7s. 6d.

———— Dictionary of Greek and Roman Biography and Mythology. Woodcuts. 3 Vols. 8vo. 5l. 15s. 6d.

———————————— Greek and Roman Geography. Woodcuts. 2 Vols. 8vo. 80s.

———— Classical Dictionary for Schools, compiled from the above works. With 750 Woodcuts. 8vo. 18s.

———— Smaller Classical Dictionary, abridged from the above Work. Woodcuts. Crown 8vo. 7s. 6d.

———— Classical Mythology for Schools. With Translations from the Ancient Poets. With Illustrations. 12mo. 3s. 6d.

———— Complete Latin English Dictionary. With Tables of the Roman Calendar, Measures, Weights, and Money. 8vo. 21s.

———— Smaller Latin-English Dictionary, abridged from the above Work. 12mo. 7s. 6d.

———— Latin-English Vocabulary; for Phædrus, Cornelius Nepos, and Cæsar. *2nd Edition.* 12mo. 3s. 6d.

———— Copious and Critical English-Latin Dictionary, compiled from original sources. 8vo. and 12mo. (*In the Press.*)

———— Principia Latina—Part I. A Grammar, Delectus, and Exercise Book, with Vocabularies. *6th Edition.* 12mo. 3s. 6d.

———————————— Part II. A Reading-book of Mythology, Geography, Roman Antiquities, and History. With Notes and Dictionary. *3rd Edition.* 12mo. 3s. 6d.

———————————— Part III. A Latin Poetry Book. Hexameters and Pentameters; Eclog. Ovidianæ; Latin Prosody, &c. *2nd Edition.* 12mo. 3s. 6d.

———————————— Part IV. Latin Prose Composition. Rules of Syntax, with Examples, Explanations of Synonyms, and Exercises on the Syntax. *Second Edition.* 12mo. 3s. 6d.

———————————— Part V. Short Tales and Anecdotes for Translation into Latin. 12mo. 3s.

———— Student's Latin Grammar for the Higher Forms in Schools. Post 8vo. 6s.

———— Smaller Latin Grammar for the Middle and Lower Forms, abridged from the above Work. 12mo. 3s. 6d.

———— Initia Græca, Part I. An Introduction to Greek; comprehending Grammar, Delectus, and Exercise-book. With Vocabularies. 12mo. 3s. 6d.

SMITH'S (Dr. Wm.) Initia Græca, Part II. A Reading Book. Containing Short Tales, Anecdotes, Fables, Mythology, and Grecian History. Arranged in a systematic Progression, with a Lexicon. 12mo. 3s. 6d.

———— Initia Græca, Part III. Greek Prose Composition. Containing the Rules of Syntax, with copious Examples and Exercises. 12mo. (*In preparation.*)

———— Student's Greek Grammar for the Higher Forms in Schools. By Professor Curtius. Post 8vo. 6s.

———— Smaller Greek Grammar, for the Middle and Lower Forms. Abridged from the above Work. 12mo. 3s. 6d.

———— Smaller History of England. With 68 Woodcuts. 12mo. 3s. 6d.

———— History of Greece. With 74 Woodcuts. 12mo. 3s. 6d.

———— History of Rome. With 79 Woodcuts. 12mo. 3s. 6d.

———— Classical Mythology. With Translations from the Ancient Poets, and Questions on the Work. With 90 Woodcuts. 16mo. 3s. 6d.

———— Scripture History. With Woodcuts. 16mo. 3s. 6d. (*In preparation.*)

STANHOPE'S (Earl) History of England, from the Peace of Utrecht to the Peace of Versailles, 1713-83. *Library Edition.* 7 vols. 8vo. 93s. Or *Popular Edition.* 7 Vols. Post 8vo. 5s. each.

———— Life of William Pitt. With Extracts from his MS. Papers. Portraits. 4 Vols. Post 8vo. 24s.

———— Miscellanies. Post 8vo. 5s. 6d.

———— History of British India, from its Origin till the Peace of 1783. Post 8vo. 3s. 6d.

———— "Forty-Five;" a Narrative of the Rebellion in Scotland. Post 8vo. 3s.

———— Spain under Charles the Second. Post 8vo. 6s. 6d.

———— Historical and Critical Essays. Post 8vo. 3s. 6d.

———— Life of Belisarius. Post 8vo. 10s. 6d.

———— ———— Condé. Post 8vo. 3s. 6d.

ST. JOHN'S (Charles) Wild Sports and Natural History of the Highlands. Post 8vo. 3s. 6d.

———— (Bayle) Adventures in the Libyan Desert and the Oasis of Jupiter Ammon. Woodcuts. Post 8vo. 2s.

STEPHENSONS' (George and Robert) Lives. By Samuel Smiles. With Portraits and 70 Illustrations. Medium 8vo. 21s. Or *Popular Edition* with Woodcuts. Post 8vo. 6s.

STOTHARD'S (Thos.) Life. With Personal Reminiscences. By Mrs. Bray. With Portrait and 60 Woodcuts. 4to. 21s.

STREET'S (G. E.) Gothic Architecture in Spain. From Personal Observations during several journeys through that country. Illustrations. Medium 8vo. 50s.

———— Brick and Marble Architecture of Italy in the Middle Ages. Plates. 8vo. 21s.

SULLIVAN'S (Sir Edward) Princes, Warriors, and Statesmen of India; an Historical Narrative of the most Important Events, from the Invasion of Mahmoud of Ghizni to that of Nadir Shah. 8vo. 12s.

SWIFT'S (Jonathan) Life, Letters, Journals, and Works. By John Forster. 8vo. (*In Preparation.*)

SYBEL'S (Von) History of the French Revolution, from the Secret Archives of Germany. Translated from the German. By Walter C. Perry. Vols. 1 & 2. 8vo. 24s.

SYME'S (Professor) Principles of Surgery. *5th Edition.* 8vo. 12s.

STUDENT'S HUME. A History of England from the Invasion of Julius Cæsar to the Revolution of 1688. By DAVID HUME. Corrected and continued to 1858. Woodcuts. Post 8vo. 7s. 6d.
*** Questions on the above Work, 12mo. 2s.
———— HISTORY OF FRANCE; from the Earliest Times to the Establishment of the Second Empire, 1852. By W. H. PEARSON, M.A. Woodcuts. Post 8vo. 7s. 6d.
———— HISTORY OF GREECE; from the Earliest Times to the Roman Conquest. With the History of Literature and Art. By WM. SMITH, LL.D. Woodcuts. Crown 8vo. 7s. 6d.
*** Questions on the above Work, 12mo. 2s.
———— HISTORY OF ROME; from the Earliest Times to the Establishment of the Empire. With the History of Literature and Art. By Dean LIDDELL. Woodcuts. Crown 8vo. 7s. 6d.
———— GIBBON; an Epitome of the Decline and Fall of the Roman Empire. Incorporating the Researches of Recent Commentators. Woodcuts. Post 8vo. 7s. 6d.
———— BLACKSTONE: a Systematic Abridgment of the Entire Commentaries. By R. MALCOLM KERR, LL.D. Post 8vo. 7s. 6d.
———— MANUAL OF ANCIENT GEOGRAPHY. By REV. W. L. BEVAN, M.A. Woodcuts. Post 8vo. 7s. 6d.
———— MODERN GEOGRAPHY. By REV. W. L. BEVAN. Woodcuts. Post 8vo. (In the Press.)
———— OLD TESTAMENT HISTORY; From the Creation to the Return of the Jews from Captivity. Maps and Woodcuts. Post 8vo. 7s. 6d.
———— NEW TESTAMENT HISTORY. With an Introduction connecting the History of the Old and New Testaments. Maps and Woodcuts. Post 8vo. 7s. 6d.
———— ECCLESIASTICAL HISTORY. Containing the History of the Christian Church from the Close of the New Testament Canon to the Reformation. Post 8vo. (In preparation.)
———— MORAL PHILOSOPHY. With Quotations and References. By WILLIAM FLEMING, D.D. Post 8vo. 7s. 6d.
———— ENGLISH LANGUAGE. By GEO. P. MARSH. Post 8vo. 7s. 6d.
———— ENGLISH LITERATURE. By T. B. SHAW, M.A. Post 8vo. 7s. 6d.
———— SPECIMENS OF ENGLISH LITERATURE. Selected from the Chief Writers. By THOMAS B. SHAW, M.A. Post 8vo. 7s. 6d.

TAIT'S (BISHOP) Dangers and Safeguards of Modern Theology, containing Suggestions to the Theological Student under Present Difficulties. 8vo. 9s.

TAYLOR'S (HENRY) Notes from Life—on Money, Humility and Independence, Wisdom, Choice in Marriage, Children, and Life Poetic. Fcap. 8vo. 2s.

THOMSON'S (ARCHBISHOP) Sermons, Preached in the Chapel of Lincoln's Inn. 8vo. 10s. 6d.
———— Life in the Light of God's Word. Post 8vo. 6s.

THREE-LEAVED MANUAL OF FAMILY PRAYER; arranged so as to save the trouble of turning the Pages backwards and forwards. Royal 8vo. 2s.

TREMENHEERE (H. S.); The Franchise a Privilege and not a Right, proved by the Political Experience of the Ancients. Fcap. 8vo. 2s. 6d.

TRISTRAM'S (H. B.) Great Sahara, or Wanderings South of the Atlas Mountains. Map and Illustrations. Post 8vo. 15s.

TWISS' (HORACE) Life of Lord Chancellor Eldon, with Selections from his Correspondence. Portrait. *Third Edition*. 2 Vols. Post 8vo. 21s.

TYNDALL'S (JOHN) Glaciers of the Alps. With an account of Three Years' Observations and Experiments on their General Phenomena. Woodcuts. Post 8vo. 14s.

TYTLER'S (PATRICK FRASER) Memoirs. By Rev. J. W. BURGON, M.A. 8vo. 9s.

VAMBERY'S (ARMINIUS) Travels in Central Asia, from Teheran across the Turkoman Desert on the Eastern Shore of the Caspian to Khiva, Bokhara, and Samarcand in 1863. Map and Illustrations. 8vo. 21s.

VAUGHAN'S (REV. DR.) Sermons preached in Harrow School. 8vo. 10s. 6d.

WAAGEN'S (DR.) Treasures of Art in Great Britain. Being an Account of the Chief Collections of Paintings, Sculpture, Manuscripts, Miniatures, &c. &c., in this Country. Obtained from Personal Inspection during Visits to England. 4 Vols. 8vo.

WELLINGTON'S (THE DUKE OF) Despatches during his various Campaigns. Compiled from Official and other Authentic Documents. 8 Vols. 8vo. 21s. each.

———————— Supplementary Despatches, and other Papers. Vols. I. to XII. 8vo. 20s. each.

———————— Civil and Political Despatches. Vols. I. and II. 1812 to 1825. 8vo. 20s. each.

———————— Selections from Despatches and General Orders. 8vo. 18s.

———————— Speeches in Parliament. 2 Vols. 8vo. 42s.

WHITE'S (HENRY) Massacre of St. Bartholomew. Preceded by a History of the Religious Wars of the Reign of Charles IX. Based on a Personal Examination of the Metropolitan and Provincial Archives of France. With Illustrations. 8vo. 16s.

WILKINSON'S (SIR J. G.) Popular Account of the Private Life, Manners, and Customs of the Ancient Egyptians. *New Edition*. Revised and Condensed. With 500 Woodcuts. 2 Vols. Post 8vo. 12s.

———————— Handbook for Egypt.—Thebes, the Nile, Alexandria, Cairo, the Pyramids, Mount Sinai, &c. Map. Post 8vo. 15s.

WILSON'S (BISHOP DANIEL) Life, with Extracts from his Letters and Journals. By Rev. JOSIAH BATEMAN. *Second Edition*. Illustrations. Post 8vo. 9s.

———————— (GENL. SIR ROBERT) Secret History of the French Invasion of Russia, and Retreat of the French Army, 1812. *Second Edition*. 8vo. 15s.

———————— Private Diary of Travels, Personal Services, and Public Events, during Missions and Employments in Spain, Sicily, Turkey, Russia, Poland, Germany, &c. 1812-14. 2 Vols. 8vo. 26s.

———————— Autobiographical Memoirs. Containing an Account of his Early Life down to the Peace of Tilsit. Portrait. 2 Vols. 8vo. 26s.

WOOD (SIR W. PAGE) On the Continuity of Scripture, as Declared by the Testimony of Our Lord and of the Evangelists and Apostles. Post 8vo. 6s.

WORDSWORTH'S (CANON) Journal of a Tour in Athens and Attica. *Third Edition*. Plates. Post 8vo. 8s. 6d.

———————— Pictorial, Descriptive, and Historical Account of Greece, with a History of Greek Art, by G. SCHARF, F.S.A. *New Edition*. With 600 Woodcuts. Royal 8vo. 28s.